The Devil in Texas
El diablo en Texas

bp

Bilingual Press/Editorial Bilingue

General Editor
    Gary D. Keller

Managing Editor
    Karen S. Van Hooft

Senior Editor
    Mary M. Keller

Assistant Editor
    Linda St. George Thurston

Editorial Consultants
    Barbara H. Firoozye
    Ann M. Waggoner

Editorial Board
    Juan Goytisolo
    Francisco Jiménez
    Eduardo Rivera
    Severo Sarduy
    Mario Vargas Llosa

Address:
Bilingual Review/Press
Hispanic Research Center
Arizona State University
Tempe, Arizona 85287
(602) 965-3867

The Devil in Texas
El diablo en Texas

Clásicos Chicanos/Chicano Classics 5

Aristeo Brito

Translated from the Spanish by
David William Foster

Bilingual Press/Editorial Bilingüe
TEMPE, ARIZONA

First Spanish edition © 1976 by Aristeo Brito and Editorial Peregrinos, Tucson, Arizona.

ISBN 0-927534-05-3
Printed simultaneously in a softcover edition. ISBN 0-927534-06-1

Library of Congress Catalog Card Number: 90-80917

PRINTED IN THE UNITED STATES OF AMERICA

Cover design by Robin Ravary and Christopher J. Bidlack
Back cover photo by A. Taylor

The Western States Book Awards are a project of the Western States Arts Federation. The awards are supported by "Corporate Founder" The Xerox Foundation, the Lannan Foundation, Crane Duplicating Service, and the Witter Bynner Foundation for Poetry. Additional funding is provided by the National Endowment for the Arts Literature Program.

Acknowledgments

This project is jointly supported by grants from the Arizona Commission on the Arts, a State agency, and the National Endowment for the Arts in Washington, D.C., a Federal agency.

The editors also express their appreciation to Crane Duplicating Service for its generous donation of the bound galleys.

While the towns of Presidio and Ojinaga exist in the Rio Grande Valley, the characters and situations in this novel are fictional and none exist in real life or are based on persons living or dead. Any resemblance to real situations or to persons living or dead is purely coincidental.

About Clásicos Chicanos/Chicano Classics

The Clásicos Chicanos/Chicano Classics series is intended to ensure the long-term accessibility of deserving works of Chicano literature and culture that have become unavailable over the years or that are in imminent danger of becoming inaccessible. Each of the volumes in the series carries with it a scholarly apparatus that includes an extended introduction contextualizing the work within Chicano literature and a bibliography of the existent works by and about the author. The series is designed to be a vehicle that will help in the recuperation of Raza literary history, maintain the instruments of our culture in our own hands, and permit the continued experience and enjoyment of our literature by both present and future generations of readers and scholars.

The Devil in Texas/El diablo en Texas was originally self-published in 1976. The book met with considerable enthusiasm from critics, some controversy among readers in Presidio, Texas, but mostly, unfortunately, was neglected because of lack of distribution. With the encouragement of the editors of the Bilingual Press/Editorial Bilingüe almost from the day we moved in 1986 from Binghamton, New York, to Tempe, Arizona, Aristeo Brito decided to revise his book and simultaneously agreed for us to translate it into English and publish it in a bilingual, English-Spanish edition. During the summer of 1989, the manuscript was completed, including its masterful translation by David William Foster, just in time to submit it to the biannual book awards competition of the Western States Arts Federation. Mira no más que this book, so beautifully written, so lastimosamente forgotten, won the prestigious Western States Book Award for fiction on the basis of its English translation. The jury consisted of Jorie Graham, Elizabeth Hardwick, William Kittredge, and N. Scott Momaday.

I cannot think of a more instructive reason for the existence of the Clásicos Chicanos/Chicano Classics series than the "all's well that ends well" destiny of Aristeo Brito's hauntingly beautiful novel.

We at the Bilingual Press/Editorial Bilingüe are proud of the ultimate confirmation of this book by a jury of prestigious peers and by what the series has been able to accomplish in the never-ending struggle to recuperate and to maintain our culture, our literature, our heritage, and our identity. It is results such as this one that keep our morale high and make the struggle worthwhile. And so for this century and into the next, le brindamos para nuestra querida raza esta bellísima y ahora, finalmente, consagrada novela del compañero y carnal, Aristeo Brito.

G. D. Keller

About the Author and Translator

Aristeo Brito was raised in Southwest Texas. His poetry and short stories have appeared in numerous journals and anthologies, and his first collection, *Cuentos i poemas*, was published in 1974. The original Spanish-language edition of *El diablo en Texas* appeared in 1976. He has been actively involved in the promotion of Chicano literature in organizations such as the Modern Language Association, and he has lectured and read widely from his works throughout the United States and in Spain and Mexico. He has also received grants from the National Endowment for the Humanities and the National Endowment for the Arts. Brito received his Ph.D. from the University of Arizona in 1978, and he is presently Chairman of Languages at Pima Community College in Tucson, editor of *Llueve Tlaloc*, the college's bilingual literary magazine, and teacher of creative writing.

David William Foster is Regents' Professor of Spanish and Director of Spanish Graduate Studies at Arizona State University. In addition to his translations of Chicano literature, he has translated Argentine fiction and published numerous scholarly works on contemporary Latin American narrative and theater, with an emphasis on Argentina. His current research concerns cultural texts in Latin America focusing on gay and lesbian identity and the relationship between sex and violence. *The Argentina Generation of 1880: Ideology and Cultural Texts* was recently published by the University of Missouri Press, and *From Mafalda to Los Supermachos: Latin American Graphic Humor and Popular Culture* was published by Lynne Rienner Publishers in 1989.

Contents

To all the Brito family

Stasis and Change Along the Rio Grande: Aristeo Brito's *The Devil in Texas*

Charles Tatum

The United States-Mexican border that stretches for two thousand miles from the West Coast to the Gulf Coast has several major twin cities where commerce and tourism thrive. Thousands of Mexican citizens cross into this country daily to work in American homes, agricultural fields, construction sites, factories, restaurants, or wherever they can find what is usually menial, low-paying, and backbreaking work. The fortunate few who have obtained work permits go about their tasks without the constant fear of being picked up and deported by U.S. authorities. Those who cross illegally must keep a constant vigil for the familiar green Border Patrol vehicles that they have come to associate with fear and disruption.

Bureaucrats, the media, social and law enforcement agencies, and others often refer to the Mexicans who choose to come to this country without legal authorization as undocumented workers. This euphemism serves to dehumanize and hide the bitter reality that thousands have left homes and families, often deep in Mexico's interior, to travel north to the United States in search of a living wage. It also serves to divert our attention from the horrible conditions under which these Mexican citizens have crossed into the United States and the indignities and physical abuse that many of them have suffered.

In addition to those who cross the border primarily to work, many Mexicans and Chicanos go back and forth frequently to renew family relationships and visit friends. Unyielding government regulations and restrictions sometimes make such contact difficult to sustain, especially for Mexican citizens coming to the United States, but such obstacles have done little to prevent it.

It can thus be said that the U.S.-Mexican border is for many a temporary inconvenience, a line created by treaties and regulated by national laws and international accords to discourage or, at best, to channel, human commerce. Despite the resolve of politicians and self-appointed protectors of the American Way of Life, Mexicans and Chicanos alike will continue to defy the artificial boundary thrown up almost 150 years ago to discourage traffic of those considered to be unacceptable to partake of this country's natural wealth.

Aristeo Brito grew up on this divisionary line that separates Texas from Chihuahua in the small and isolated West Texas community of Presidio, which sits by itself on the Rio Grande (what Mexicans refer to commonly as the Río Bravo) hundreds of miles downriver from El Paso. Its only companion is the equally tiny Mexican village of Ojinaga situated directly across the river. Like Presidio, it too is hundreds of miles from a major Mexican city. This is indeed a desolate place where the river seems to have dumped much of its saline backwater and upstream debris before moving on to the Gulf of Mexico. It is hot—so hot that it is frequently the hottest place in the continental United States during the summer—dry, dusty, and generally inhospitable. One descends into the Presidio-Ojinaga lowlands from the relatively mild climate of low mountain ranges on both sides of the border. Both countries seemed to have destined this spot on their shared border as a reminder to travellers of how lucky they are to be from elsewhere.

Yet, despite its inhospitability and isolation, Presidio-Ojinaga has had a part in the bitter, often violent conflicts that have erupted along the Texas-Mexican border for over 150 years. It seems that every mile along the Rio Grande from El Paso/Juárez to Brownsville/Matamoros has been contested at some time since 1836 when Texas declared its independence from Mexico. The much-feared Texas Rangers, a paramilitary constabulary created by politicians in Austin to keep the state's Chicano population in check and to keep out foreigners (i.e., Mexicans), ranged up and down the border terrorizing both citizens and non-citizens, especially when Anglo interests were threatened. Emma Tenayuca and Homer Brooks describe the role the Texas Rangers had in the introduction and implementation of Anglo commercial farming along the Middle and Lower Rio Grande early in the twentieth century: "Texas Rangers, in cooperation with land speculators, came into small Mexican villages in the border country, massacred hundreds of unarmed, peaceful Mexican villagers and seized their lands. Sometimes the seizures were accompanied by the formality of signing bills of sale—at the point of a gun" (Montejano 367).

The Texas Rangers left a bitter legacy among Chicanos, a legacy captured in the popular mind in hundreds of *corridos* and anecdotes transmitted orally from generation to generation. *Los rinches*, a term of opprobrium, were seen as little more than legalized assassins and henchmen who carried out Anglo-directed repressive acts against the Chicano citizenry. The contrasting views of the Texas Rangers are captured in the following early twentieth-century popular songs. The first is a Texas Ranger Patrol song; the second is from the *corrido* of Jacinto Treviño, a popular Chicano hero known for his guerrilla attacks against repressive Anglo law enforcement bodies:

> O bury me not on the lone praire-ee
>   where the wild coyotes will howl o'er me!
> In a narrow grave just six by three
>   where all the Mexkins ought to be-ee!
>
> Come on you cowardly Rangers;
> No baby is up again you.
> You want to meet your daddy?
> I am Jacinto Treviño!
> Come on, you treacherous Rangers;
> Come get a taste of my lead.
> Or did you think it was ham
> between two slices of bread? (Montejano 102)

Brito grew up in Presidio-Ojinaga at a time when the memory of *los rinches* was very much alive and rekindled by the seemingly lawless acts of their latter-day counterparts, the United States Border Patrol. Chicano youths at Presidio High School (where he graduated as class valedictorian in 1961) did not have to stretch their imaginations to relate to the fear and loathing their elders expressed toward the Texas Rangers; the Border Patrol were vigorous defenders of the Rangers and modern practitioners of their unwritten mandate to preserve a repressive class system and an exploitative economic order along the border.

Brito recounts how one day soon after he had graduated from high school he suddenly became aware of the terrible conditions in which most of Presidio's Chicanos and Ojinaga's Mexicans lived.[1] Like many of his generation he had come to accept these conditions as natural and unchangeable, vaguely aware of the class and economic infrastructure that created and perpetuated them. He had seen the border towns' static and oppressive atmosphere as unconnected to external forces, something you either accepted and lived with or fled, but not as a situation with which to come to grips or try to change.

The building of a bridge over the Rio Grande between Presidio and Ojinaga was a momentous event that changed forever life for Mexicans and Chicanos on both sides of the border. Up until the construction of the bridge, they had gone back and forth by boat with relative ease; now, suddenly, the Border Patrol began to prevent these "illegal" crossings, thus channeling traffic through the regulated and controlled bridge access. Brito thus joined a community that highly resented the bridge and the restriction of movement that it brought the Spanish-speaking population. Visits to the homes of family and friends in Ojinaga were always potentially troublesome because the Immigration and Naturalization officials at the bridge would often harass non-Anglos.

Like so many other Chicano families in the Presidio-Ojinaga area, many of Brito's relatives had spent years picking cotton, vegetables, and fruit in the region's irrigated fields, low-paying work they turned to due to the paucity of other opportunities. Many of these fields were on land once owned by Mexicans but slowly appropriated by Anglos after the 1848 Treaty of Guadalupe Hidalgo. Brito himself had spent much of his childhood and adolescence picking, hoeing, and weeding, performing backbreaking work under a merciless sun in an area that averages less than ten inches of annual rainfall. An Anglo-controlled economic system and hostile natural elements thus conspired to perpetuate a two-class society, one consisting of middle- and upper-class Anglo landowners as well as a few non-Anglo retailers and the other consisting of disadvantaged Mexican and Chicano workers.

Brito's father had been active in Presidio's Civilian Conservation Corps during the Second World War, and despite his efforts to support the war effort at home, he was inducted into the Army. He refused to serve and was sentenced to four years imprisonment. Many years later during high school, Brito himself tried to enlist in the military but was refused due to low scores on an intelligence aptitude test. Excluded not because of his native abilities but due to his low literacy in English—a problem shared even today by thousands of Chicano youth raised in Spanish-speaking homes—he then devoted himself to becoming literate in both Spanish and English. He graduated at the head of his high school class and received scholarships to continue his education at nearby Sul Ross State University in Alpine, Texas. He graduated with distinction and was accepted into the graduate program in Spanish at the University of Arizona in Tucson. He had left Presidio-Ojinaga for college returning only for brief visits with his family. He had resolved never to live there in part as a reaction to a series of negative experiences he had suffered as a child and adolescent.

A factor that influenced his change of heart was the Chicano Movement. Its spokespersons from the mid-1960s to the early-1970s had succeeded in educating Chicano high school and college students about their own history, culture, and place within American society. Like thousands of other Chicanos during this period, Brito was profoundly affected by the Movement's ideology and the often violent confrontations between activists and the police on campuses and in the barrios throughout the Southwest and California.

Finally, in 1970, in the middle of his doctoral studies, he decided to return to Presidio-Ojinaga to assess the impact of the Chicano movement on his people. He discovered to his astonishment that very little had changed. His family, friends, and acquaintances had heard only distant rumblings of the great social upheaval that the rest of the country was going through. He found what he had abandoned: a static Mexican-American community mired in its past, relegated to second-class citizenship and exploited by a dominant Anglo ruling class. There seemed to be little inclination to change, to resist years of economic and social oppression.

In the face of this overwhelming sense of stasis, of the present being the same as the past and the future unlikely to alter Presidio-Ojinaga or its Spanish-speaking population in any significant way, Brito decided to postpone his doctoral thesis to give himself over to creating a fictionalized version of his community's history from the mid-1800s forward. He set about the task of scouring Presidio County's archives in search of data. He talked to dozens of older Chicanos who shared with him hundreds of anecdotes and fragmented memories that their parents and grandparents had, in turn, shared with them. He began to be aware that the unchanging physical appearance of the town was reproduced in their view of history; it became difficult for him to determine if a given occurrence had taken place one hundred years ago, fifty years ago, or ten years ago. His informants did not seem to be either aware or particularly concerned about historical accuracy or chronology. In addition, they very naturally gave their tales a mythic and fantastic cast that was very different from what Brito had expected. After months of listening patiently and feverishly filling numerous pages with notes, Brito set about writing his work, which he entitled *El diablo en Texas*.

Structure and Content

Brito divided his novel into an introduction and three sections. Each of the three sections is situated in a different period of Presidio's history: 1883, 1942, and 1970. In the introduction, a first-person narrator introduces us to the town of Presidio where he was born and raised. His emphasis on its aridity, barrenness, and isolation foreshadows the general state of abandonment in which the town finds itself at an indeterminate time in the present when the narrator introduces us to it.

The opening passage is strongly suggestive in several respects of Juan Rulfo's novel *Pedro Páramo* and of his short story "Luvina." Rulfo intentionally blurs in his longer work the line between life and death, reality and fantasy. He populates his fictional town of Comala with lost souls, *ánimas en pena*, condemned to wander the desert landscape in search of release and relief from their earthly purgatory. They walk among the living talking to them and to each other as though their worlds were one and the same. In a like manner, Brito's narrator tries to capture Presidio's essential qualities: It belongs both to the land of the living and the land of the dead, for "being born there is like being born half dead" and tourists flee the town when they hear "the empty sound of suffering souls" who congregate to talk among themselves.

As Rulfo does in creating the mythical town of Luvina, Brito endows Presidio with a phantasmagoric quality that he reinforces throughout the rest of the work. It is a town in the process of decay, unable to help itself and dying of its own passive resignation to its demise. The striking imagery of death and desolation of the first section serves to enhance the novel's essential qualities. As in Rulfo's Luvina, the church, the very center and dominant symbol of the town's spiritual health, is falling apart. In addition, the town has no doctors, no pharmacies, and no medicine. Death is everywhere evoked in the following images: "the remains of crumpled bodies, bodies perforated like a sieve through which the water irrigates the fields green with drunken sweat"; "a child waiting on a swing, thief of the wind, a child who hears the sighs in the water, in a fortress trembling with the howling of funereal dogs at midday."

Using the same striking imagery, Brito introduces in the first section the sociohistorical elements that permeate the rest of the novel: the dominating presence of the Border Patrol searching for and punishing those who have come north from Michoacán and elsewhere to find work; the humiliation of Americans of Mexican descent whose families once owned the fields they now work; the huge profits for Anglo landowners generated by the hard labor of Mexican illegals and Chicano poor; the indignities of poverty; the indebtedness to Anglo-owned businesses; and the exploitation of Mexican and Chicano laborers by members of their own culture who have sold their soul to the "Man."

The use of highly evocative language and the imagery of the introductory section combine to form a mosaic of the forces, both external and internal, that have conspired to keep the Chicanos of Presidio in a suspended state of apathy and inaction. The description of the devil, a mockingly playful (but deceptively harmless) trickster who dances to the beat of popular 1950s music, is an important part of this mosaic. He is an incarnation of the

allegorized evil that enhances the cyclical nature of life in Presidio
and the novel's essential quality of stasis.

While Brito does not present chronologically the novel's char-
acters and events, he is faithful to the historical record of conflict
along the Texas-Mexican border during the latter half of the nine-
teenth and the first part of the twentieth century. The first sec-
tion, "Presidio 1883," focuses on Ben Lynch and Francisco
Uranga. The first is an Anglo landowner who has come to the
Presidio-Ojinaga Valley to make his fortune raising cotton and
crops on stolen land worked by Mexican illegals and poor Chi-
canos. The second is a Chicano journalist/lawyer who tries to rally
his people to resist Anglo colonialism.

Don Benito—Ben Lynch's acquired Spanish name—and his
fellow Anglo interlopers go about the job of eliminating systemat-
ically the Chicanos who oppose them. Don Benito marries Rosa-
rio, Francisco Uranga's sister, and tries to ingratiate himself with
the Spanish-speaking population. We learn that he has conspired
with Lorenzo, a young ambitious Chicano, to deceive his own
mother into selling her land to the Anglo and that he treats his
workers despotically and disdainfully as though they were children
to be rewarded or punished. For example, early in the first section
Don Benito hosts a barbecue for his workers who have labored
hard (and cheaply) in his fields, but the same day he lures and
then executes several men who have stolen his horses. The local
Texas Ranger unit, under the command of a Captain Gray, is only
too willing to assist him to control "his" Mexican workers and to
eliminate troublemakers.

Francisco Uranga, Don Pancho, is depicted as a tragic figure
who has dedicated his life and profession to seeking justice for his
people. He has harangued them and denounced the Anglo com-
munity in the columns of his newspaper, *The Frontiersman*, de-
fended victims in court, and urged his *raza* to resist submitting
themselves passively to the oppressive and greedy Anglos. All to
no avail. Only the dusty copies of the newspaper will bear witness
to his tireless efforts. In a long, reflective interior monologue to-
ward the end of his life, he becomes painfully aware that the Mex-
icans of Ojinaga and the Chicanos of Presidio have actually lost
ground and their cultural dignity over time. His own town has
spurned him for stirring up trouble with the Anglos, for speaking

out too forcefully and too frequently against injustice and govern-
mental corruption. Don Pancho's one triumph has been to con-
vince the Mexican government to refuse Ben Lynch's request to
export Mexican workers to pick his cotton fields.

Don Pancho's desire to spur his people to action is fulfilled by
his son, who becomes politicized when he learns of his brother's
death. Reyes Uranga organizes a guerrilla band that resists Don
Benito, his men, and the collusive Texas Rangers. He eludes cap-
ture by staying on the Mexican side of the river where he enjoys
popular support.

The first section of *The Devil in Texas* reflects the historical
record accurately but not in a linear or detailed fashion. Rather,
Brito documents the Texas-Anglo arrival and subsequent coloni-
zation of Presidio-Ojinaga in a highly fragmentary narrative richly
textured with symbolic and mythic elements meant to evoke
rather than reproduce events along the Texas-Mexican border
from the mid-1850s through roughly the first four decades of
the 1900s.

The second section, "Presidio 1942," is similar in its focus and
intent. While it is also deeply rooted in the sociohistorical reality
of the border, Brito infuses this section with the same qualities
found in the first. These qualities will be discussed shortly after a
brief summary of the second section's content.

The Texas Rangers have been phased out and replaced by
equally arrogant U.S. Border Patrolmen who also serve as a para-
military force to support Anglo interests on the border by control-
ling the ebb and flow of illegal immigration and harassing
American citizens of Mexican descent whenever it is necessary to
assert their authority.

The social structure of Presidio has changed in fundamental
ways from the earlier section. An evolving Chicano population
has lost much of its cultural pride and defiance of the foreign cul-
ture. Rather than occupying professional positions—like Francisco
Uranga—and owning land—like Francisco's wife Paz—they now
depend heavily on seasonal work in the Anglo-owned agricultural
fields. Moreover, Chicanos, rather than performing all the monot-
onous physical labor themselves, are employed by Anglos to con-
tract, transport, and supervise illegal Mexican workers who cross
the border in ever increasing numbers. Teléforo and his son Chale

keep a tight reign on the undocumented workers in their charge, occasionally threatening to report them to the Border Patrol if they do not produce. Chicanos, themselves oppressed, act as sur- rogate enforcers of Anglo authority and oppression, an integral el- ement of the colonialist labor system now firmly established in the Presidio-Ojinaga Valley.

Work and money are scarce. Most of the young men flee the Valley for larger nearby towns, Texas cities, or beyond, never to return. The few young men who stay squander their hard- earned wages at the bar, the movies, the pool hall, or in Ojinaga's whorehouses.

The Catholic Church plays an active role in maintaining the oppressive social structure. Presidio's priest preaches suffering, sub- missiveness, and acceptance of one's lot in life rather than strug- gling to free oneself from social and economic bonds, passivity, and injustice: "You have to suffer in order to inherit eternal life. That's why Christ loved and suffered. He set an example for us, and you've got to follow it."

Reyes Uranga's son, José, is now a grown man and married to Marcela. Like the children and grandchildren of many other of Presidio's original Chicanos, he has become a sharecropper on the land once owned by his family. His wife is pregnant with the child who throughout much of the second section is the first-person narrator who speaks from his mother's womb commenting on his parent's actions and feelings and reflecting on the town's past, present, and future.

This narrative device allows Brito to present economically a wide range of internal and external realities while maintaining the novel's gradual forward motion. Brito endows the fetus, who gives us a running interior monologue during much of the latter part of the novel's second section, with an unusual wisdom and percep- tiveness, which allows him to function as a substitute for a tradi- tional omniscient third-person narrator. An example of his wisdom is illustrated clearly in the fetus's following comment about his mother's difficult pregnancy: "She's carrying one hun- dred years, just imagine . . . one hundred years of history in her belly. Her sickness is words that can't come out from here, from inside. They stay stuck in the mouth of her stomach until they make her vomit." Brito describes the fetus as a seed that has been bouncing from womb to womb for a hundred years looking for a place to take root and chosen, as a kind of Christ figure, to lead his people out of their valley of sorrow.

In addition to providing a running commentary about contemporary events and to reflecting about the past, the unborn child's prophetic vision also serves to foreshadow his return as an adult to Presidio and the role he will play in its destiny as its authentic chronicler, its true poet/writer. He warns us to beware of poets who, like false prophets, sing the beauty of Presidio and lull its dwellers into a false sense of euphoria. "Some day soon, I will light a match and burn their [poets'] feet. Some day they will not sleep because the night will weigh heavily on them, like a ball chained to their feet or like a hard rubber ball. The bodies of the tired laborers will writhe in their beds and their bones will crunch." Marcela dies in childbirth. Her unnamed son grows into adolescence, leaves Presidio, and then, in the novel's third section, returns.

The presence of this anonymous character gives the second and the third parts of *The Devil in Texas* a highly autobiographical cast, for, as already mentioned, the author subsequently goes home to write about the town's history and future, using the novel as his voice. Also highly autobiographical is José's arrest and imprisonment for refusing to be drafted, just as Brito's father had done.

In the novel's short third section, "Presidio 1970," Brito has the narrator talking with his father who has died recently and will soon be buried. The son comments movingly and understandingly on his father's decades of toil in the fields, his refusal to kill his brothers in war, and his false hope that his lot and that of his people would someday improve. He expresses great tenderness for the wrinkled, emaciated old man to whom the land, time, and the Anglo have dealt many blows. The narrator decides to stay in Presidio, at least for a time, knowing that "The flame has got to be lighted, the one that died with time."

Formal Aspects

We have already briefly referred to the phantasmagoric quality of Presidio-Ojinaga that suggests the infernal world of spirits of

Juan Rulfo's *Pedro Páramo* and the physical, psychic, and spiritual abandonment of "Luvina." Like the Mexican author, Brito skillfully weaves into the sociohistorical dimension of his novel a rich texture of symbols and images that allows the work's mythic dimension to reinforce its social themes.

The most important of these symbols is the devil himself, who appears throughout the text associated with a series of other symbols that together constitute the novel's mythic/religious structure.[2] Brito does not depict the devil as a nefarious and mysterious force but as a character with quasi-human traits who lives among the people mocking them, making their lives difficult, disguising himself, and taunting and tormenting them at the most unexpected times. The image of this playfully evil figure has its roots in the folk Catholicism that Arnoldo de León describes as typical of the *tejanos* (Texans of Mexican descent). According to a traditional legend called "The Devil's Grotto," indigenous to the Presidio-Ojinaga area, Satan wreaks havoc on the people for their pagan ways. Finally, a priest uses a cross to overcome him and deliver the people from his power once they have converted to the Christian faith. They then are allowed to enjoy good health and abundant crops (Arnoldo de León 160 and 165). Brito, however, gives this native-born folk/religious tale a very different twist. His devil dwells in the deepest part of a cave "situated in the depths of the sierra of Santa Cruz." He emerges from this cave/grotto to dominate the entire Presidio-Ojinaga area. His dominance is represented by a very long swing mounted on a peak overlooking the valley below.

Rather than being redeemed by the triumph of good over evil as in the legend, the people of Presidio-Ojinaga have been condemned to a hundred years of hell. Presidio, which means jail in Spanish, is metaphorically this hell, a hell dominated by the presence of the devil in his multiple forms: "A stifling night, an oppressive night, a night that chokes people. Pale skulls of squeezed-out sap, skulls lost on the dry land of the cotton fields. False plants watered with sweat. Stuffed worms. Presidio, prison, hell. A devil laughing silently. Shhh!"

Significantly, the novel has no counterbalancing presence of a benevolent God. Within Catholic doctrine, the Pope and the ecclesiastical body of cardinals, bishops, and priests are his representatives. In *The Devil in Texas*, however, the parish priest, rather than mounting a spiritual campaign against evil, participates in the townspeople's remaining locked in endless poverty and oppression. He preaches acceptance and long-suffering rather than resistance of this earthly evil that has surrounded and dominated their lives for a hundred years. The priest, and through him the Catholic Church, rather than protecting his flock from evil as does the priest of the "Devil in the Grotto" legend, delivers them to the devil. He does so by cooperating—if not consciously than at least inadvertently—with the Lynch family and the other Anglos to keep the Chicano population powerless.

The complicity of the Catholic Church in maintaining the status quo is, of course, a common theme in much of Chicano and Latin American creative and social science literature. Except for the priests, the nuns, and the faithful who believe in and practice the tenets of Liberation Theology, the Catholic Church has historically cooperated with social and political elites to deny the faithful their basic human rights.

The powerlessness of the Church in the face of evil is demonstrated dramatically in the second section when the devil, disguised in a blond wig and a Stetson hat, enters God's very sanctuary and appears before Marcela right after she has received Holy Communion at Mass. He winks at her and then disappears, leaving her emotionally distraught, a state from which she never recovers.

Brito's use of the devil is clear: The Chicano population of Presidio lives an eternal hell that is not the result of the vague theological notion of Man's fall from grace but rather was created by the arrival of the Anglos. Further, no supernatural figure will deliver them from their valley of tears. Although the return to Presidio of the anonymous narrator in the third section does suggest a Messianic intervention, Brito seems to indicate that the Chicanos of Presidio must redeem themselves through social action and resistance by throwing off the bonds of oppression. The devil who lives among them is not, then, merely a fantastic and magical figure but the Anglo himself: Ben Lynch (who is identified explicitly as the "Green Devil") and his descendants; the Texas Rangers; the United States Border Patrol; the FBI that pursues José; the sheriff; the landowners; and all the other agents of oppression. Brito merely draws on the folk/religious tradition to reinforce the novel's underlying social theme.

The imagery associated with the devil is quite involved and extended throughout the novel. He is represented as both a human-like figure who disguises himself in various garbs—a handsome stranger wearing goat's feet at a dance; a railroad stationmaster; a dandy who attends parties; a fancy Texas cowboy who appears before Marcela—and as the classical biblical serpent. In the latter guise, Brito associates him with the serpentine flow of the Rio Grande that separates Mexico and the United States, Mexicans from Chicanos. He is described variously: early in the novel he is "laughing in his waterbed"; "master of the rivers"; and a serpent that tries to devour the illegal workers who wade across the river's swirling waters.

At the same time that we associate him with the menacing watery obstacle that separates family from family, we also view him as the creator of the bridge that spans the river: "The bridge was the work of the devil. (The bridge is the devil's rainbow: two goat's feet with each one planted in a graveyard. The bridge is a slide to make you die laughing, right, Jesús?)" This apparent contradiction between the bridge as obstacle and the bridge as joiner is explained simply by the fact that the structure gives Anglo authorities the ability to control human traffic from the Mexican to the Texas side of the border. Whereas before, Chicanos—Jesús, son of Don Pancho, for example—ferried their own across the river on rafts, now Anglos control the crossing. The juxtaposition of the river and the dual images of bridge and the devil's swing from one side to the other forms a cross. But rather than serving as a redemptive symbol, it mocks and defies the very positive meaning the cross carries in the folk/religious tradition. Rather than warding off evil, it embodies it.

In addition to the devil and the bridge, the town's fort plays an important symbolic role in *The Devil in Texas*. The first Spanish army detachment built it on a hill overlooking the valley in 1683 to defend against marauding Indians. At some point in the ensuing two hundred years it was abandoned after having ceased to function as a military stronghold. It was then used by people seeking high ground and refuge during sporadic flooding of the Rio Grande. After 1883, however, the fort assumes an especially ominous character for Presidio's Spanish-speaking population because it is there that Ben Lynch has massacred twenty-six of his

Chicano ranchhands for stealing horses. Their spirits now are said to roam from room to room mixing freely with devils who some believe also inhabit the site. Brito's description of the abandoned fort precedes a long section in which the souls—*ánimas en pena*—talk among themselves:

> There, near Presidio, the fort rises up at the place they call the Barren Hillside like a crumbling castle. It is an adobe castle without doors that the wind uses like a clay whistle, and there is always someone who goes by at night there with his hair on end and insists the castle is haunted. There are spirits and there are devils that roam from room to room. The unbelievers deny it, saying that it's a bunch of lies, but what is certain is that you can feel history. The legends of the people are the pages of a book that have been torn out and cast on the pyre.

Several anonymous voices then proceed to record for us the popular legends about Ben Lynch's arrival in the valley, his machinations to deprive the people of their land, the involvement of Lorenzo and other Chicanos in selling out their own people, the massacre, and so on. The voices refer to events in a roughly chronological fashion, the overall effect of which is to give an overview of the suffering, exploitation, death, and abuse that has occurred all along the border from the late 1880s forward. Jesús, one of the wandering souls, prophesies the birth of his nephew who in turn fathers the anonymous narrator of the the last part of the novel's second section.

Along with the devil, the fort as the lost souls' dwelling place, is another of the novel's folk/religious elements. As in the case of the former, Brito manipulates the latter's traditional meaning for his own novelistic purposes. Unlike the *ánimas en pena* of Catholic lore who wander about their earthly purgatory wailing and bemoaning their fate, the souls in *The Devil in Texas* are, like the devil himself, playful and mocking. They go about taunting each other and, especially, Ben Lynch, seeking their revenge on him without fear of retribution. In death all the souls who inhabit the fort are equal.

The Devil in Texas within Contemporary Chicano Literature

It is unusual that although the United States-Mexican border plays a dominant role in the history of Chicanos in this country it has not become an important literary space in contemporary Chicano letters. This is not to say that many writers do not touch on historical, cultural, linguistic, and psychological issues of immigration, the undocumented worker, the exploitation of cheap labor, and living in the breach between two countries. For example, José Antonio Villarreal in *Pocho* and Richard Vásquez in *Chicano* use the trek northward from Mexico to the United States and the border crossing as an essential phase in their fictional families' assimilation and acculturation into American society. This is also the case of Ernesto Galarza's autobiographical work *Barrio Boy*. Such writers treat the border ambivalently, for while its crossing usually represents renewed hope for a better way of life, it is also associated with the loss of one's national and cultural identity, the exchange of the familiar—however undesirable that may be—for the unknown.

Writers such as John Rechy, who deals more directly with living along the border, also view it ambivalently. This is nowhere more clearly set forth than in his first novel, *Cities of Night*, in which the young male protagonist leaves his native city of El Paso to embark upon his search for a place in which he can escape intense self-examination. El Paso is at once a source of fond nostalgia and the cause of his unhappiness. Other writers such as Ron Arias, in his novel *The Road to Tamazunchale*, refer fleetingly to the border.

Perhaps the closest parallels to Brito's use of the border as literary space are found in some of the novels of Rolando Hinojosa's Klail City Death Trip Series; in Miguel Méndez's *Peregrinos de Aztlán, The Dream of Santa María de las Piedras*, and a few of his shorter works; and in a few of Estela Portillo Trambley's short stories.

Rolando Hinojosa's fictional Belken County is located somewhere in Texas's Lower Rio Grande Valley, hundreds of miles downriver from Presidio-Ojinaga. While Hinojosa does not incorporate the Mexican dimension of the border experience as directly as Brito, it is implicit in the lives of his characters who have strong family ties in Mexico dating back to the Spanish Escandón

Expedition of the late eighteenth century that founded many of the settlements on both sides of the river. Also implicit are the rigid class structure and colonial labor system that Brito reconstructs so vividly in *The Devil in Texas*. The interaction between Chicanos and Mexican nationals and the particular dynamic of drug smuggling along the border form the basis for Hinojosa's recent detective novel *Partners in Crime*.

Miguel Méndez's novel *Peregrinos de Aztlán* is a complex world of oppressed Yaqui Indians and Chicano barrio-dwellers on both sides of the Arizona-Sonora border. While the specific historical experience that is this novel's backdrop is different, it has in common with Brito's work the same substructure of socioeconomic oppression rooted in both colonial Mexico and a profit-driven Anglo cheap labor economy. Most of the novel is narrated by Loreto Maldonado, an old Yaqui Indian who brings into focus the more than half a century of his people's collective suffering. Through other characters such as El Cometa, Pedro, El Vate, and Lorenzo, Méndez reveals the seamy underbelly of life in border barrios, a tenuous existence perpetuated by both upper-class Mexicans and wealthy Anglos for their own selfish economic interests. The participation of the Yaqui Nation in the Mexican Revolution, which subsequently betrayed them, is linked to the Chicano participation in the Vietnam War. Like Brito, Méndez experiments with language as well as temporal and spatial fragmentation. Anonymous speakers populate both novels and there is a close tie between Méndez's wandering *peregrinos* [pilgrims] and Brito's *ánimas en pena*. In his second novel, *The Dream of Santa María de las Piedras*, Méndez uses the border as a divisionary line between two worlds that are equally corrupt and doomed: a technologically superior but valueless U.S. society and a moribund Mexican rural society forgotten by the Mexican Revolution and the bureaucrats far off in Mexico City.

Estela Portillo Trambley, an El Paso-based writer, uses this West Texas border city in the title story of her collection *Rain of Scorpions and Other Stories*. Her story is set in Smelter Town, a community of Chicano industrial workers close to El Paso that lives under poisonous sulphur dioxide clouds spewed out by the local smelter. Somewhat like Brito's anonymous narrator who returns to Presidio in search of an intangible inner peace he eluded

by fleeing his roots, Portillo's Fito, a Chicano militant, concludes
that he will find his freedom in Smelter Town, not in some vague
notion of homeland divorced from social reality.

While contemporary Chicano writers such as Hinojosa, Mén-
dez, and Portillo Trambley use the literary space of the United
States-Mexican border, in Brito's work it becomes a more encom-
passing, more totalizing reality. Because his intent is to probe and
render poetically the static character of a small Chicano/Mexican
river community over its hundred-year history, it is only appropri-
ate that his treatment of this space be fuller and deeper than that
of the other writers. Presidio-Ojinaga is, after all, the protagonist
of *The Devil in Texas.* Ben Lynch, Francisco Uranga, José, Reyes,
Marcela, the Texas Rangers, the Border Patrol, the souls of the
departed, and the anonymous narrator himself are merely support-
ing actors who perform different roles on its historical stage. The
props on the stage have changed somewhat from the nineteenth
century, but the stage itself has remained constant.

Brito is not the only Chicano writer who incorporates fantas-
tic, magical, and folk/religious elements to give his narrative a
mythic quality, but he does it as well as any other. Perhaps the
closest parallel to *The Devil in Texas* is Ron Arias's *The Road to
Tamazunchale*, a novel which, because it takes place in the main
character's dreams, has an illusory, ambiguous quality. Like Brito,
Arias creates a splendid combination of social commentary and
artistic contemporaneity. Just as Fausto Tejada journeys back and
forth at will in time and space, a Peruvian *llama* herder and his
flock appear mysteriously on a Los Angeles freeway, and a small
cloud moves about in a cloudless sky, Brito has an unborn child
speaking wise and prophetic words from its mother's womb, the
souls of the dead roaming the halls of an abandoned fort, and a
ubiquitous devil appearing in different disguises and swinging from
a mountain top over his domain.

In addition to his original use of the border as literary space
and his manipulation of fantastic elements, Brito excels among
contemporary Chicano novelists in his artful incorporation of dif-
ferent linguistic registers in *The Devil in Texas.* While it is not
apparent in the translated text, the original Spanish version re-
flects the author's keen sense of language. Salvador Rodríguez del
Pino, in his study of the novel, has listed several distinct levels:

standard Mexican Spanish; regionalisms; Texas English; Texas Spanish; the argot of the 1950s *pachuco;* and even an example of the Tarascan Indian group (Rodríguez del Pino 105-106). Like Miguel Méndez and Rolando Hinojosa, Brito was concerned about giving an accurate and authentic view of the border Chicano; the successful use of an authentic language to fit different individuals and situations aided him immensely.

The publication of Brito's novel in its English version is sure to capture the attention of a reading public eager to learn more about Chicanos in general and about our literature in particular. Readers of *The Devil in Texas* will not be disappointed, for they will discover in the following pages both a fine piece of writing as well as an example of the social commitment that has characterized Chicano literature since the mid-1960s. It is our strong hope that after finishing this work, the reader will go on to explore the great variety and inviting panoply of literary offerings by other Chicano authors, authors who, like Aristeo Brito, add an important dimension to contemporary American letters.

University of Arizona

Notes

[1]Salvador Rodríguez del Pino provides an excellent biographical overview of Aristeo Brito in his book *La novela chicana escrita en español: cinco autores comprometidos*. (See "Works Consulted" for the full citation.) The biographical information provided in this section draws extensively from Rodríguez del Pino's work.

[2]Justo S. Alarcón has done a very interesting and perceptive study of the role of the devil in *The Devil in Texas*. He focuses on the multiple metamorphoses the figure of the devil undergoes during the course of the novel. (See "Works Consulted" for the full citation of Alarcón's article.)

Works Consulted

Alarcón, Justo S. "La metamorfosis del diablo en *El diablo en Texas* de Aristeo Brito." In Francisco Jiménez, ed. *The Identification and Analysis of Chicano Literature*. New York: Bilingual Press, 1979. 253-267.

Barrera, Mario. *Race and Class in the Southwest. A Theory of Racial Inequality*. Notre Dame: University of Notre Dame Press, 1979.

Brito, Aristeo. *El diablo en Texas*. Tucson: Editorial Peregrinos, 1976.

de León, Arnoldo. *The Tejano Community, 1836-1900*. Albuquerque: University of New Mexico Press, 1982.

Lewis, Marvin. "*El diablo en Texas*: Structure and Meaning." In Francisco Jiménez, ed. *The Identification and Analysis of Chicano Literature*. New York: Bilingual Press, 1979. 247-252.

Martínez, Julio and Francisco Lomelí, eds. *Chicano Literature. A Reference Guide*. Westport, CT: Greenwood Press, 1985. 77-83.

Montejano, David. *Anglos and Mexicans in the Making of Texas, 1836-1986*. Austin: University of Texas Press, 1987.

Rodríguez del Pino, Salvador. *La novela chicana escrita en español: cinco autores comprometidos*. Ypsilanti: Bilingual Press, 1982.

Tatum, Charles. *Chicano Literature*. Boston: G. K. Hall, 1982.

The Devil in Texas

I come from a small town called Presidio, which means prison in
Spanish. It rises up dry and barren there, in the farthest corner of
the earth. I'd try to describe what it's really like to you, but I can't,
because it appears in my imagination as an eternal vapor. I would also
like to capture it in an image for an instant, like a painting, but my
mind becomes filled with long shadows, shadows that whisper in my ear,
telling me that Presidio is a long way from heaven. Being born there is
like being born half dead. Working there means attending to one's tasks
silently, unconcerned by the fear of the tourist who comes to town and
leaves frightened by the empty sound of suffering souls he hears. Per-
haps these voices are what keeps me from portraying my village as it
really is, for when they speak to me they shatter my head and soul as if
a mad dog had played with me, leaving the remains of crumpled bodies,
bodies perforated like a sieve through which the water irrigates the fields
green with drunken sweat and laughter stifled by some damn uniforms
with maps of the U.S. on their right arm, searching for those who soak
themselves in the river that fertilizes the devil's eyes plants mocking the
people and a Holy Child playing marbles on his knees while he waits for
his father to come back from prison, an unknown scarecrow, a child
waiting on a swing, thief of the wind, a child who hears the sighs in the
water, in a fortress trembling with the howling of funereal dogs at mid-
day, and the child dies at night, the old woman cries, a fetus thinks at
night, night, night as long as infinity, a heavy night, monotonous like
lying history the same as the prostitutes, although they have good reason
and history doesn't, because in the pens on this side Ojinaga's skinny
cows fetch a good price, to be fattened at the expense of others, and the
church meanwhile is falling apart every day except on Sunday, as well
as the houses of cheese and chocolate gnawed by rats because there is no
cement and the ancient privies, thrones of the Catholic kings now made
of tin siding and the bathrooms in the open air in the middle of winter
wrapped in canvas so the eyes can't penetrate or in a bathtub in the
middle of the room on Saturday to sprinkle the dirt floor, dirt-land with
mounds of firewood forbidden to all except the renter who knows the
bounty of the Lord who has stores that give credit for food and rationed
gasoline, but medicines are not sold in the pharmacies because there are
no doctors, only leaves of laurel, rosemary, rue, and mint for the chil-
dren with upturned rheumy eyes, and the mothers feel as if they were in
labor when they eat chorupes, beans with wild quelite, and deviled meat
with azadero but penicillin cures all ills amen when the trucks loaded

*with the humiliated spit at the blasphemous sun with the stench of ap-
proaching death, a smell that penetrates, penetrates, penetrates the
melted, hunched-over, broken-down spine, almost almost embracing the
melon that if you eat it it'll give you cramps if your body doesn't go
limp on you it slips away and your mind flies away in the sultry air but
be careful because they pack you off in the refrigerated Santa Fe car
and they carry you off to Disneyland while the government map asks
you if you're legal from the land sown with brothers of your brothers of
your brothers amen and the border bridge closes at midnight so a lock
can be put on hell even though the whole river used to being an owl
slips through and you don't even need the sun any longer because
you're a plant, you're barren, worn-down land, and the devil is tired of
laughing in his waterbed because the good father went at midday up the
mountain in a procession to banish him so they say and so the doors
would open along the whole river and people could cross without fear
and the cross on the top is blessed at the same time the devil is getting
ready to go out dancing and the crazy dudes can hardly sit still in the
drugstores with jukeboxes playing Elvis Presley Fats Domino Little Ri-
chard and the blob that creeps and you ain't nothing but a hound dog
finding your thrill on Blueberry Hill dancing alone with pointy shoes
with taps tapping tap tapping shoes down the street unpaved no sound
lowriders dragging their two pipes with fender skirts, skirts to cover their
shame God save us, save us, the chickens say in the chicken coops of
the houses when the cantinas close and the pool table with its broken
pockets but still ten cents a game after Tarzan movie over Tarzans wild
all over, shouts, blows on the chest on the chest of Tarzan the monkey
man who came to save the poor Indians in a school where they were
taught to fragment languages by a goatherd who taught sciences because
he knew how to drive them into dried-up pastures because the pumps
stole all the water traca traca trac the whole night long until they sucked
air and died because the cotton gin never stopped, with its whooooooo it
sucked up the trailers called the Chancla and Mocha and Golondrina
names given by the people like a stamp of possession fifty-fifty while all
the tenant farmers proud of being bosses of the lands that used to belong
to them "I pay with tools, poison, money, you kick in your life and you
give me half, that okay?" because you go and you go as hard as you
can as hard as you can and you don't earn a thing the whole year but
"how about bringing in the crop of your life? you'd never seen a thou-
sand dollars all in one place they lie safe in a piggy bank while you*

don't pay bills that add up to fifteen hundred dollars and you buy a truck without gasoline to carry your workers because you're the boss, proprietor, symbolic sower and you help the less fortunate work like dogs when you pay them part of the crumb that belongs to you from the crumb your boss paid you you humble slave, never knowing when you stepped on someone else's head it meant other peoples' heads would get stepped on in turn, God forgive them, because over on the other side, a dog's life, "hell my friend, where from?" "from Michoacán" dressed in clothes made from bags of flour and sandals with rubber soles that say Goodyear which Presidio never knew, to you, Presidio the fortunate, and to you, father who art from Presidio, Amen.

Presidio 1883

T HE SNAKE, STRETCHED OUT like a tiger's tail between the
candles that had gone out a long time before, begins to
wiggle. The playful critter's smiling because it's the master
of the world, master of this abandoned chapel, master of the rivers,
of the towns situated across from each other, master of the people.
And that makes it feel good.

Now it slithers along over the scapularies and the relics, nu-
merous limbs and heads and all shapes of metallic human bodies
and slips down onto the floor. With its tongue darting out it snakes
slowly outside through the battered door and begins to climb to-
ward the roof of the chapel, strangling the base of the Holy Cross.
It rests for an instant in this position and then wraps itself around
the top part of the cross. Now comfortably entwined, it gazes out
over its surroundings. Nothing has changed, it thinks, since the
friars made their way down the river many years ago. It remembers
that from the very beginning they tried to cheat it, wrest its do-
main away, the valley that they gave the name of La Junta de los
Ríos, the meeting of the rivers. But only time is permanent, it
thinks. What is left of that church and that mission? Nothing.

From up there it imagines the Presidio-Ojinaga valley to be like a
green arrowhead outlined by the rivers, and it is pleased with its
imagination. Then it focuses on Lynch's fields, where heads pop
out from time to time, and it smiles with pleasure. This time the
heads are like roosters sunk among the waters of a scummy lake.
The image suddenly fades with the whistle of the train crossing
the bridge, and the serpent observes how, just when it's about to
cross over to the Mexican side, it comes to a brief stop. Then it
continues in slow motion, and the serpent smiles again. What an
imagination! The river and the train: a crooked and drunken
cross, a serpent cross, a melting cross. But it quickly tires of the
game of images and begins to think about what it heard yesterday.
That tomorrow more people are coming from the interior to work
in the fields of Presidio. Stupendous! And like a child with a new
toy, the serpent rapidly slides off contented. Then it begins the
descent to the base of the mountain where its cave is located.

CHAVA THE IDIOT FAILED to hear the four soldiers singing. But
their shouting at the mules made him jump and come out from
behind a mesquite tree. Then, as if he'd seen a ghost, he threw

away the skin from the banana he was eating and ran off with his hands over his ears. He didn't stop running until he reached the corner where the widow Nieves lived. Meanwhile, the soldiers were laughing uproariously over the scare they'd given the idiot until he had disappeared. After their attack of laughter died out, the mule driver ordered one of them to go announce their arrival.

"Tell Ben we got the merchandise and that we'll meet him over there at the fortín."

Sam answered by touching a hand to his cap and spurred his horse off toward the nearby house of the landowner on the outskirts of town. Meanwhile the covered wagon continued toward the fort.

Chava knelt for a long time behind the Nieves house with his eyes covered. Between Hail Marys and fits of trembling, he sang a song about a pretty little fish that refused to leave the water because its mother had told him that if he left the water, he would die right away.

When the woman heard him, she came out of her house and told him he could take his hands away from his eyes. The idiot answered her that the dead men on the mules made him hurt and that he wanted his mother.

"Stop all that right now. Would you like something to eat?"

". . ."

"Well, if you want to eat, come on in and stop biting the fingernails you don't even have."

The woman went back in, and Chava continued to pick at his face. He tried to pull out the few hairs on his chin where the skin was about to start bleeding, and he spent a few moments in serious concentration working at it. But then he began to talk to the dead, his mother Pancha, Aunt Cuca, and his fiancée Rosario. Then he decided to proceed down the street, barefoot and half naked under the 120-degree heat. "Pretty little fishy, don't you want to come and play with my hoop? We'll go out into the yard. My mother told me not to go out." But little by little Chava's song faded away along the road.

"DON'T KID YOURSELF, NEIGHBOR. Don Ben did real well this year with his harvest. That's why he's going to throw a party. Otherwise he wouldn't . . ."

"Come on, neighbor. Do you mean to say that the man has no heart?"

"No, all I mean is that it's to his advantage, since now he can afford it, and our old folks deserve it."

"You're right. They really break their backs."

"Ramón says that this time he is going to shine at the party that . . ."

"Right. He told Chindo to kill three large calves so there would be enough. There'll be two dinners. . . ."

"Really? And where's the bash going to be held afterward, neighbor?"

"Special people are coming over from Marfa. They say he even ordered five barrels of beer, the one with the star."

"But, listen, weren't they going to hold the dance there in the fort, too?"

"It doesn't look like it. . . . According to Jorge, the guy with the big snout, they're going to play in the park."

"I'm sure not going to miss it. I'm all excited, and even though my old man isn't here, I still plan on showing up. What about you?"

"Come on, do you think I'm a stick-in-the-mud? If you go, I'll go with you."

"Let's go, then."

As soon as Ben received the message, he immediately began to saddle the horse.

"No, Ben, please don't do it, for the love of God."

"And for the love of a dead dog," the old man answered as he mounted his horse.

The woman didn't answer, left alone with the sound of the hooves ringing in her ears. When the man disappeared around the bend in the road, she locked herself in, cursing her husband's anger. Rosario felt like going out into the road and shouting at the people to hang him. But she still hoped that Ben's heart would soften, and that made her calm down. She busied herself by ordering the servants to clean the tables and the party tablecloths. Ah! and that damn curtain that he'd had her make. Only Rosario knew what its purpose was, for behind it the evil of man would be hidden. She shouldn't ever forget it, he told her, but she was unwilling to take it from the cabinet, as though this action would stop the anger of her old man. Perhaps he wouldn't come for it, perhaps . . .

"PERHAPS WE SHOULD try to . . ."

"No. You do as I say."

"Sir, our orders . . . It would be better if . . ."

"No."

"Captain Ramsey said some innocent . . ."

"You tell the Captain I'm going ahead as planned. He'll get the damn thing back tomorrow. Now just help me get it into that room."

The soldiers unloaded the small cannon and rolled it toward the center of the room where Ben wanted it. Then he asked them to aim it toward the door leading to the dining room. Those who had betrayed him deserved no better than this, because they were thieves. Those bastards would see how they were going to pay for betraying him, the horse thieves.

THE NAME OF THE HORSE THIEF was Jacinto, and he had never thought about the possibility that someone had squealed on him. Thus when Lorenzo, Ben's foreman, crossed the river to bring him the invitation, he didn't hesitate at all in accepting it.

"But why so . . ."

"You deserve special treatment, Mr. Jacinto. Mr. Ben sent me expressly because he considers himself very grateful. No one has helped us so much like you and your companions. You don't forget something like that. So call them together; the party's waiting for you there. Your dinner is a special one, at eight o'clock."

Lorenzo was right, Jacinto thought, although the old tightwad would still be as miserly as ever. Otherwise, why would they be robbing him? Only in that way, by robbing him, were they able to pay themselves for the trouble they went to without receiving a just wage. But maybe Ben finally recognized the workers' worth and as a consequence invited all his friends. And by the time he'd added them up, there were twenty-five.

THAT AFTERNOON EVERYONE had a great time at the fort. But it seemed strange to them that only the salon used for serving was open. Nor could they understand why other guests like Jacinto

and his men had been invited to eat later. Meanwhile, Don Ben-
ito Lynch, all decked out and smiling like an angel, chatted
among the people. And thus, little by little, they forgot about the
locked doors. Besides, the food was as good as the beer, and, car-
amba, the dancing that followed!

When the sun went down, the people scurried out into the
yard where the Frontiersmen where getting ready to play, and by
eight o'clock the fort was vacant. Only the special guests were left
waiting for their reception. Meanwhile Chava, who had not
wanted to eat, continued to crouch behind a nearby dwarf oak as
though he had taken root there. He was still trembling, pensively.
He remained there until the loud shot of the cannon made him
run out hysterically. On the other hand, the people at the dance
didn't even hear the muffled pistol shots that finished off those
who were left still living. The only thing that ran through the
dance that night was the rumor that a handsome stranger wearing
goat's feet had been dancing.

"IN THOSE DAYS people sowed wheat, corn, things like that to be
harvested before September because then the river would come
and they would have to abandon their shacks out in the fields
and come to the fort. The fort would be completely filled by poor
people who had lost their shacks.

"Once when I was still a little girl, we planted there in the
field where the best harvest was taken. We had a chile field that
gave regularly because we really worked it. There was always
someone to buy the chile cheap, but it was enough for us to get
by. Lorenzo had a very destructive cow. He put it in a pen, and it
would crawl out itself. It would get out, do its damage, and the
next morning it would be back in the pen. When it would get
into the irrigated chile, it would trample the shoots, and the cow
stayed fat by doing us in. So Papa complained many times to
Lorenzo, but Lorenzo would never admit that the cow did any
damage, always asking, 'But where's your proof?' The proof, of
course, was the tracks: Papa would follow the tracks back to the
pen, but Lorenzo wouldn't admit to it. My papa always told him
very clearly, 'Look, you'd better watch out, because I'm going to
catch her, and you'll have to pay me for all the damage—go on,
just take a look at what she's ruined. Just look at how the ears of

corn are bent.' But no, Lorenzo's always been a real devil. Anyway, my papa went to speak to Fermín, who was the judge in those days. Fermín went to advise Lorenzo, but he got the same 'Where's your proof?' Dad told Fermín, 'We have a dog that can catch her. I'll turn the dog loose on her, and, I promise you, when he catches her the cow won't come back.' Fermín said that was fine, because he'd already told Lorenzo to control the cow or he would have to pay for the damages the animal had done, and he hadn't gotten anywhere, either.

"Well, we heard the cow. The dog obeyed my brother's orders very well, so my father spoke to him and told him the cow was out. He said, 'Turn the dog loose on her,' and he'd no sooner said it than he turned the dog loose on the cow. What a barbarian! He tore her snout to pieces and made her jump the fence. But he didn't let go, because once he'd sunk his teeth into an animal, he wouldn't let go.

"The next day, Lorenzo showed up at the house with a 30-30, cussing my papa out. My papa said, 'Hold on a minute, I'll be right there.' Then my papa went and grabbed a two-barreled shotgun. He said, 'Come on, let's see who goes first.' Well, Lorenzo backed down. And that's how the thing went."

"Nobody leaves this world, Daughter, without paying for his crimes."

"Why is Uncle Lorenzo that way, Mama?"

"Because he's full of the devil."

"But he only brought the message, Doña Mónica."

"That's not the only thing he's done, Eduvijes. You just be sure, Lorenzo is going to pay dearly for this."

"Don't you think, Daughter, that we were that hard up. This land that Ben owns belonged to my mother Mónica, my aunt Paz, and to Victoria and Zenobio. They owned the land from here almost down to the river. In those days, my aunt Paz was mentally ill. Apolonio Varela, married to Aunt Victoria, lived in Marfa, and they came to take her to work for a while. My aunt had a small suitcase where she kept her papers to the land, and they never realized they had taken the papers away with them. She resisted being there for two or three days, but they made

her sign the papers, selling to old man Ben. It was all because
of her son Lorenzo.

"At that time your uncle Zenobio and the others hired a law-
yer, Francisco Uranga, who we all called Don Pancho. But they
told him they couldn't pay him because things were bad. But no,
he told them they could pay him later. And then Ben's lawyer
came in on the other side, but Don Pancho won. He said he
could sell Aunt Paz's part and do whatever he wanted to, but
nothing more. So Ben and Lorenzo, my aunt's son, came to an
agreement. Ben greased the man's palm, gave him money, and put
him to work in the riverbed. And when Papa went to work in the
fields in the morning, Lorenzo had already knocked the wire fence
down. Then they asked him why, and he said that it was because
he was going to make it straight. That if we had beat them that
time, we weren't going to again. So Uncle Zenobio, Papa, and
the rest believed that since he was going to put up a berm so the
river couldn't get in, it was to their advantage. Lorenzo was the
slick one, and he screwed things up. He was so heartless that he
cheated the crazy old woman, his own mother. May God forgive
him, Daughter."

No ONE EVEN KNEW how they got to Presidio, but the fact is that
they were riding horses and shouting. They came from the south
of Texas with one idea: to bury the people alive and to thrust
them even deeper into hell. And even though the invaders had
come to the darkest corners of the earth, they knew how to be
creative. In Presidio they discovered that the land and the people
had lucrative possibilities, but some of them had to be buried first.
A few months later, they went straight down to the river to drown
the launch operator, Don Pancho's son, in the water. First because
he had struck Ben, and second because there were larger interests
in the transportation of people. But the only thought on Jesús's
mind was his sister Rosario. What business did that bastard gringo
have dating her? Come on! Stay the hell away! So one night they
buried Jesús under water, filling the launch and his body with dirt
so the two would stay submerged. The stone hung from his neck
would make sure of that. Meanwhile, his lawyer's diploma was
only good for Don Francisco to wipe his ass with, since the case
was thrown out of court. And the worst part was that his daughter

ran off with the gringo before the year was out. Shit! Not only down, but out as well! But from now on, watch out, you bunch of bastards! Later, his brother Santamaría continued to ferry people across even after they said there would soon be an international bridge, and as soon as it was built, people would have to use it to get across. But Santamaría, armed with a carbine, ignored that law because people preferred the launch. Go through the check-point and show papers? Go straight to hell. The bridge was the work of the devil. (The bridge is the devil's rainbow: two goat's feet with each one planted in a graveyard. The bridge is a slide to make you die laughing, right, Jesús?)

"The Lynches have their history; the old people, anyway. They killed people like barbarians. There were some poor people work-ing for them, and when they tried to leave after a year, they took their pay with them. Sure, I'll pay you, they would tell them, but then they would take them away and kill them. People didn't pro-test because there was nothing to eat. Things were very bad. Around here we had to get by on cups of atole or whatever. So what could anyone do about it? Sure, there were men like Papa who weren't bothered by having to kill someone. And so there were men like him who could do whatever they wanted to with anyone they wanted to, but they would think about not leaving the families all alone. Because anyone can be courageous. But Papa was all tied down with us. Otherwise, how long would the Lynches last? You could just chop their heads off and cross over to the other side. Because don't think there were only Lynches around here. I can still remember how that Captain Gray used to kick ass. He belonged at that time to the Texas Rangers. He was real mean."

Don Pancho couldn't understand the broken message that Chava the idiot was giving him, so he did his best to calm him down. Once he had calmed down a little, he opened the store's storage room and spread a sarape over the bags of beans so Chava could lie down. At least he won't spend the rest of the night wan-dering around in a daze, Francisco thought. Then he put the chain on the door and went home to his house-store-printshop, certain that truth would come out with the light of day.

But the night turned out to be a long one for Pancho. A few hours later a pair of eyes full of pure rage showed up at his door. Reyes handled the carbine as though it were made of paper; at the same time he poured out of the corner of his mouth the story of what happened at the fort. When he finished, the old man invited him in, but Reyes refused. He said he preferred to go find out the truth, since Chindo's word was often unreliable.

"Okay, but don't go doing anything foolish."

"That creep'll get his."

"Make sure first, Son, and be patient."

"That's what I'm going to do, make real sure."

"Then we'll talk about it. But don't forget, Reyes. It's never too late as long as you're still alive."

"Okay, old man."

Don Pancho went into his private office and there among books and piles of newspapers, he set about struggling against his cynicism. He meditated on his life and his career, which had been a real disaster. Nothing more. Failure, crashing failure, period. The dusty newspapers and books that surrounded him were the last vestiges of a fight he'd lost. Proof of his creative age? Even the question was stupid. He remembered how his own destruction matched the town's, how the two had been reduced to an insignificant microcosm, but one replete with history. For his part, he had been spurned by both governments because of his strong sense of justice. There was nothing left of the efforts he had made during his time to ensure basic human rights, and the only thing that consoled him was unearthing his truth buried under the dust. The issues of *The Frontiersman* he had saved in his office said it all. Perhaps someone would come someday and read them, but that would be after he was dead.

He remembered very well his first year of practice, because it was in that same year when the world he had built in the air during his studies collapsed around him. Reality, damn it, was something else. Life was lived by shouting and waving hats. He had soon realized that the career of a lawyer was not quite so illustrious, and even less when it was practiced in a town of impoverished conditions. Then he came to realize that the best way to help others and to help himself would be through journalism, and he immediately began to publish *The Frontiersman*, a small newspaper that was read not only by those who needed to read it but also by other publishers in the Southwest. His undertaking grew strong when to his surprise he began to receive newspapers from California, Trinidad, Colorado, Laredo, New Mexico, and from places where he never even suspected there were Mexicans. In time, the publication became a strong voice with one concern: polemics, denunciation, and protest over the life of Mexicans in these areas. Soon his words were being picked up by newspapers in Mexico, and the Mexican government did not take long to recognize Francisco Uranga's benefit to the country. He received his appointment as consul with great enthusiasm. The exact words? "To serve as representative of our citizens abroad as appropriate in the defense of their rights and principles as designated by the treaties between Mexico and the United States." Just as soon as he had received the appointment, he began to order by priority the tasks to be undertaken. First, the clarification of the question of properties that had been usurped in the Presidio valley and to discover how to validate claims on lands that had little by little been rolled away like a rug. (But he remembered that by that time it was already too late because the legal archives were written in another language and bore another seal.) Later, he would pursue the complicated question of citizenship, and for that he would have to contact the other consuls in the Southwest. And he would have to find quickly a more efficient way of arranging the repatriation of all those individuals who wished to go home, but who thought that the Mexican government had abandoned them. Another of the causes, and here he was emphatic, was the need to combat the insolence on the part of those who considered themselves the law, and crossed the border without prior authorization. This point was one of the touchiest, because he had seen numerous cases in which the person being pursued was taken out of Mexico in order to try him in a foreign court and in a foreign language. Yes, it was necessary to clarify the law of extradition so trammeled by the conqueror, although he knew that it was a very difficult task. On other occasions, the opposite occurred: the person accused by the Mexican authorities could not prove that he was a citizen of the United States, even when the treaty said that anyone not repatriated within two years would be considered a citizen. And the papers? They had vanished into thin air. Where are you from? From the land, sir. From wherever I can make a living.

It did not take long for Pancho Uranga to realize that he was
in the same whirlpool. Between the accumulation of paper and
the confusion, he lived as though sick and lost at sea. He ended
up with his hands tied with frustration, transformed into one of
those persons who know so much about how the world works that
they smirk as if to say: Jerks, what did you expect? God's blessings
wrapped in a blanket? Get it straight; humanity is rotten to the
core. And each time the devil won out, the thorn dug deeper,
and by the time he tried to extract it, it had already poisoned his
soul. By then he had taken up the pen as a sword. His writings
appeared in his own paper, *The Frontiersman,* in *The Tucsonian,*
The Spanish American, The Zurtian, The Voice of the People, and
forty other newspapers that were coming out at that time: "I
roundly denounce the usurpation of the lands and I support the
White Caps for having shown their weapons"; "I put my name to
the resolution of the unified Spanish American press which con-
demns the governor of New Mexico for calling us 'greasers' in the
English-language press of New York and who now has the nerve to
threaten us"; "I protest the filibustering expeditions of opportunis-
tic Yankees"; "I condemn discrimination in the workplace, in
schools, and in public establishments"; "I support the defenses
mounted by the Mexican Alliance"; "with anger and love I la-
ment the dissolution of our people and I weep for its future"; "I
am a partisan of the radical element of workers in San Antonio,
California, and New Mexico, not because I know they have
achieved something, but because it proves that we are still alive
and that there will be something for us to fight"; "I am suspicious
of the justice and the sentences meted out by judges that are
guided by the opinions of prejudiced witnesses; moreover, I know
that Manuel Verdugo was not guilty. I found out afterward that he
was sentenced to die in El Paso"; "I condemn the sale of black
slaves in Fayetteville, Missouri"; "for the information of the editor
of the aforementioned rag in Guadalajara, my efforts to repatriate
our people are genuine. And I do so because I know the sufferings
experienced in a country that is considered the best example of
democracy, and I also would have you understand fully, via exam-
ples, that our people here are not a bunch of tamale vendors, as
you so grossly describe us. The survey I print here contains the
number of persons of Mexican descent, and you should know that

of all those who responded, only four are in the business of selling tamales, and not because they are lazy but because of the adverse fortunes they have experienced. I have on numerous occasions appealed to the Mexican government to provide the money to provide transport for those who want to be repatriated, as well as to allot them a parcel of land; otherwise, what guarantee is there that they would live any better if they returned to Mexico? The problem now has its roots in the fact that the Chinese are willing to work for less wages"; "I would have the gentleman, who speaks without any basis when he says that those of us who are from here are the poorest and uneducated, know that, if we concede that he is right that the working family lives poorly, that doesn't mean we are uneducated. We recognize our circumstances and do what we can about them. Now, explain to me, Mr. Publisher, why you believe that these working people are the ones who least seek to be repatriated? On another occasion I would like you, instead of spewing out nonsense, to set yourself to thinking a little more. We, my colleague, do not wish to move from this land that we have always considered our own, and if I make the effort to repatriate some people, it is because I am moved by the hope that the Mexican government will help us"; "I would remind the governor of Chihuahua that he made a big mistake by conceding vast areas of land to the settlement companies, since all they do is take over the natural resources. In time these companies will go the same way as the great overlords who now exploit the poor mercilessly"; "I denounce publicly the misguided deeds of the consul in El Paso, who cooperated with the sheriff in the extradition of Rufino Gómez. The hundred pesos they paid him under the table will not serve to calm his conscience after the accused has been sentenced"; "I would never have believed that one of our own (from Laredo) would comment so unfavorably on the poetry that we publish in the literary section, and even less so over its being written in 'bastard' Spanish. We regret very much that these attitudes are so deeply rooted. Why is our colleague so blind to the facts? Better, why doesn't the gentleman lodge his complaints with the educational system or the federal government, which promised to respect our language and our culture? If there were schools where our maternal tongue were taught, perhaps you would have no reason to complain. But this is an ideal. You'd be

better off to spend your energies in assuring the well-being of your
children, since God knows they need it, rather than showing the
same attitude of superiority that we have experienced for so long."

Thus he pricked sensitivites with the tip of his pen, and it
wasn't too long before both governments considered him an en-
emy of harmony. By the time he defended the cause of Catarino
Garza, who provoked the uprising of workers in New Mexico
against the landowners and the government of Chihuahua, he had
ceased to be consul. It was a miracle he wasn't killed, although in
those days he would have preferred it, because nothing mattered to
him. The town he had defended with love now turned its back on
him, and that was what hurt the most. Some, as soon as luck
went their way, came down on him. "Old troublemaker, leave well
enough alone. Things are going well, and you threaten our posi-
tion with your stupidity. So either you shut up or . . ." *The Fron-
tiersman* died a death without glory. People were right, history
stops for no one. (History flows like water. Sometimes calm,
sometimes with the devil riding it, making it swollen and rabid.
Then it brings forth a deformed hand that stretches its fingers out
to infinity. Then the water's hand withdraws and becomes a claw,
leaving only a trickle in the bed of the Río Grande. Then the
people on their eternal migration return to form a twisted cross, a
miserable cross of flesh and water.) And since the history of my
race is that of the river, I thought, I am going to build a launch to
ferry them across. This will help me support myself, but I will
charge only those who can pay. It will also give me the opportu-
nity to guide people by setting them on the best road. "Go this
way and be careful with this and that, and if he doesn't give you a
job, follow the river until . . ." But before I do that, I'll gather my
belongings, my books, and move to Ojinaga. I will build a house
near the river on the other side, in order for our history not to be
washed away in the water. Many years after, when I lost Rosario
and I found out they were going to build the bridge, I wasn't even
surprised. Not even when I heard that they had drowned my
Jesús. My wound began to bleed again when he was buried a mess,
and I swore I would avenge him. But I couldn't, and I thought
you would avenge him, Reyes, being his brother. I didn't want
really to raise you to be an assassin. The weapons would come
later, and these only as a last resort. What I wanted to give you

first was book-learning, but not out of those that tell false stories. That's why I had you study with Mariana, my teacher, and not in that hovel of a school where they drill you with the idea that you should cut off the roots of the language that gave you birth. Then I would send you there to Presidio, but only after you knew the truth, why things are the way they are, when you would be proud to be a son of the people. But as you well know, you turned out a failure. I don't know why you were that way since childhood, Reyes. When I sent you to Mariana, after only a few days she came to tell me you had hit her back after she had struck you. I never even wanted to see your face. You didn't want to go to school, even though it earned you a lot of whippings; do you remember, Reyes? I still don't know how you learned what you do know. Perhaps from my books that you read on the sly, because I never saw you bother with anything. You're lazy and a bum. Busy yourself with the firewood so you can buy and sell or go help your uncle Santamaría with the launch, I told you, but no, you'd show up in the afternoon with food, firewood, and money. "And where did you get that money?" "I sold fish to the gringo down the bridge." "I told you not to go messing around with them! Damn kid!"

THE GALLOPING OF THE FIVE horses was cushioned by the loose sand of the river. The horsemen drew up to the shore, plunging themselves into the mud until they could reach the water. The boy Reyes was playing absentmindedly, and he didn't hear a thing because of his splashing in the water. The men looked at each other and smiled, ready to give him a good scare, but at that moment a horse couldn't fight off a tickle in his nose and snorted. The boy jumped like a fish struggling against the hook, and the men burst out laughing.

"Just look at the little devil. Come over here. Where are you from?"

"From here, from that house over there."

"Who's your father, and what does he do?"

"Francisco Uranga, Don Pancho, the man who runs the launch."

"Do you know this place well? Do you know where the gringos live?"

"Yes. This is where they killed my brother."

"Why did they kill him?"

"I'm not sure, but they say because it's against the law not to use the bridge."

"Fucking bastards. They still believe this land belongs to them. Just because it's on the other side of this damn puddle. And what the hell are you doing hanging around here?"

"I was fishing."

"All you're going to catch is a cold, dumb kid. Do you want to go with us? What do you say, boys? Can we use him?"

"Sure, why not, Chief?"

"Come on then, get dressed, and congratulations."

"No, sir, I don't want to go with you, and my father wouldn't . . ."

"Cut that stuff out. What the hell good is there in hanging around here?"

"Ramón, hand me that good one. There you are. Now then. Listen, I just know this is going to turn out right."

"The kid looks like an owl with such a large carbine and his eyes popping out, Chief."

They all laughed. Reyes didn't know that at that moment his brother Jesús was coming alive in him and that the indignation of half a century would begin to take shape that very day.

"I DIDN'T WORK IN SHAFTER, but when I was a girl, my sister Camila married Cipriano Alvarado and said, 'Don't stay here, let's go.' Then she sent for me and my brother Chente, but I told her real clear, 'I'm not going to spend all my time with you.' She said, 'Fine. Whenever you want to come, I'll go for you.' There were a lot of people in Shafter in those days, along with a lot of money because the silver mines were working. The men earned so much that even my little brother got the fever, as little as he was. But that's how it was with the poor. They died. When they went down into the mines, they came out sick, the poor devils. I think that's what my brother Chente died of."

"WHY DO I HAVE TO DIE, Eduvijes? Sister, I'm only twelve years old. That's no reason to cry. You've done what you could. I only want to know what life is like when you grow up. But you're grown up. Tell me, is life pretty, like it is when you're a child? That's how it seems to me, Vicke. . . . Vicke, your name, Eduvijes, is pretty, too, but I like Vicke better. . . . Last year when my dog died, I felt very bad, if only you could've seen me, because his eyes were very sad and he was still wagging his tail. Did you know that dogs wag their tails when they're happy? Is it true that he was happy, Vicke? When he was dying? Even when I'd hit him, he'd wag his tail. Are grown-ups like you? I felt very bad before he died, because I had hit him too. And before he died, I promised him I wouldn't do it again. Because I believe that no one has the right to hit you, to strike you, and if they do, you ought to hit them back. Because then you die and go to heaven without getting even. Well, that's what I used to think, Vicke, but not now. Because I believe that if the dog is so full of love like that, people must have even more. I say that because I feel more love than the dog, Vicke. Is that how it is with you? Damn it! You're crying! Don't cry, Vicke. Give me a smoke. I've never smoked, but now I want to see what it's like to smoke. Come on, light it for me. I wish you could wipe this sickness away, Vicke, the lump I have here in my chest. It sure hurts. Look, touch me here. I wish you could remove it. I want to cry, Vicke, but what would Don Jesús say? It would make me feel ashamed. What did he use to say? That men don't cry. Is that true, Sister? I wouldn't tell you this if he were here, but look, once I found him crying behind a tree. I never knew why, but if he saw you crying, he would carry you in his launch. Do you remember, before the bridge was built, how he would take people from one side to the other? I used to have a lot of fun with him. In those days we were all equal. It's not that we aren't anymore, but things have changed since they built the bridge. It's funny, Vicke. People feel apart. Aren't bridges supposed to be for just the opposite? Before, we could go see Grandma and Grandpa without . . . What are those papers for, Vicke? Why do those men ask for them all the time? Who are they? Have you ever seen the devil, Vicke? Is it true we're in hell? It's sure hot here, but this isn't hell, right, Vicke? My grandma told me that the devil lived in that cave where we went, do you remember? I don't believe it, because it's been blessed up there on the sierra. But they told me that he came to do us evil, that he was all over the river. Vicke, you're not talking. My chest hurts a

lot. Bring me a warm rag, please. This cigarette is no good. I
thought it would take the pain away. Why am I sick, Vicke? Why
don't they make me feel better, please? When you come back,
Vicke, get me into bed. I'm not comfortable here on the floor.
I don't know why they put me down here. Vicke, I don't want
to die!"

NIGHT STRETCHES OUT toward infinity. Like a black and sticky
piece of gum that envelops the river, the trees, the fields. Then it
reaches down to the houses and wraps itself around the people,
gluing them firmly to their beds, the floor, or wherever they were
caught sleeping. The silence is also dark and monotonous. Then
the moon comes out, emerging with the rhythm of the violins,
and the gum turns into mercury, laying a slippery coating down
over the universe. The river is platinum-colored, the leaves of the
poplars are silver, and everything is silver-colored like a snowy
night in other climes.

    Silver gives dimension to the night. It lengthens and multi-
plies the night. The moon is not death. The moon is life for the
people swarming around the river. The shadows take on life under
the moon. There is the moon, eating a cactus fruit, casting the
peels to . . . Moon, give me some, give me what you are eating.
You are my life and my adoration. I am you, moon. Your shadow.
I am the body that lights up the night, that stretches the night
out. I am a man of night, I am the life of night. I am the son of
She Who Weeps, and my name is Reyes, sons of bitches. I am the
brother of Jesús of the river.

IN THE DEEPEST PART of the cave situated in the depths of the
sierra of Santa Cruz, a ray of light falls on a still pool of water.
The serpent uses it as a mirror, a mirror that now reflects a hu-
man face. The image contemplates the mask full of laughter; a
dark blue suit, a cap to cover his pointy head where horns are
usually seen, and some shiny boots, also black. The boots don't fit
right on his rooster feet, but that's not important. It's only for a
few hours. As a final touch, the "stationmaster" serpent takes
down an oil lamp set aside for this occasion. Now he's all ready to
show up at the train station. Later, he'll exchange his mask for
that of a ranch hand, but only when he's ready to receive the five

hundred souls of the workers coming in from the interior. Once
outside, the devil in human form mounts his burro and heads him
toward the station.

The train station for beyond the grave is almost empty when
he gets there. That's strange, since there are always swarms of
people waiting for trains. Perhaps they've finally realized they
never run on time. The ticket seller confirms this to him. "The
train's running a few minutes late," he says. That's what he says,
but the devil knows very well that the word "minute" doesn't
mean a thing. That's why there are warnings fastened to the wall:
*Trains running to paradise leave on the hour, but their arrival depends
on the will of God.* The other warning corresponding to the line to
hell is also emphatic: *These trains run according to the will of man
and arrive when least expected.* Dumb, stupid people. It looks like
they never read what's obvious.

It's the first time the devil in human form has been in a train
station, and he feels the same expectation that a passenger or a
spectator experiences. He has also heard that the trains run late,
and since he's not used to waiting, he begins to have doubts about
himself. Now he's not so sure he heard the announcement right,
that today and at this hour the workers would arrive. "No, it's not
possible for me to be wrong. I'm real sure that the travelers de-
parted. There's never any doubt about that. But perhaps? . . .
The devil-man goes over to read the announcements to see if by
chance the information they contain will ease his doubts. "Let's
see. . . ." He reads, but it doesn't really help. Just stupidities:
". . . return tickets are not sold on the line to paradise; children
under seven travel free in their mothers' arms; there are no re-
duced fares; only good works can be carried as baggage in order to
avoid being detained; travelers of any nationality are allowed as
long as their passports are in order; the central ticket office is
open around the clock." Fools! Nothing more! The line to para-
dise went out of business a long time ago. The devil then moves
on to the announcement concerning hell: "No discounts, no mi-
nors, passengers may travel with as much luggage as they want,
but they must leave everything but their soul behind. . . ." Ah!
Here it is! ". . . *those who travel on this line may continue on the line
to paradise if a priest stamps that they've confessed on their tickets be-
fore changing to the death train.*" Son of a . . . ! Can it be possible?

What if the train got stopped out there, precisely for this reason?
Could there be some miserable party-pooper? Could there?

"The train's pulling in on track number five."

The few people begin now to stir while the masked man stands
there astonished. He hasn't even heard the puffing of the train.

"Please, ladies and gentlemen. Exercise caution. Please do not
approach until the train has come to a complete stop."

The devil stationmaster, lamp in hand, follows the bunch of
people so excitedly that he has forgotten to change his clothes.
"Now to detour those wearing huaraches," he thinks.

The passengers begin to get off the train. One, two, three . . .
then two . . . then . . . one. . . . They can be counted on one
hand. The train is empty. No, it can't be. The stationmaster
doesn't know what to think, and he stands there for a long time
until no one else gets off.

"But where are all the other people?"

"That's all there are, sir."

"Look here. There were supposed to be . . ."

"I told you there are no more. Don't pester me!"

The stationmaster turns red with anger and makes a screeching
sound as he smashes the lamp against the track. Then he lets
loose with a fart that could never have smelled human, disappear-
ing like a flash into the heavens. The burro is left braying for its
master, while at the corner of the station the Los Pepenados group
sings: "The devil went for a walk . . . and they gave him choco-
late . . . it was so hot that he burned his craw . . . it was so hot
he burned his craw . . . but ay, hah, hah, hah . . . hah hah hah
hah . . . but ay, hah hah hah hah . . . hah hah hah hah
hah. . . ."

THE FIVE HUNDRED ACRES of cotton were about to be lost because
of a lack of pickers. It had been Ben's first blow, and the situation
grew worse when the people from Presidio demanded a penny
more for each pound picked. There was no way to explain who
had had enough influence to cut him off. Besides, the "incident"
at the fort was so insignificant in proportion to the business he
conducted that he had forgotten it that very night. Previously, an
act of justice like this had not kept the water from flowing calmly
and lucratively. Why should it be different on this occasion?

What could have happened? Why had the government refused to allot him the five hundred souls he'd requested? He had no answer. He could not explain how the excursion that Governor Jones, his friend, had made to Mexico had failed.

Only Francisco Uranga and his son Reyes had the answer, and when the latter read the news in Marfa's *Century*, the tears flowed. They were tears of triumph that had waited for so many years, and they were tears of pleasure because his triumph had been double. The Mexican administration knew full well the mistreatment of its workers, but there were always more beneficial moves, and it was easier to hide things with money. Hell! It was just because of that that Don Pancho couldn't believe it. To have brought them to their knees was almost unbelievable!

How had it happened? When he had learned that Jones would almost certainly be the next governor of Texas, Francisco had gone to Marfa to shake his hand. There, the day he had come to play the clown in public, he had found out about his "international" intentions. He immediately availed himself of the newspaper fraternity to begin to pick away in earnest. First, he informed the publishers from around here: Rodríguez of the *Zuriago*, Sifuentes of the *Laredian*, Armenta, Armendáriz . . . from then on he'd become the voice of a network that had no boundaries. It had been easy. To make public the massacre at the fort and, right after, to outline Jones's excursionist plan.

They waited for Jones at each stop in Mexico and hammered him with the same question: "Is it true that the Mexican suffers in Texas, more than in any other state, discrimination in the workplace and in other public establishments? Is that business about the massacre in Presidio true? I'm asking this question because so-and-so corroborates that . . ." By the time the Governor reached the capital three days later, his head was spinning. Martínez-Vega, the consul in Matamoros, had shown up at the official convention and requested the floor. First he gave the details and background of how he had confronted the governor himself, and then he went right on to read a list of accusations. Finally, he read a resolution signed by the principal Spanish-language publishers of the Southwest. The pressure and the scandal assumed such proportions that the corrupt policeman Alcalá had to refuse publicly Jones's request to export workers to the State of Texas. It was quite a joke, Francisco thought, that only weeks before, the Mexicans in Arizona had heeded the call of the governor of that state. "We need the support of every good citizen for our crops not to be lost." The first ones to turn out had been those who spoke Spanish, forming troops of people to salvage the harvest on Sunday. One paradox after another. Christ!

BENITO LYNCH WELCOMED THE NEWS by slaughtering a kid goat that had gotten in his way. Later, like Don Quixote, he rode by on horseback, knocking over the tents that he had bought for the occasion. They couldn't even stand him at home for those five days.

Nevertheless, Benito had not allowed himself to be beaten. He ordered Lorenzo to announce to the local workers that they would get the raise they requested. Meanwhile, since he was in a bind, he would personally go over to the other side to insist that they be paid a good price for harvesting the cotton. After the man had made his offer before the various assemblies, Reyes, for his part, gathered his comrades together and ordered them to make another, contrary, announcement publicly, written in the form of a warning: "Crossing the river is forbidden for anyone who intends to work in Benito's fields. Any act that supports the cause of this criminal will be punished severely. The Coyote." No one showed up in the fields on the second day, except for Lorenzo, who brought the announcement to his boss's house.

"And who is this Coyote?"

"I don't know, boss. It's the first time I've heard the nickname. But what I find out is that there's been a band of thieves for some time and they have no qualms about going after what they want."

"So, that's the way it is, huh? Fine. You go to Mexico and announce that I will pay four cents for each pound picked and that I will provide complete armed protection."

He went on to inquire about the whereabouts of the Coyote. He didn't care who he was. All he wanted was to waste him.

Lorenzo was back that same day before too long. He brought two items of information: first, that he had succeeded in obtaining twenty nighttime pickers for him, pickers who were a little unsure about even wanting to do it. In any case, he had told them if they decided to come, one of them should come and say they're coming at night. The second item of news was that the Coyote was none other than Reyes Uranga, his brother-in-law. No kidding! Reyes, the quietest of the whole pack of hands. Reyes? That made him laugh.

Benito lost no time in going into action. He got in touch immediately with the sheriff in Marfa for him to come and help out, and by the third day he was already poking around the houses and outskirts of Presidio. Then, after they found nothing on this side, the ten rangers crossed the river to the Mexican side and went up to the sierra where they supposed that Reyes and his band were hidden. But they came away from there, too, with empty hands. Thus, the following day they announced they were leaving, preparing their departure with dimmed lights, and by night they returned to see if by chance . . . But Reyes had not swallowed the hook.

Nothing happened the fourth day either, but a wetback showed up at night at Ben's house to tell him that the twenty that had been recruited were on their way. But it would not be that night, but the following one. So Ben prepared the sacks and left them by the trunk of the fat tree near the water pump. Benito did not tell Lorenzo that the wetback had come, out of fear that the plan would be discovered. Neither the wetback nor the pickers knew they were the bait. The strategy was simple. To get Reyes where he was weak, by mistreating the people a little bit, and if he had any balls, the bastard would come out in the open. What Benito did not know was that Reyes himself had practiced with the pickers the day before. Did they want to work? Okay, then either fish or cut bait, he had told them. They would have to cooperate. So what if they got hit by a bullet? They'd get what they deserved.

BENITO SMILES as he walks among the dark houses. Not even any dogs are barking, or maybe he can't hear them. He smiles with triumph written on his lips. His smile, made from a grimace that fools no one, is as clear as an X-ray. The rider moves among the blocks of prosaic adobe. Adobes that were made at one time from new straw and that now look like useless cornstalks. Anybody who'd want to make poetry of this is a liar. All the houses lack is a cross in front of them to be cemeteries. Nevertheless, now and

then one of them wards off death with little flowers and a veranda
in front. Then the dusty, unblack-topped street. The green devil
smiles because they've all been tricked. The devil manipulates
puppets. The devil plays with human life. And human beings
never understood how he made it into their midst. He was like a
gust of wind that blows between their legs, making them trip.
Others say that it was a dream from which they had awakened
naked. When they awoke, they had placed themselves in the
hands of the gentleman, who had promised them relief and had
made good. He had given them work on their own land, and the
people began to feel life again in their stomachs. Then he paid
them in advance, and they paid it back into his hands. "Every
family gets a box of food as a Christmas gift, and I'll have a bar-
becue when the harvest is over. But don't forget, vote for me,
vote Democratic." In two years, the vassals had crowned a king
they called the "Green Devil."

A stifling night, an oppressive night, a night that chokes peo-
ple. Pale skulls of squeezed-out sap, skulls lost on the dry land of
the cotton fields. False plants watered with sweat. Stuffed worms.
Presidio, prison, hell. A devil laughing silently. Shhh!

Benito appeared like a ghost at the door of the house. Then he
glued his lips to the jamb and called quietly . . . "Pst! Lorenzo!"

The barking of the dog inside the porch answered him, and
Benito jumped back.

"Shut up, you bastard!"

"Hey, who's there?"

"It's me, Ben."

"Wayda momen."

"That's okay, Lorenzo. Don't get up. I'm only here about the
pickers. They're near the river. Go by later, okay?"

"Okay, Don Benito."

The Green Devil moved away like a shadow.

Lorenzo did not go to bed then. The appearance of Ben at this
hour had left him restless, so he went outside to smoke a cigarette.
Crafty old guy, bastard. If he weren't paying my salary, I would
have bailed out already. The problems he brings me. One of these
days I'm going to wake up stretched out in the river, plugged by
my own people. And people are right, I'm bad to them, but the
fact is that they get you from all sides. If the old goat helped the

poor people instead of paying them shit, he wouldn't have any problems. Jerk. Some day he'll change, after I'm good and dead.

ALREADY IN THE MIDDLE of the field ten riders appear and surround old Ben. He tells them the basics: the pickers will be in the section indicated by the fat poplar, but to be on the safe side, wait for Lorenzo. The latter didn't need a pistol to convince him he should serve as guide. Just don't go too far. Then we'll see what happens, he tells them.

The man digs his spurs in and disappears into the night. It's been a long day.

THE WHISTLE ON THE OTHER SIDE of the river shatters the silence. It reaches the ears on the Mexican side. Quickly various figures jump into the river and lose themselves among the cotton fields. Like frightened criminals they run toward the poplar tree to grab the bags and disappear again into the ditches. They tie the bags to their waists and begin to devour the plants like locusts. Bush after bush is stripped. *Shas. Shas. Shas.* The bags fill up. They cast the bag over their shoulders like a giant sausage and place it alongside the ditch.

This night the pickers are especially wary and move filled with fear. Worse, they don't know if it's the waiting or not being sure if the Coyote will come. For that reason some of them have started in the middle of the rows and have picked toward the river.

The men drag themselves along under the moonlight. They twist and turn among the plants. The green plants, with their white buds, look like Christmas trees. The pickers try to climb to the top just like elves. But they can't escape the long tail that ties them to the ground. Now the serpent, tied to their waists, tries to devour them with its open maw, but it can't. The picker stuffs it with cotton, cocoons that will leave it full so it will leave the people alone. The rapid, rapid hands get all scratched. Perhaps some miracle will transform the cocoons into small gold coins. But it's all no use. The devil carts them away. The devil multiplies. Then another serpent comes along, as hungry as the other one and then another and another, until one night God's blessing pays them for the misery they don't deserve. For now the platinum-colored pickers will continue to slither among the green sea and white serpents. White tufts, poof, greenbacks. Green eyes, green teeth. Rotten, the soul rotten, green, green. Green sea, green bodies, green death, decomposition.

FRESH DEATH in an upholstered coffin is nice and warm. The body can lie down in it, enjoy the warmth of an electric blanket. But these moments are short-lived because then the evening's dew takes its place and envelops the body in cold. That is when the soul emerges with the will to prolong life. It slips along the upholstery like a cat seeking warmth, but it's all useless; the coffin's no longer warm or tender. The soul is like a mother who loses her son in a storm, and the wind carries her far away from her lost child. That's what happens with Chente. The dawn's breeze transforms his soul into a long trail of cigarette smoke, blowing it over toward the fort, where so many other souls have been deposited.

OUTSIDE, BEHIND THE HUT, the men squatted on their haunches around a bottle. As the couples would arrive at the house of the deceased, men and women would separate and go off in different directions. The women would go in; the men would enlarge the circle. With the warmth of the bottle and Levario's animated tongue, the men often forgot why they were there.

Inside, there is a wafting odor of wax, but it is soon blanketed by the dust rising from the dirt floor. No faces can be seen in the dying light of the candle. Rather, there are bodies wrapped in black dresses and shawls like fishnets. The women who were able to find a seat stare off into space. They are like mummies, tired of fingering their rosaries. It looks like they are trying to make the beads rounder and, at times, as if someone had wound them up, they begin to pray out loud. The murmuring lasts only a few minutes; then there is a leaden silence, a silence interrupted by a huge and bothersome fly. The fly buzzes twice around the coffin of the deceased and lands. Silence takes over again. The women get up to go out for some air and others come in to take their places on the benches. Shrouded rows contrast with recently whitewashed walls. Roberto, Eduvijes's fiancé, comes and goes, comes in and goes out, asking the men to help him bring chairs from their houses because more people are likely to show up. Thanks to Chito, Levario, Don Francisco, and Reyes, who came and left early, everyone's helped him out. Poor Vicke didn't even have time to make her dress, sweep, make arrangements. But everyone helped out. The coffin, placed on top of two buckets, was donated by Levario, despite the fact that he was so repulsive. You had to know him to stand him. He was one of those persons who only need to open their mouths to give you a pain in the ass. The announcement on the door of his "coffin factory" says it all: DIE IN STYLE . . . WITH LOMELI COFFINS. But he had a good heart. Roberto remembers the time he went to fetch a coffin for the little angel:

"Who was it this time?"

"Chentito, Vicke's brother."

"Ah! May he rest in peace, since he never got any here. The kid was born sick. He almost died when he was six months old, and the worst part is that all they gave him to eat was crackers with coffee. Let's see, how about these, they're the best ones. He'll sure go to heaven in style with this one, right? Heh, heh. With this upholstery he can fly pdq. Take it, no charge, and tell Vicke many happy returns, hah, hah. That's right, tell her I'll stop by to see her tonight." (That's the reason, you talk too much, and because you are what you are, you rub people the wrong way, jerk. Maybe also because you joke about death, making fun of it. Look at you, dressed in your best, with your bottle of tequila ready to yak all night long. That's what you'll do until your wife Virginia stops you cold and drags you drunk off home. I don't like you because you're a parasite of death.)

"Thanks, Levario. God bless you."

THE HUT IS LITTLE, but the whitewash makes the two rooms look bigger. The percale curtain covers the opening where the door should be, although the light shines through as it does from the priest's side of the confessional. Vicke, sitting on her bed, observes the movements with dull eyes and then casts her gaze on a candle that threatens to go out as it projects the heart of Jesus along the wall. Christ accompanies Vicke in her suffering, a suffering that flickers in tune with the dancing light. The Holy Child, with his luxurious garment, is also present. Now Vicke moves her gaze to the portrait of the dead little angel and then to the image of the Holy Child. Once, twice, three times. Many

times, until the two images become one. She studies and com-
pares them. The curly hair, the smile, the joined hands. "Ay, no,
no, the picture is missing a hand!" And she recalls that it was be-
cause of the wind last night. She remembers that when the statue
fell, her brother was dying, the poor thing. She had picked the
statue up from the floor, as he had ordered her to, and no sooner
had she done it when the child became very talkative. When she
brought him the warm cloth he'd requested, he asked her to take
him by the hand, and then be began to remember things. "Let's
see, Vicke, I'll bet you don't remember this: there's the moon . . .
What's that business about the moon eating prickly pears if it's
made of cheese? I believe that if it were true, it would've already
melted, don't you think so, Vicke? There's the sun drinking so-
tol. . . . Listen, Vicke, do you think things in heaven are like us?
That's why I'm not afraid of the night, are you? When you go
outside, I don't . . . the snake in the sea, in the sea, around here
you can . . . Listen to me, Vicke, do you remember the song
about the pretty little fish? . . . in clear water flowing from the
fountain . . . playing with my hoop . . . my mama told me not to
go outside or I'd die right away. . . ." And that's how Vicke had
spent the night. Listening to him, singing to him, answering him,
making his lips into a smile until the wee hours when he slipped
off to sleep. When he could no longer awaken, the smile still
stamped on his little face, she sent for Roberto. Her love came as
quick as . . . "My God, give me strength. I only want to know
why you do these things to little children. You know they are little
angels and do no harm. Why did you take this little boy instead of
me? Punish us, kill us adults, but not them. Why do you do it?
Why have you left me so alone, alone, alone?"

Levario's jokes become more and more gross and drunken.
They filter in through the window as though making fun of the
Our Fathers and the Hail Marys. Like a gas chamber, the hut is
suffocating in bodies, candles, night, nausea. Dizziness. Vicke feels
sick. "My deepest sympathy, no. My deepest sympathy, no. My
deepest sympathy, NO! My deepest sympathy, NO! NO!" The NO
grows larger like two inflated balloons. NO. They slowly grow
larger in Vicke's mind until the balloons cannot fit in the two
rooms. Then they spill out through the window and get even big-
ger. Finally the thorn of suffering pops them. "Nooooo!" Vicke

begins to cry. Long sobs mixed with NO. Outside the conversation stops to receive Vicke's suffering through the ears, but liquor has already stopped them up. Is that not why they drink on these occasions? Ah, old cowards! Why aren't you men enough like the women? Why can't you take it like they can? Only Levario's dog answers as though he were mindful of the suffering. His howling accompanies the woman.

"Shhht! Shut up, mangy dog!" Levario kicks him. The dog, with his tail between his legs, moves around the drunken men and then lies down again alongside his master. The talking drops in pitch.

"Poor woman, her parents died just two years ago, one right after the other."

"At the time of the long trek to Marfa?"

"Yes, then. I also remember that the kid got real sick. His face was all red from coughing so much."

"What was it?"

"Well, no one knows, but they say he picked it up over there. Others say that he caught something in the mines when he worked there."

"Poor kid. They should never have let him go."

"Poor Vicke, because she's the one who always took care of him."

"They say that Don Benito and Doña Rosa were over to see her earlier."

"Good grief! The Boss?"

"Yes. When he wants to be, the old guy is okay. He's the one who built these rooms for Vicke on his own property."

"Sure. There's no doubt about it. I helped him do it, although at the time he told me it was to store alfalfa bales, but since it didn't work out . . ."

"So, there you are. I heard just the opposite, that he built them for Vicke because he owed something to her dead parents."

"Really? And what was that?"

"No one knows, but I believe that there's something to it, because when the soldiers came, they didn't cart her off to El Paso. I mean, only to Marfa, but then Ben went over and brought her and Chentito back."

"Well, who knows what the deal is, but if they came to see her, there must be something . . ."

Thus the night fills with life, while inside the remains of death beat against people's breasts. They jab, wounding like a pin. Vicke dozes off from being so worn out, and she dreams nightmares. A luminous little point that turns into an indecisive bat. Then it drops down on the wake like a blind comet. Vicke sees it first as tiny, but then it grows larger, more and more and more, then PLOP! It smashes into her forehead. The beating of its wings in her eyes and on her arms makes her tremble. The bat departs. The woman opens her eyes. Levario stumbles in and goes over to Chente's body. "My God, get that drunk out of here, get him home to bed. Make him respect the little angel, for God's sake." The drunk draws near, while the eyes of the women try to stop him but can't. He begins to feel the coffin. With a sensual pleasure he runs his hands over the cloth. No, it isn't the body that moved him to draw near. It's his work, his coffin. He's so fascinated that he forgets that the coffin is mounted on two pails and he leans against it. The body moves to one side. The man attempts to stop it, but he's drunk. The two fall to the ground with a dry thud.

"Aaaaaaay! Have pity, don't hit him. It'll hurt him! No! Chentito, my beloved Chentito!"

Roberto, who has just come in, runs to help the women who are helping to resettle the coffin on the pails. Then he takes Levario by the arm and pulls him outside.

"Go on, now, Levario. It's time to go. And don't come back." His tone of voice is that of repressed anger.

"Alll I tttried to do was to touch the coffin. . . ."

"Go on, I told you!"

His wife Virginia comes out mortified, saying over and over again how sorry she is, and takes him home. Meanwhile, inside they are rubbing Vicke's neck with alcohol to calm her. She cries for a few moments and then falls back into the snares of sleep.

THE BURDEN REYES WAS UNDER could be felt among the men. He had just come from the wake for Chente. A "Good evening, fellows" and then silence. Rufino, alias "the Cricket," goes up to him.

"What's going on, Chief? You look like the one who's dead."

"Well, what do you expect, buddy? But it's not because there's one little angel more, but because I can't make any rhyme or reason out of this life."

"Come off it, Chief. Look, here's your favorite song."

"Well, let's hear it."

The Singing Cricket wasn't about to get any prize for this song either, but the ballad of Joaquín Murrieta wasn't half bad when accompanied by a well-tuned guitar.

"Gentlemen, I'm Mexican, but I understand English. I learned it from my brother, backwards and forwards, and I can make any American tremble at my feet. I came . . ." Reyes is no longer listening. Reyes's mind expands and overflows his rancor. The kid who had just died is nothing but another in the line of ignoble deaths that include his brother Jesús. For . . .

". . . songs I have sung, punishing Americans, and for the noble and simple Indian. . . ." (Bitch of a life that doesn't even respect the innocent. But I won't leave without making them pay dearly.) "When I was still a child, they left me an orphan, with no one to give me any love, and they killed my brother . . ." (. . . And as long as there is injustice and I see old people mistreated, I will go on, by God, I will go on . . .) "My destiny is now no other, watch out, neighbor. . . ."

"WATCH OUT, BUDDY, don't let your mind wander."

"Eh? Hell, I was just about to doze off."

"Don't tell me you want to miss out on this one."

"Who said anything about fear? It's just my age, friend. You might say I carried you away in diapers, don't you remember? Right from the bridge. Shit, what a struggle you put up. But just look at where you are now."

"What do you expect, man? In those days, I didn't even know where chickens laid their eggs. But now that I see things up close, it's hard to take, you know? It makes your soul steam."

"If they come, we'll just have to scare them. So they'll know who we are. But we'd better not let things get out of hand like that other one did. He really gritted his teeth."

"Well, I guess it's about time for us to go on over. From here we'll go by foot, so watch the horses. And wait until Cricket starts to sing."

THE TEN RANCHERS, following Lorenzo, also dismount about ten yards from the poplar. Then, under the command of their chief,

Chester, they suddenly grab Lorenzo and put a handkerchief over
his mouth, tying his hands to his saddlehorn. Then they tie his
horse, along with the others, to a wooden stake nailed on the
corner of the pump. They keep under cover until they reach the
poplar, and once there, they fire into the air first and then the ten
spread out among the ditches after the people.

The Cricket sings. You can soon hear the sounds of splashes in
the water. Reyes and his men cross the river as if it were some-
thing natural. They get to the tree unfazed and unhurried, where
they calmly listen to the dry kicks to the body of the one who ran
away backwards. *Umph. Umph.* The riders remain passive in the
face of his struggling. And then . . . "Waaaaater, fellows!" Cricket
yells, and then the firing starts. The men don't shoot to kill, but
the surprise makes Ben's henchmen run off scared, leaving the
work unfinished. That's what Reyes wants. Then his men take out
their whips and chase after Chester and his band, beating them
until they collapse exhausted.

Lorenzo, meanwhile, has managed to goad the horse with his
spurs until he succeeds in breaking the reins. But he doesn't want
it to gallop because his hands are still tied. He makes a great effort
to speak, to beg them to have pity, but he can't because of the
gag. He manages to loosen the knot on his hands, but Rufino
discovers him, and he just manages to apply the spurs when the
latter comes up alongside and knocks him to the ground. Then he
rolls him downhill and plunges him into the water without realiz-
ing the man isn't saying anything. He dunks him once, twice,
three times. His body is limp. Rufino finally leaves him lying
there and goes to attend those who have been beaten.

"Hey, Manuel, what you got there?"

"Old man Rentería. He still hasn't come to from the thrashing."

"Well, try pouring some water on him."

One by one the pickers huddle together under the fat poplar,
some not so worked over as the old man, others with only their
mouths open. Reyes goes over to where someone is lying moaning
in the irrigation ditch. He discovers a boy shivering. He holds his
hand out to him. It looks like the boy is winking at him, but the
bruise is too purple for it to be a joke.

"Just look at the beating you got. Come up here. And now you'll
know next time not to think it's so great. Don't think for a minute

you're going to get paid for your work or the beating. Here, dummy. Take this money and . . . try to earn it some other way."

They went over to where Lorenzo was, just where they'd left him on the sand, on his stomach. Rufino rolls him over himself. . . .

"Listen, chief, I think we went too far with this one. Hell and damnation, it's Lorenzo, buddy."

"Well, nothing's to be done. May God take him and forgive us, buddy."

THERE, NEAR PRESIDIO, the fort rises up at the place they call the Barren Hillside like a crumbling castle. It is an adobe castle without doors that the wind uses like a clay whistle, and there is always someone who goes by at night there with his hair on end and insists the castle is haunted. There are spirits and there are devils that roam from room to room. The unbelievers deny it, saying that it's a bunch of lies, but what is certain is that you can feel history. The legends of the people are the pages of a book that have been torn out and cast on the pyre. . . .

COME ON, FELLOWS, let's hear it for Don Benito, the guy with the goat's beard. Come on, everybody. . . . Don Beniiito, Don Beniiito, Don Beniiito, let Don Beniiito sing, let him yell, Don Beniiito, let Don Beniiito laugh! . . ."

"And where'd you get the idea to cheer him?"

"Because yesterday I saw him walk by with his dandy's clothes on, with one paw on the ground and the other one touching the white beard on his chest."

"He's got a lot of personality."

"No, the little old goat of Presidio's got money and guts."

"Once more, fellows, Don Beniiito, Don Beniiito, Don Benito, the one who owns the store . . ."

"Don Beniiito!"

"Don Benito, the one in the graffiti in . . ."

"Don Beniiito!"

"In the restrooms, on the walls in the streets, on the bankers' checks, on the backs of the cattle . . ."

"Don Beniiito!"

"In heaven and hell, on the lands of Vicke's parents who lost in the county court . . ."

"Don Beniiito!"

"On the parchments, Don Benito the landowner, Don Benito the soldier . . ."

"Don Beniiito!"

"May he be praised, let's all the dead say it."

"May he be praised!"

"For his works and his property, for freeing us from the Man."

". . ."

"Yesterday I remembered I saw him go by with his chest so puffed out that I got the idea to give him a scare. No, I wanted to give him a thrashing if I could have, but the old man couldn't take it, may God remember him when he dies."

"Hold on. Let's all raise our hands and pray for him before he joins us in the fort."

"No, let's give him another scare, for his cleverness with the poor, for his thievery, and for his killings."

"Stop! Be quiet, for the love of God. I can't stand so much name-calling. He was young, he didn't know any better. He was a military man. There was war, people were afraid, there was conflict between governments, he was only an employee. Back then in '63 they told him, come on over here, boy, where the mighty river twists and turns."

"Eeny-meeny-miny-mo . . ."

"And Captain Gray told him, all the cats are black, watch the river from this side, cross over if you need to."

"The troop passed through here and went on toward Chihuahua. Don Benito returned with a soldier's glory."

"Let's hear it, fellows! Don Benito went to war . . ."

"Riding on a bitch, the bitch dirtied itself, and Benito licked it clean."

"And then he got in among us, he conquered lands, he set up a store, he gave everybody jobs."

"Shut up, loud-mouths. We all share in the blame. How many times have I told you to demand your rights and watch out for the wolves and protect your papers?"

"What did we know about the American government?"

"Okay, but why didn't we band together in those days? Why? . . . Go on and see if you jerks can figure out why. When the treaty was written, land rights were assured in writing. Then claims were made, a

lot of claims, to the federal committee. What happened? Of over a
thousand, seventy were approved. The rest were paid for at a dollar-
fifty an acre. Call that justice? Bunch of assholes . . ."

"And you, Don Rubén, what happened to your claim?"

"No, well, death came to me very soon, and just what I thought
happened. My poor old woman, what was she to do? With a
long-barreled pistol she put up a fight, but she went mad, or better,
started to. May God forgive that traitor Lorenzo who also cheated her.
I don't know what kind of deal they made, but there in the courthouse
Lorenzo convinced her to sign over to him. Couldn't do anything. The
dumb broad signed, and after a while she's no longer the owner, but the
government is going to pay her for everything they've taken away. But
let's drop the subject. It wasn't her fault, and I probably would've done
the same thing. . . ."

"I remember her. When I came to these parts, I worked for her."

"And what are you doing here?"

"Well, sir, I came to seek the life I couldn't find on the other side."

"Where are you from?"

"I'm Melchor from Michoacán, sir. I come from far away. They
told me that life was better in these parts."

"But you're real young. How did . . .?"

"Well, sir, I died in a fire here at the fort. I never thought I
would die so soon. I begged and begged the Virgin for her to let me see
my mother, but as you can see, sir, that wasn't possible. I wanted to
show her I had learned to write and that she should be proud of me."

"And what's that piece of paper burned around the corners you're
carrying, Melchor?"

"Just look, sir, it's a poem for my mama that I didn't send her.
When they burned me, I put it in my mouth because it was the only
part of my life worth anything."

"Read it, Melchor."

"Ah, sir, you'll just laugh."

"No, man, why would I laugh? Read it, read it. Right, fellows?"

"Have Melchor read his poem! Have Melchor read his poem! Have
Melchor read his poem!"

"See, man? You have an audience. Come on. And please hold your
head up just as if your mother were listening to you."

"Okay, here it is. It's called Saintly Mother:

You who in your misery made every effort to console me
and to give me the thrashing I deserved,
you who lighted two candles to the saint there in Igualapa
When I fled far, far away from you,
you who are and were very good and long-suffering,
Accept my thanks and my love,
for I can't give you anything but this bunch
of fresh-cut flowers, some from the fields
and the freshest ones from the floating gardens,
Accept them, sweet, good little mother,
Accept them, pretty, saintly little mother,
may God bless you today on your saint's day.
Oh, do you remember all of my bad deeds?
Well, you know they weren't on purpose.
Maybe it's out of longing,
Maybe it's out of trust,
Because I carry your name in my heart
Like your sacred little soul of lilies
Pretty little mother, good little mother, saintly little mother.
You've been good all your life,
You've shed tears for all my sins.
Now on your saint's day all I can give you
is this bunch of freshly cut little flowers
some from the fields and the freshest
from the floating gardens
Accept them, sweet, good little mother
Accept them, pretty, saintly little mother
and hug me tight, bless me a lot
for my spirit sings to you on your saint's day. . . ."

"Long live Melchor!"

"Looong may he live! Now have the Indian Melchor sing. Have him sing! A cheer, fellows . . ."

"Have him sing! Have him sing, have him sing, have Melchor sing! Have Melchor sing, have Melchor sing . . .!"

"*Tzitzi, curapi, tzan en an tzetzas et tzana por su me cuaria . . . ca que tzan tzin, por tunque lo ña miri curiñaaa . . . cinnamon flower, I sigh and sigh because I remember youuu . . . I sigh and sigh because I remember youuu, aza guera, aza sentí . . . because I remember you. . . .*"

"Another! Another! Another!"

"Ay, ay, ay, ay, tlazita mutzi caraquia, itzle cuicho, itzla cochitl, aim pero ro quimooo . . . tzama ri cuaria, maqui ni qui ni quia, matzen flor azul, matze pere tzaratzin, male ña quim pa ña quiii . . . ay, ay, ay, ay . . ."

"What're they saying, sir?"

"That they're singing."

"Ah, yes . . ." (The languages become mixed together, become mutilated like pieces of the soul.) "A pretty song . . ." (Other languages are drilled into you like with the point of a pencil and then they turn the pencil around to erase your own as easily as though the soul were written on the piece of paper. Then the language stretches out like a cord and wraps itself around your body, turning you into a ball just like what happened to the cat.)

"Why so serious, young man?"

"For no reason at all. I was just thinking . . . (that justice is a tongue stretched out like a long thread that life grasps onto and ties into knots).

"Why do you wear that cap on your chest?"

"Just out of habit. I tried to stop the blood I was losing."

"Was it a fight?"

"No, it was a bullet that they fired at me when I was running."

"Were you a wetback?"

"No, sir. It was when things got rough back in 1930. Do you remember when everybody was starving to death?"

"Of course I remember. I was in Los Angeles in those days. They said we were making things worse, and they began to throw us out in droves. I remember that in August of that year, it came out in the newspapers that they had thrown 82,000 out. But the funny thing is that they realized too late that we were the only ones who were not asking for help or for food. Things were really mixed up in those days. The immigration service got involved in things without authorization, and they began to make a sweep of people. I remember poor old Anselmo, how he cried because they yanked him out of the house where he'd lived for more than fifty years. But that's all a long story. Tell me, boy, about what happened to you, but first take that cap away from your chest. It looks like you're begging forgiveness. . . . Ah, shit! What a hole! I can see why you keep it covered. Come on, tell me."

"Well, what happened is that my parents emigrated when I was six years old. My papa found work on young Ben's ranch, which had previously belonged to his father, and he considered himself happy, although I had to help him out after school. Life went on like that until 1931, just like you said. The government got the idea that we were a nuisance, although they said they were throwing us out because they felt sorry for us. What they didn't want to understand was that it was worse over there. One day they showed up at home and examined our papers. My papa had emigrated with his papers all in order, but they told him that I was illegal and that I would have to go back to the country where I was born, Mexico. And if I didn't, the whole family would have to return. My mama begged and cried, and my father complained, but it was of no use. And I liked school so much. Well, in any event, I went to live with my grandparents, but I couldn't stand it. After six weeks, and despite my grandmother's warning, I got up real early to cross the river. (Grandma, I'm going over to the other side. No, child, don't cross the river. The field on both sides is dry. Don't cross. Can't you see the spiders are weaving a web to catch you under the water? Can't you see the green chiggers will get into your bones?) It was still dark, but trembling with fear and all alone, I dived in. . . . (Heavy shadows, like dying fish . . . splashing in the water . . . tracks that sink away.) My grandma didn't want to let me come, and as I walked along the road I seemed to hear her telling me to turn back. . . . (Green shadows, your pupils the color of the sea . . . the weeping willow is crying bitter tears for you . . . turn baaaaack!) But I crossed over anyway, like an echo in the mountains. It seemed like everything was against me, because I no sooner was on the other side when it started to get darker and to lightning. . . . (My eyes clouded over with gray clouds and a black sky . . . the earth trembled under my feet, the sky broke into pieces, luminous machete blows.) Then I really got scared, because if it rained I wasn't going to be able to go on, and I think it was fright that made me keep going, even though I knew that I couldn't protect myself if the rain caught me in the middle and I lost my way. And that's what happened. The rain caught me when I was only halfway across the field . . . (pelting my face, whiplashes on my back. Run! Take cover! Turn baaaack!) and the worst part is that it soon turned to hail and I began to be covered with bruises. (Tears, rain, icy ammunition. Have mercy!) My cap was useless, and like a madman I started to run while I cried. I don't even remember how I

*found the tree (under the sad weeping willow I shivered while the drops
falling on the leaves of the plants applauded). I made my body into a
ball and cried for a long time until I fell asleep. In the morning I started
to walk again, but my heart was heavy, as if the whole world were
making fun of me. And when I got there, I cried in my mother's arms
like a child. (And you, Mama, you gave shape to time fathoming the
transparency of the sea. You liked to gather the waters of the lagoons
and rivers in your round pupils. And although the rivers no longer
flowed as before, you mended with the rocking of your chair. Don't you
remember how I tickled your ribs, and that's how you filled the arroyos
of your skin? A laughter of multiform water overflowing your linen
petticoats. Life without measure. Teeming seas. A transparent sky that
cuddles in your lap.)"*

"I can see all that. But, then, how did they shoot you if it didn't
happen then?"

"Ah, that was later when I started working, since I was no longer
going to school. I was all alone in the fields cleaning up when the
patrol appeared. The same ones. I believe that if it had not been for
this hate, they wouldn't have recognized me. The fact is that they
immediately came over to me. I just asked them to at least let me
get my clothes and say goodbye. Well, they said fine, and tossed me
into the car. They took me to my home, and they waited for me in the
car till I took care of my business, and even though my parents raised
a ruckus, it was no good. When I came out, I noticed that one of
the patrolmen was drinking some water from one of the faucets a little
ways off. The other seemed to be sitting in the car dozing. I don't know
what came over me, but I got the idea to run, knowing that I couldn't
get away. The one drinking water saw me and fired his gun to scare
me. But then he started to run, and when he saw he wasn't going to
catch me, he steadied himself so as not to miss. And like a fool I turned
around to face him, and suddenly I felt the cold next to my heart. But
I didn't feel any pain, just a huge surprise. I remember that I acted
scared because when the two came to put the handcuffs on me, I
held my joined hands out to them. Then, handcuffed, I picked my
hat up and put it over my heart. They helped me get up and I walked
with them to the car, but my legs said no. I think that my hat tried
to cover the hole my life was flowing out of. But how can a hat hold
on to your life? All of us who are going to die are funny, don't you
think so?"

"*That's for sure. But what are you doing here? You're not from Presidio.*"

"*I'm from the world, sir. Like death. What does it matter if you're from here or from there? Ignorance is enormous, and it's all the same. Poverty, too. The reality is the hole I have here, sir.*"

"*I am reality, gentlemen.*"

"*And who are you?*"

"*I am Jesús of the river, I am of the water.*"

"*You're nuts, you're of the earth like all of us.*"

"*Of neither ashes nor of clay. I lived in the water, and I died in the water. I am all water.*"

"*And why are you in the fort if you're made of water?*"

"*Because the fort is made of glass. It's an aquarium.*"

"*Sure, right, nutball. An aquarium with doors of crumbling adobe. You're ridiculous.*"

"*No, the doors are made of voices.*"

"*Ours?*"

"*No, the devil's.*"

"*That's not true, they're ours. They're cries, the whistling of men who want to cross the river. They are speaking to you, Jesús.*"

"*No, they're the sirens of the sea. They love me, which is why they call to me.*"

"*Yes, they want you. Dead.*"

"*No, they want me to tell them fairy tales.*"

"*Just your old stories, Jesús. What are they going to want your idiocies for?*"

"*Because my stories are the truth. I am also a siren.*"

"*How so, Jesús?*"

"*Because my body is in Presidio, but my soul is in the river.*"

"*Didn't it go to heaven?*"

"*No, because it's dried out on me, and I want to go on living.*"

"*In a hell like this one?*"

"*Yes, to smother the flames.*"

"*But how, just tell me, are you going to do that if you're dead?*"

"*I am going to rise again. I will call myself Joseph.*"

"*Your son?*"

"*No, my brother Reyes's son, and I'm already singing, gentlemen: 'My pride is to have been born in the humblest barrio . . . (this guy's a real nut. I hope he shuts up fast) . . . the day the people let me down is the day I'll die.'* "

THE FEW TOURISTS who by chance filter into Presidio looking for old things are lucky enough to find a blond relic named Mack. He's assumed to be the expert on the history of Presidio, the fort, and Ben Lynch. So that by the time they leave Nancy's Café, they know all about the number of hangings and fuckings and all those things human beings are capable of. The rest is easy. For a few dollars he'll organize an excursion to the fort. And there he makes them form a semicircle before going in so that . . . But better let the old fart tell it himself. . . .

"YES SIREE, OLD BEN came to this part of the country from his dad's in Alabama. Guess he got tired of driving them dark folks over there and so headed fer San Antone. Ben was still young then, and I guess them wild hairs of his stood up when he heard 'bout the trouble with Mexicans. The story 'bout the slaughter at the Alamo made him mad aplenty. Now I ain't sure when he get to San Antone, but I know he arrive too late. Musta been a sight when he ride into town. You should see a picture of him, here, see? Big, and tall in the saddle, with all that fair hair abristling in the wind. Anyway, he got there a day after all this happened and he sure got burnt up when he hear about Crockett and Bowie died. Couldn't do nothing about, though, just get mad over the whole mess. He wasn't received good either by Mrs. Caulder because she got a patio full of dead, stinking . . . bodies, so she give him a piece of her mind, thinking he had took part in the killing. But he told her different and help her get rid of most of the carcasses. Young Ben was a hell of a cowpoke. He was pretty happy-go-lucky kid them years, but I ain't saying he had no sense in him. He was hard-working and never give his boss reason to talk. He was a tough hombre those years; sure he could sing and yodel, but people wasn't going to mistake him for no sissy. He could fight damned near anybody and boy, could he ride. He could ride broncs till they spilt over, tired as hell. And them bulls, you would think he was born on 'em. But his rough and tough ways don't mean he wasn't brought up right. Hell, no. His folks reared

him good. They tell him 'bout the Lord, and the right living, and
all that 'bout being a loyal and proud man. Sure he was ornery—a
few fights once in a while, but who ain't when you're that age?
And 'specially when you come to a town of . . . people with dif-
ferent folkways and no care fer law and order. I mean, you know,
he come to San Antone fer that there reason. He learned pretty
quick how to deal with 'em in the canteenas and he wouldn't let
no man beat 'im. And he already know 'bout how conniving these
critters can be with knife and all, you know what I mean. Fact, I
heard the reason there ain't no Indians in this part of the country
no more is cause these folks beat 'em at their own game. The first
time he fight, he fight five of them at once and he licked 'em
clean. And when he whipped 'em pretty good, that's when he got
his reputation. He didn't need no gun; the bastards would disap-
pear like shitflies . . . pardon the expression . . . and after that
they would turn yellow and run. Oh yeah, they knew what he
stood fer. Anyway, guess it was about that time that things started
getting pretty stinky down the Rio Grand and they start organiz-
ing the Texas brigade and other lawful organizations to clear up
the mess. You know, horse stealing, cattle rustling, killing white
folks. People nowadays don't pay much attention to the service
these constabulary, Texas rangers they call 'em, give to their
country. Remember, there wasn't no law to protect the citizenry,
so they take it in their own hands. Sometimes when there wasn't
no courthouse judge around, a noose on a tree was enough fer
'em. Hell, with all these desperados running wild, they had to do
something, hoosegow or no hoosegow. Sure, they made some mis-
takes, but hanging innocent people was rare. And although they
crossed the border and followed them outlaws clear to hell, there
was not enough of them to clear up the mess. Anyway, to make a
long story short, the rangers went recruitin' by way of San An-
tone and they hear of Ben's reputation soon enough. In fact, they
found that the only bad habit he had was seeñoritas and tobacco
chewing, so they hired him. But first they talk to his boss directly
and of course there wasn't no problem. Mixin' with them don't
spoil 'im. So he pack his saddlebags with dried beef and off he
goes (come a ti i yippi yippi yea, come a ti yi yippi yippi yea, 'tis
cloudy in the west and looks like rain and my old slicker's in the
wagon again . . . on a ten-dollar horse and a forty-dollar sad-

dle . . .) I ain't sure what good he done over the Valley by the
Rio Grand, but next thing, he show up in Presidio. It was about
the time the government start getting pretty worried about border
troubles so they start moving soldiers up and down the river. Ha,
ha, but I cain't figure why they sent soldiers to Presidio 'cause it
was just a poor Mexican settlement and there was no white folks
yet. All they find was poor people and a few savages, Jumanos,
they call them. They say the name's Mexican, which means hu-
mans, and I guess that's true, hee, 'cause they sure as hell didn't
cause no trouble. That's funny. Sometimes you cain't tell the dif-
ference between Mexicans and Indians. They mix up pretty good,
ha, and they sent the whole company to fight and there was none
to fight. Truth is, they only find a forteen built of adobe by Span-
ish soldiers, long time before, and it look like it never been used;
yeah, this one here you're seeing. They say it was a custom to
build them everywhere they went, just like the Alamo in San An-
tone, but this one here wasn't no beauty. Sure doesn't look like it
can even hold water out . . . fact, you probably could blow at it
and it'd fall. Anyway, they find themselves this Presidio del Norte
with nothing to do, so they move up to Marfa sixty miles away
where there was white folks already. But Ben stayed 'cause he was
smart. He know what he was doing but, you know, this is where
the story become different. I mean, Ben was different. He
changed, no doubt about it, 'cause he married a seeñorita. By this
time he was pretty savvy in the language and took to marrying.
Of course, she was different too, educated, pretty, clean—you
know what I mean. But I ain't saying he was a turncoat, though.
He still loved law and order. He always done good like he used to.
He never quit being a ranger, either, and he could run anybody
out of town that give him reason to. One night when he was
acourting Rosary, he got pistol-whipped pretty bad by his brothers,
but he got even soon enough. But that's what I mean, he become
different 'cause he didn't hold no grudge. He learn how to love
these people. I guess that's what love does to you, get soft in the
guts. Anyway, he was a well-respected feller by the community,
and of course they couldn't help it 'cause he was kind to them. He
gave 'em work and food, everything, and of course they look up to
him like a daddy. He learned how to handle 'em and I say this
'cause next thing, he own a hell of a lot of farmland and long-

horns. Fact, he even take over the forteen and use it as a office
once his business went good and the soldiers had move out. He
started using a lot of Mexican help and from here he would pay
'em with all them wads of bills. Yup, Ben was a good old critter
with a big heart; you have to admire a guy like him. Sh—hell, he
even made a big barbacoas and invite the whole lot of them to
eat. He was fair if they do the job, but if they fail or trick him,
boy, he would turn meaner than a . . . angry mama bear. It ain't
no bu—lie, either. But people remember more than good deeds.
For example, he never forget Paz, the old lady that sell him the
land. He done a lot of favors fer her, and even after she died, he
took in her daughter Vicke once she lost her husband. Anyway,
people remember old Ben Lynch. He was hard-working, kind,
law-abiding, etcetera, and all them qualities that an hombre
should have. And I ain't saying all about him is true, though. But
damned near all of it . . . Okay, folks, let's go in . . ."

"MY DAD FRANCISCO WORKED in Ojinaga on a farm, sharecropped,
and he raised a lot of wheat. We were no longer needy because my
mother worked making tortillas and took in washing to feed those
of us who were little. Then he got this field and we were no
longer hungry. He raised beans, squash, and lentils, and he put
everything aside. When we joined him, it hadn't been long since
he'd picked the corn, some huge ears, and he put it in a large
trough there next to the house. He made a large bunker with
poles to store the corn. We left quite a bit behind when Pancho
Villa came. We couldn't take any of it. We came here because
Pancho's horses ate it all. A terrible loss. We left the odds and
ends we had, our sandals (we didn't have shoes), our beds, every-
thing got left behind. All we came with was a burro, with a
wheelbarrow, and a large pan filled with bread dough. That's what
we took with us, and we came here to the fields to make tortillas,
where everybody camped out. We also brought a skillet and a fry-
ing pan and some spoons, that's all.

"The burro walked on ahead with our belongings, with us be-
hind. By the time we got to the riverbank, the water was way up
on us because the river had risen. All those who knew how to
swim went on, and those who didn't stayed behind over there.
Lord, what a mess it was that afternoon. Carmen Chávez's brother

came along with another man when the heavy shooting began in the town. They made a raft without really knowing how to. They made the raft to cross the river, but they drowned. Yes, it was sure a terrible mess. We got across because our house was up on the hilltop. All you had to do was to descend the hill, and there was the river. A lot of people crossed over and camped in the woods. People crossed at different points. People scattered, and we ended up in the village of Puerto Rico to live."

"WHEN THE 1910 REVOLUTION broke out, the soldiers would grab people and put them in the army, so almost everybody living in Ojinaga went over to the other side. And since we were out of work, we were nothing but vagrants, as they say. Things were a bit rough, so we survived by fishing. The river was real low, the water very clear and clean, and where there were deep parts we would go with sticks and make noise so the fish would come out and we could spear them with the sticks. The day they grabbed us that's what we were doing.

"We had come in the morning, me, my little brother, who was this high, Francisco Brito, my cousin, and Chamalía Heredia, who was my uncle. We fanned out into the river, and with our sticks we were scaring the fish. My uncle didn't go in, but stayed up on the cliff, since from there he could see whether the fish came out or not. The water was very clear, and he would tell us whether they were coming up. And after a little bit we could hear the sound of the horses over there toward Quivira. It was an advance party going from Ojinaga to where they were fighting in Mulato. Then Chamalía asked us if he should speak to them, but I told him no because the way the revolution was going, who knows what they might do to us. Well, he did speak to them. He yelled to them, and they rode on over. No sooner had they gotten there than, with their rifles in their hands, they grabbed Chamalía. Then they told us to get out of the water, but we headed for the other side (it really bothered me, for example, that I couldn't go and that they took my brother along, as little as he was. He was really a small fry) but they fired after us. We had to get out of the water, and they tied us up right away. They treated us real bad. They told us that we were Madero supporters and that we were passing supplies to the Maderistas. Eduardo Salinas, who was their chief, ordered them to tie us up with the ropes from the horses. They hobbled us and put us barefoot in the mesquite trees. Then he said they were going to shoot us. There was a cemetery there in Quivira on the top of a hill, and he ordered them to take us up the hill in order to kill us there. They accused us of something we couldn't even understand. Sure, we knew about the revolution, but we weren't involved. Well, they took us there, and all except two of them left for Mulato. They stayed behind with us on the hill. It was real hot and we were barefoot, the whole bit. Well, they concurred and got my brother, since he was the littlest, to give us his clothes and then they dressed us there on the hill. Although they had the order to kill us, they didn't, and one of them did something for us that was real nice. Because, you see, all of us kids would get together on the other side at night and have mock battles. Some from Loma Pelona and others from Terronal. We'd set palm fronds on fire so we could fight each other with lighted torches. Some were Maderistas and others were government troops. That night the Maderista boys named me their captain. Then we used a piece of paper to write out checks to pay the soldiers, and since I was the chief, it was only natural that I had all those papers in the pocket of my pants. They had amounts written on them when we were grabbed.

"I can truly see why God is very great. I was really worried then, but there was no way out. The soldier who went for the clothes frisked me and took everything out of my pockets. But he didn't show it to anyone, for if he had, I wouldn't be here telling about it. Just imagine what would have happened to me. Oh, Lord! But I didn't say a thing, just pretended I was mad and ran away from them. Well, they sent us to Ojinaga, and as soon as the women and soldiers saw us prisoners they started to say all sorts of things to us. Then they let go of us and tossed us in the jail, and we slept there that night. They held us the next day, too. About that time, my grandfather Cleto Heredia, who was sheriff of Presidio County, realized they were shooting at us from the other side and brought pressure to bear. So three days later they let us out and even offered us a safe-conduct pass to the other side. Then I said to my uncle Chamalía, 'See how mad they were? Come on, let's go join up with the Maderistas.' And we did. So that's how I got into the revolution.

"When they did Madero in, I went with Villa. I was a soldier until 1915. In 1915 I left and crossed to the other side, but meanwhile always working for the party until 1920, when things were wrapped up. I was involved with Villa in many ways: I carried provisions, clothing, just about everything. I had crops to tend so it wouldn't be noticeable. I was there in the middle of the field, near the river, and there I sowed my crops. I crossed Hipólito, Villa's brother, over to the U.S. He was living in San Antonio, but they kept an eye on him so he couldn't even stay home. And you have to be real careful about the Americans, because all they care about is what is convenient for them. For money or whatever, they're the ones who brought him over to Marfa, when I took him in. He and other generals stayed at my house, and from there I led them on a march to join Villa's men. I worked like that until 1920 when the revolution ended, along with my people, in accord with him, and when we had to go see him, we crossed the river at night. And so we were always going back and forth.

"Villa was a real devil when he took Chihuahua. He was very clever. We attacked, but we weren't able to make our way in that first time. Since it was the capital of the state, all the soldiers were bivouacked there. So, Villa got the idea to give a false alarm. We grabbed the telegraph operator in Villahumada and made him call Juárez, since it was part of Chihuahua, saying that they were asking for troops in Chihuahua. It was a trap because he called Juárez then and they sent some trainloads of soldiers. When they were on their way, we struck and really whipped them. Then Villa called in that he was going to attack Chihuahua, and turned back and attacked Juárez and took it. That was important because it left Chihuahua hemmed in from all sides. The only outlet was through Ojinaga because we only had a handful of men there. By the time the governor realized that, he came with the millionaires and the troops. They all ended up here.

"The few of us that were here wandered the hilltop with cattle, and when we came into Ojinaga we didn't realize the enemy was in town. Except that my brother-in-law Luis Cortez and some other men from Ojinaga came over to the place the workers gathered and told us. They saved our lives.

"A few days later, we met with the people Villa had sent on ahead, about two thousand, and meanwhile the troops in Ojinaga were swarming all over the place. There wasn't enough room for the enemy, and they spread out over the fields and toward Mulato. Well, first we advanced on the troops in Mulato, and we caught them at the entrance to the small canyon. But a lot of them got away to the other side through El Polvo. We intercepted them at the Alamo arroyo, and engaged them in battle. The next afternoon we surrounded Ojinaga, but they were fierce. There was nothing we could do. There were only a few of us, although it was later said that there were eight thousand of them. Well, we attacked three times, but no . . . There were three large holes surrounded by sandbags where everyone was standing. They killed a lot of us. We retreated in defeat. Three days later, Villa arrived with his men, Maclovio Herrera, Rosalío Hernández and others. Well, even with all these people, we couldn't lick them. But Villa was a real devil, and I remember as though it were yesterday how mad he got for having put his men in such a position. And things were real tough. They had chopped down all the poplar trees and put up barbed wire so riders and their horses couldn't get through. He told us right out: don't pay them any heed, fellows. By morning, God willing, by this very hour, we'll be sitting down to the dinner they're going to fix for us. We have to take them before dinner. No sooner said than done, as it turned out. He gave everyone orders, and they all fanned out on foot. There were a few officers on horseback behind them, but this was for when the attack took place, with the order that anyone who turned back was to be shot. So no one tried to run. But people moved out of sight, and everyone had a sign and countersign. The sign: the exposed body, hatless, the hat here on your chest and the sleeve rolled up, and then the countersign. There were many who got the sign but not the countersign, and those who didn't were killed.

"In any event, it seemed by design that when the sun set, a wind with a lot of dust came up and you couldn't even see your own hand. So by the time the enemy realized what was happening, we were on top of them. And I remember it as though it were today, how we ate their dinner. Let me tell you how that night we set to making coffee with water drawn from a small arroyo nearby. All of us in the barracks drank the coffee, and only the next day did we realize that we had made it from blood. It ran, was still running, because a lot of people had fallen into the large hollow.

When they had run out, a lot of them fell dead and wounded right there. They was a lot of blood flowing, and that's what we used.

"The next morning we woke up to see how many there were and to turn them over. Trucks and wheelbarrows picked up people from the town. They gathered them up and dumped them there where the tank is, the one they call the horseshoe. There was a very deep hollow there, and it was full to the top with the dead. They were carting them off in droves all day long. . . . As you can imagine, the story is a long one. . . ."

Presidio 1942

T HE RABBIT, BUNCHED UP into a ball, is sleeping peacefully. He can't imagine why his dream is so pleasant this time. Like a baby's smile, he enjoys the landscape of row after row of lettuce. The rabbit is happy because he's dreaming about eating, crouching down without any worries. Damn! How tough his life is, especially when the humans show up all excited and shooting at him with their rifles. Trucks shining their spotlights looking for his ears, and then suddenly, bang . . . bang . . . bang. Poor brother rabbits. Some are bounty for the dogs, others for the wolves. But tonight the moon rabbit wraps into himself like a happy fetus and dreams. . . .

The moon dresses itself in bitterness and viciousness. It's in a bad mood because it hasn't rained and because the universe is burning in all directions. The Río Grande is only a puddle, the plants are burning up, and the people, burnt-out particles, begin to stick out in the river. The moon hates when it cannot detain them, when there is not enough water to cover their mouths. This is also why the moon is angry. Because the people do not stop their coming and going. That's why it growls.

"Jump! Go on, damn moocher!"

The rabbit's lodgings tremble with the shouting of the moon, and it makes him jump to the ground. Then, startled, he runs off as though he heard the barking of the dogs behind the bushes. Suddenly he feels a slight pain near his tail. He imagines a tiny bullet that moves slowly throughout his whole body like the tickling of a leg that has gone to sleep. He can't get up. He tries to wiggle his head, and it feels as if he doesn't have one. Now, even his eyes feel heavy. Is he dreaming? He half remembers that deep into the night he felt tired and he lay down there by the cave to get his energy back a little bit, but he can't remember when sleep overcame him. And now this strange sensation. The paralysis he felt before has reached his tongue. He tries to look around, but he can only see his body, which is about to burst. The swelling is extreme. He no longer knows what to think, and he doesn't know whether he's still dreaming or if he's out of his mind. Nor is he sure if it was a bullet that he felt on his flank or whether he simply fell so hard from his perch that he hurt his body. Now in the middle of his drowsiness he can barely make out the snake moving toward him with ritual movements. The snake from the low sierra of Santa Cruz closes in on him with his mouth wide open, and he's not certain if the serpent is laughing soundlessly or if he wants to whisper something in his ear. Meanwhile, all his drowsy mind repeats is the story of a small mouse who innocently sat down in front of his hole when a cat appeared with flattering offers of all sorts of delicacies, and then the mouse emerged only to be devou . . . zzzzzzzzzzzzzz.

THERE ARE THINGS that are repeated like dreams, and my father, like so many other men, needs them to make life tolerable. This morning he has awakened dreaming of smiles. He arises from the floor with the same spirit and goes to sit down alongside an enormous belly that seems to spill over from the bed. He contemplates my mama with tenderness, but she doesn't move, not even feeling a mosquito that, sitting on her cheek, insistently draws another mouthful of blood from her. After shooing it away, my papa puts some warped shoes on that sound like the squeaking of the door. When he goes out, he is greeted by soft blows on the leg of his pants. It's Chango's affectionate tail.

The dog doesn't have to hear him say "Come on, let's go see dawn," because he will follow him as he has always done, and the two will walk together to the cotton fields. They will go to the same place where Papa José has taken us to dream so many times, and there he will sit until he's drunk with God. Then his funnel-body will begin to suck up the thousand colors emerging on the horizon. But the magic cloth quickly dissolves, and the clouds will remain completely undressed, prepared to receive the king.

My papa has always believed that the clouds are poor, deceived nymphs. He thinks this because when the sun uncovers its face, it immediately starts to laugh itself crazy. And thus, laughing and laughing, the sun injects him with the energies necessary to live. But the sun also makes fun of him, and the sun's laughter changes into the viciousness of a dog trying to eat its own tail. And Papa only comes back to reality when he realizes he's being roasted alive. Then, shaking his head without being able to believe it, he will speak to Chango: "I won't be like he is, friend. Yes, I would awaken with young bones and I would thank my fortune, but I would not burn, nor mock, nor go mad." Then on the way home, he will walk dreaming about one day living in a similar kingdom and that some day he will sleep in the Creator's house . . . in his own way.

José, after having celebrated the dawn, felt in a good mood and before going to wash his hands, gave a peck to his pregnant beloved, who was making his lunch for him. She answered him with a smile that was a little forced.

"How did my little darling wake up?"

"Fine. . . ."

"Did he give you trouble again?"

Marcela shook her head.

"You just wait and see what comes out. Then you'll forget all this."

"I hope God's listening to you, José. I want him born well."

The woman had good reason to be worried. Three years trying and nothing, until finally she had gotten pregnant. The happiness, nevertheless, had lasted briefly, since she had started to suffer right from the start. And now nine months later, it was late. The old woman Vicke, her mother, was also concerned, which is why she had stopped working in the Rocha house. Now she did the washing and ironing here.

After eating their breakfast in silence, she with a bitter taste in her mouth and he with the good mood he'd felt since Saturday, José gave her another kiss.

"Take good care of yourself, José. Be careful of the sun."

"Don't worry, my old lady." He went out.

THAT MORNING the sun laid bare the chocolate houses with such a great blast that the smoke coming from the stovepipes could not even be made out. That day the people, already scorched, would be set afire by the sun, and they would be ready to call it quits for the week by midday. Little by little the song of the birds turned into a shrill cry of anger: afterwards the cicadas would continue their own song to end up their self-destruction—insects whose bodies were found clutching the bushes.

Cars and trucks could be seen in the distance, full of workers on their way to different parts of the fields. José's buddy Teléforo was doing the same: he went sounding the horn from house to house, picking up those under his command.

Teléforo deposited the cleaners at the section of cotton that was the least dirty, and when they saw how clean the furrows were, their hearts picked up. They quickly bunched at the edge to sharpen their hoes vigorously, and when they heard Teléforo give his son instructions to take charge of the supervision while he went to check on the wetbacks he had working down by the river, they could barely contain their enthusiasm. Chale was a good fellow, and when he wanted to he let them slack off. But now he spoke to them with a serious tone.

"Okay, come on, you heard the boss. No loafing around. Hop to it or I'll report you."

"Whew, the guy's a pain. Come on, let's take his clothes off so he'll stop acting like he's the top cock," Jusito proposed, while the women turned red and quickly scrambled off among the furrows. Smart-aleck kid! Couldn't keep his mouth shut!

Chale, seeing how mad the faces of the others were, burst out laughing.

"What a bunch of shit. You believe me? This kid's not crazy, not by a long shot. Who told you I was a friend of work? Life is short, guys. Take it easy—anyway, you won't get any prizes."

They slowly set to, and after a while all you could see were heads with caps among the cotton fields. They also didn't take long in discovering the trick. Damn creepers were wrapped around the plants so that you couldn't even get across. Just one of those bothersome weeds was enough to make a mess for everyone. Hoes were out of the question. You had to crawl down on the ground and pull the root out by hand. That's how they spent the day, buried in a labyrinth like a drunk who can't find the door to his own house. The bodies showed up on the edge during the breaks, soaked bodies, with spitting faces, coughing, tossing their hoes in the drainage ditch and going over to a nearby tree. Then eternal movements of the head, toward the direction where help was to come—the yellow truck of the old man who brought their wages. But there was nothing to be seen, and then their eyes fixed on the damp female bosoms, as though the best encouragement of the world sprang from there. The feeble old men, by contrast, think about how they'll manage with the check this time, while the women miraculously put new shoes on the kids after having made a calculation of the two- or three-week-old unpaid bills. Damn

brats. Their feet are like iron. Farther off, the knot of young men
are savoring the cold bath and beers.

THE SCENE IS REPEATED on the bank of the river. With one excep-
tion: Leocadio with the pockmarked face is furious. His audience,
which normally applauds his creative gifts, is now mocking him
because his stories have the tendency to end on too fantastic or
stupid a note. Today they have been unable to swallow the true
story of the man who was so strong that he could break blocks of
sugar on his forehead. That's why he's angry.

"Don't pay any attention to those jackasses, compadre. Go on."

"No, they can go fuck themselves. They all think they're so
smart. . . ."

"I told you not to pay any attention. I know you can't be both-
ered with that stupid book-learning crap."

"Well, you know you're right, compa, because even if we have-
n't been to school, we know more than all that riffraff, right? Just
tell me what you want to know, compa, and let's see if I don't
know it."

"Well, I've always wanted to know how we humans got
started. I was never clear about that. How did all this business
start, compa?"

"Well, now you're about to find out. They say that it was very
dark and everything, and God felt very alone and on top of it
there was no light. But I believe the real truth was that He didn't
have anything to do, and one day just out of curiosity He began to
blow just like you do to get the ants all riled up, you know? And
then He said, 'Son of a bitch' and stepped back. Because the sun
lit up in His face and left Him almost blind. And He really liked
what His blowing had produced, so He went on with a moon, and
He gave her an earring for decoration. It was turning out just
great, know what I mean, compa? Then, all excited, He began
with the earth and added water. There's the proof of it, compa,
that river running there. Then . . ."

"Stop right there, compa. You're saying He did all this on His
own?"

"That's just what I'm saying, as God is holy."

"Listen, His hands must be as big as Lencho's, don't you
think so?"

"No siree, He only had to think about it, He puffed a little, and that was it."

"Hot shit! You mean to say He did everything just with His head?"

"Yes."

"So then He really scored big."

"That's right. He said, 'I'm going to think sun,' and poof! There it was, as round and hot as a stud. And the stars? The same thing. But just get this, compa, the best part was yet to come. What do you think was missing?"

"Well, the animals."

"No, man, us. The humans."

"Hold on, just hold on. And what do you think we are, compa? Nothing but damn animals. And if you don't think so, just look at Chango Pérez's face. If he isn't an animal, he's at least part animal."

"No, man, just stop right there. That's another matter. . . . But you're getting ahead of me, compa. Let me go on."

"Go on, then."

"It happens that in those days, the snakes walked on end."

"Shit!"

"Don't get scared, compa, because they didn't bite. And even more so they didn't bite God, because He's the one put them on earth that way, just like I'm telling you. So about that time He thought about making man, but He had a tougher time with him. This time He had to use His hands. He picked up a clump of mud from where the stream watered His garden, and He blew on it. And what do you think came out?"

"A woman."

"No, compa, it was a big macho man, this size, like Samson, and . . ."

"Listen, compa, I think you're mixing things all up on me."

"No, that's how it happened."

"Well, I think you've got it all backwards."

"Calm down, compa. The story's complicated."

"Sorry, a little complicated. But . . . didn't He make woman first?"

"No, I'm getting there. God said, I've got to give this man a companion, and He yanked a rib from him with His hands."

"No, compa, that's starting to sound fishy. You're just making up crap. How the hell . . . ?"

"He didn't even bat an eye. My idea is that He didn't even realize it, because don't you remember that at the beginning all He had to do was blow?"

"Well . . . she seems a little on the noisy side to me, if you want to know what I think."

"And if you think the man He did up was great, you should've seen the woman."

"But it was just the oppos . . ."

"He came up with a hot number like those beautiful daughters Lencho makes. You can imagine, and to make it worse, just think, both of them were stark naked."

"That's fine, if you say so, no problem. But in any event, no matter how I look at it, the thing's a mess. And how were they going to resist you-know-what?"

"I'm getting to it, but don't jump ahead. So God put the two beautiful creatures in that garden they call paradise, where even the devil couldn't get in. But I ain't saying there was no devil, just that God had already warned them. 'And you better be careful you don't listen to him,' He told them, and they obeyed His order."

"And what did they eat there, compa?"

"Ah, God blew them an apple tree."

"And so they spent their time eating apples! Sure!"

"No, not that, because that was a sin, but the leaves were as good and as sweet as the apples themselves."

"And so they spent all their time eating? I thought they fu . . ."

"You don't let me speak, compa. Pipe down and wait until I'm done. Then you can ask me questions."

"Okay, compa, don't get mad. It's just that I'm finding it a little hard to swallow. Go on, don't get mad."

"It turned out that since they were in paradise, they didn't feel anything was missing, like you know . . ."

"Yes, like fucking."

"A real bore. Until along came one of those snakes who said to the woman, 'Eat an apple and you'll see how pretty your cheeks'll get.' And the vain woman . . ."

"But didn't you tell me that it was like she was raised on bur-ro's milk?"

"Yes, but she lacked color. But what's important is that the snake was God's enemy. He was the devil himself. And he went and tempted her."

"Where did he tempt her, buddy?"

"Damn it, compadre. It's impossible to talk seriously with you. Don't act dumb. I want to say that he convinced her to eat an apple. Then God got real mad and threw them out. From then on they had all the things we have, problems, tastes, desires."

"You said they could . . ."

"Yes, then they could. They let themselves go and began to have children."

"You'll have to excuse me, and I know you're going to get mad, but you don't convince me. I don't buy that bit about blaming the snake. That part about blaming the snake, and worse, blaming the woman, that's just too much. How the hell do you think a stud was going to stand it without touching her thing, especially since both of them were stark naked? Excuse me, but I just don't believe it."

"Well, compadre, you can just go to hell. And don't ask me to tell you about anything. If you want to know something, go some-place else. Don't count on me, that's all. I'm gone."

"Wait, compa, don't go off half-cocked. You don't know how to talk like a civilized person. Right away you get all hot under the collar."

"Fuck off, compadre . . ."

QUIET AFTERNOONS. Striped uniforms. They rub their sunburn in the afternoon. The white lines of dried sweat on the shirts smell bad, but that doesn't matter. The people leave them on to eat the first warm meal of the day. The fevered heads eat silently, the slow movements as though they were living an eternal monotony. But then the sun fades, and little by little the bodies come alive again. The young men like Chale and Jusito go off to the pool hall, to the bar, to the movies, over to the other side to spend the last five bucks they have. By contrast, the old folks go off to do their weekly shopping and to pay what's left on what they owe. Then they return home with a six-pack, happy for the fresh air, loosening tongues that have been thick and dry all day. And nearby, behind the mesquites and guame trees, down by the arroyo, out in the field, the kids are running and yelling, feeling life. They play hide-and-seek, tag, London bridge, while elsewhere old voices, husky voices, voices and more voices continue to deny death.

Night falls, a black giant. With its silent footfalls and the desire to strangle someone. The people retreat. The buzzing mosquitos whisper in their ear that it's time to take the chairs in. One by one, patches of light appear as if by magic. The adobe huts cringe and draw into themselves with the night. That's the only way they can resist its weight.

THEY SAY THAT PEDRO, the guy who swallowed feathers, was born with a very big heart and that that's why he had to breathe with his mouth open. It was too big for him, they say, but I think that was only part of the reason. Pedro had been born with his mouth ready to laugh, and the most insignificant thing, the worst joke, would make him burst out laughing. The only time he shut his mouth was when he swallowed feathers. They had hit the ball with its insides coming out high and strong, and Pedro had caught it: with his mouth. And even then he'd laughed. That's why I don't think there was any room in him for tragedy.

Nor can I believe that his heart could just burst. His heart was made for laughing, a liquid laughter that ran down his pants. That's why after school, everyone went to the drugstore for refreshments. They would corner him so he couldn't get up, and then the jokes would begin. After a while, the whole gang would get up with Pedro in the middle, so people wouldn't see him. Because his liquid laughter would already have flowed free. Other times in the street:

"I'll bet you wouldn't dare touch his ass."

"I bet you I would. . . ."

And Pedro would sneak up behind the man real slow. Then he would run off. Peeing his pants laughing.

Tonight the gang shuts down the cantina. But tonight, even though they haven't had enough, no one buys beers. It's very simple. No one's got any money. Not fat Nalgas, who always has money from God knows where, not Chango the gorilla, who's being supported by only heaven knows who, nor dry-skinned Güero, who always has something stashed in his sock. And even then, the town won't accept that it's time to pack it in.

"Tell Louie to get his guitar and we'll go up the hill."

"No, tell him to go get his sister."

"Better yours, you son of a . . ."

"Okay, guys, cool it."

It's Nalgas the magician speaking. They calm down.

"I don't know about you guys, but I'm starving. I need to get a bite."

"Yes, but everything's closed."

"Well, then we've got a problem, right? What do you think?"

Silence. Everybody's waiting for Nalgas's words of wisdom.

"Let's hit the chicken farmer."

Everybody's eyes open a little wider, and the plan is quickly drawn: drop one of them out front of the gringo's chicken pen, enter, and wait with his hand out until a chicken perches on it. That's it, wait like a mummy so they won't get upset, and that's all. You go out, twist its neck, and ready. But who's going? Easy. There are no heroes . . . Later, one by one they turn and look at the car. Feather Gobbler is asleep. As always, with his mouth open.

"Pedro!" Louie yells as loudly as possible. Then, the rest is easy.

"I'm coming," he accepts, half asleep.

They stop quite a ways off, with the motor running. Dogs are barking on all sides. And on all sides people are sleeping as usual. Dead.

Pedro stumbles out of the car. He's quickly swallowed up by the dark. Meanwhile, the wait in the car is worse than Feather Gobbler's risk. The minutes are hours, gunshots, beheadings, death, and finally the silhouette appears with something bulky at its side. They open the door for him and he gets in, breathing hard. Then there's nothing left but the squeal of the tires on the street corner. Everybody holds in his desire to speak until they finally turn into an alley.

"How did it go?"

"Fine, but I could only get one."

Chango feels for it.

"Hey, it's sure big!"

Louie weighs it with his hand.

"Hey, you're right."

Güero holds it up by its feet.

"Son of a bitch, you brought the rooster!"

And in five minutes Pedro spills all the beer in his body. That same night they stuff his mouth with rooster feathers. So he'd pee more, they said. But nobody thought his heart would burst on him.

THE SLURPING OF THE TUBES shakes the body seated on its haunches, and until now he had not felt the weight of his head resting on his chest. Half asleep, Chonito, José's young helper, glances at the running water to make sure he's not dreaming, but he sees the dry ditch. The water must have dried up in the river, he thinks, at the same time he straightens up his body, numb from exhaustion. He can't believe he was asleep for so long, and that the sun didn't even wake him up. A brief shiver runs down his spine, causing him to walk over to the bundle formed by his shirt and hat. Then he picks up the shovel so he can cross over to the other side with the fervent hope that the water in the tilled field is done. But he doesn't have to. José, his boss, comes up.

"What's wrong, Chonito? Are you through?"

"I don't think so, Don José. The pump stopped."

"I know. I've just come from there. When I was walking over here, I couldn't hear it, so I went to see. It started again. I think we'll be done by tomorrow, don't you?"

"Yes, sir, as long as the water doesn't run out."

"I brought you some lunch to hold you until noon and . . ."

"But aren't you going to work over at the old man's?"

"Yes, but I'm going to get that kid Leyva to take care of the irrigation. I'll just fix the dam and the pipes so he'll take care of it. It's not much, really."

"Well, if you want, I'll . . ."

"No, man, the damn migra is all over the place like ants. It's better for you to leave at noon and wait for me on the other side. After they pay me I'll cash the check and pay you."

"Then about what time'll I see you, sir?"

"Wait for me there at the poplar tree around three."

"Okay, boss."

"And be careful because . . ."

"Don't worry, Don José, I know all about it."

"Okay, I'll see you there later."

In a flash José disappears in the sea of cotton by the river, while Chonito sits down again on the edge, this time to put on his misery-laden, warped boots full of pity while he cools his rear on the damp ground. The kid, despite the fact that this is the third night he's gone without sleeping, doesn't try to go fall asleep in some nearby shade. He feels happy because this time his boss is going to win out. He never tires of contemplating the forty acres of plants heavy with fruit. He might wish Sr. José could be here with him to share the precious buds beginning to burst out and kissing the water. But Chonito knows that's a lot to ask for. José, in love with a land that no longer belongs to him, José with his bowed legs must be something more than a sharecropper. That's why he has gone to join the group of cleaners headed by Teléforo.

PRESIDIO—nothing to remember except clouds and the devil. The latter skinny, the former fluffy, both slipping across the sky and making fun of the people, the animals, the plants. It never rains in Presidio, and the boom that emerges from the throat of the clouds only serves to fill the hollow of silence for an instant. But not even the echo from the Santa Cruz sierra is enough to scare the devil. The scoundrel never forgets the town. With a firm hand he squashes the mesquite and the thin brush. With both hands he squeezes the water out of the formerly mighty Río Grande, reducing it to a mirage, a puddle.

But the old goat-foot is not all evil. He has a very long swing mounted on top of the sierra, and now and again he shows up at the fiestas dressed as a dandy. On other occasions he appears in the form of a burro and allows himself to be ridden until the kids, poking around with a stick, discover he has no asshole, and then he disappears, leaving behind the smell of French cologne. Nevertheless, his favorite joke is the cat and mouse playing the hide-and-seek game. The border patrol cat, his face furrowed, waits to pounce on the mouse, whose only defense is the hunger he carries in his stomach. The mouse jumps the puddle and begins the ridiculous flight, while the devil rolls on the ground laughing.

THE SUN DRINKS HIM UP, burns him. The sun is laughing because he's drying him out. The plants, too, feel useless, not knowing what to do, while the thirsty sun drinks everything down to the last drop.

Chonito wants to cry but can't. His throat hurts, even when he's in the water up to his neck. He knows that he shouldn't move because the water will escape, and he's shaking, he's so scared. He moans. Meanwhile, the boy is turning into steam.

He continues in the same position, reliving the incident one more time. It happened so fast. After Don José had left, he had leaned on the shovel, and suddenly sleep overtook him. The jeeps of the immigration officials awoke him, and with his mouth hanging open he saw them searching about without noticing the opening in the irrigation ditch where the water had started to run out. It seemed as though he had never seen that scene, never heard the yell to "go for the riiiver" of the wetbacks and then a bunch of heads rushing toward the river. How many times had he witnessed that spectacle, the kicking ass of old guys and children or an accident like the one last month? The patrol plane had flown very low, right over their heads, *wooosh*. The man on horseback had gotten his head sliced clean off. They say he's still looking for it at night. Or last week when they found the little kid, all bloated and floating in the irrigation ditch. People said the patrolman had only wanted to scare him by ducking him in the water because he was always crossing back and forth.

After all the ruckus had died down, Chonito noticed the water running out, and at first he wasn't worried. But then he got nervous and started shovelling like mad. The water was carrying the earth away, and the hole was getting bigger. He shovelled until his blisters were bleeding and then, since he couldn't think of anything else to do, he took his shoes off and got into the water, jamming his body into the opening. That's how he'd have to stay, waiting for Don José, who would not be long in coming back, for it was already close to one.

His feeling of anguish vanishes when he thinks what a man he is. He can handle everything now, although he's barely twelve years old—the hoe, the shovel, picking, packing, everything. And since he knows he can do things like a grownup, he feels proud of himself. But then he returns to the situation he finds himself in and he feels ashamed. What will Don José say? He had been so dumb. Water is so scarce, and if old man Lynch sees it running out on the road, he'll get mad. What a jerk, I didn't see what was happening.

Now he begins to feel sleepy again because of the fresh water running around his arms, his legs, his neck. The murmur of the water lulls him, but he resists because he feels so strange, like he's floating on air, as though his waiting will never end. Like that time when by accident the tractor had started to roll. He didn't know what to do except to go around and around in circles until it ran out of gas. A drunken eternity went by until he got the idea to ram it into a trailer. Then he had run off to his house. But that time he'd found a solution. Not like now. Now he would have to wait and wait and wait. . . .

José has to shake Chonito hard to get him to come to, and when he finally opens his eyes, he starts crying. Then the boy, all numb, lets himself go on the man's chest. But after José has gotten over his fright, he can't help but smile, and the kid, when he sees him smiling, stops crying and pulls away roughly. Then he runs off toward the river. Meanwhile, gales of laughter strike against him, stopping only when he reaches the banks of the river.

THE DEVIL IS FEELING PLAYFUL, but at the moment the only thing he can think to do is look at his body in the mirror. Standing there naked, he sees he has no sex and no hair. From the front his sex looks like that of a newborn girl. He turns around but can't find his anus. He tries now to think of a simile, a metaphor to describe his beautiful body, but he can't find a "happy comparison." He thinks and thinks, and the only thing that comes to mind is a series of questions. The failure upsets him so much that it puts him in a bad mood, and he looks around for some other way to entertain himself. Immediately, he dons a clown's suit and looks at himself again in the mirror. Bah! That game is too childish. It's not worth anything outside. He's got to be more serious about his jokes, and he's got to continue to mock human life.

Now he uses a black brush to accent his pointy eyebrows and then he immediately stretches out his arm to scrape some sky blue. This he rubs in his pupils. As a final touch to the upper part of his body, he puts on a blond wig and a Texas hat. Then he looks for a suit to cover the rest, and finds a dark green one, his favorite. When he's got it on, he grunts his way into some boots to cover his rooster feet. There, he's ready! On the way out he winks at himself in the pool he uses as a mirror. Outside, he climbs on his swing . . . but . . . hold on a moment! He almost forgot! But there's still time. So he doesn't worry about it. He hikes himself up high, high, until he can reach a star. He quickly plucks it and places it where his heart should beat. Ready! The devil is ready to continue his eternal joke.

To GET TO PRESIDIO you have to go along a narrow road of guame and mesquite trees. With the air glued to your eyelashes and a sluggish mind, your body drops away from you and falls into a well that was never completely dug out. Or you slip down a funnel. Before you fall you sit on the top of a hill to see, in the background, goat droppings, houses that look all alone in the vast agricultural terrain. Houses of poorly tended adobe, houses that beg God for mercy. Houses: old shoes abandoned in a sun that shrivels everything. Like a drunk, you let go of the top and then you let yourself slide down a road that divides Presidio in half. Like a rolling wheel, Johnny's Bar, Texaco, Ron's Lumber, Harper's (they bored through Harper's forehead so he'd give up the loot). Phillip's 66, Juárez General Store. Slowly cruising.

"What about the downtown? What about life?"

"Ah, this is Presidio, mister. Don't ask any more questions, because I can't answer them. What about what? Ah, yes. The people are down by the riverbank, among the rushes, under the bridge, on top of the bridge."

"And what's across the border? Mexico?"

"Yes, mister, Ojinaga." (Presidio divided in two by time.)

"Reyes Uranga?"

"The second house, the one with the chicken coop. But he doesn't live there during the day, only at night."

"And the youngster?"

"José? Oh, he's something else again. If he's not at home, go look for him among the cantaloupe, the lettuce, the cotton, under one of the harvesting bags, or leaning over a shovel downing tacos and Kool-Aid. Maybe down at the packing shed. By the way, who are you?"

"George Evans from Marfa. I want to speak to him, understand?"

"Is anything wrong?"

"No, nothing. I just want to talk to him."

"Well, if that's the case, you'll find him among the Santa Fe refrigerator cars playing ball in Jones's packing shed with workers with chapped and sweaty hands and baggy clothes."

"Where?"

"You mean where is he? Well, look, just follow the same road to the outskirts, and there where the cow pens are, that's where Jones's packing shed is."

"Thanks a lot."

"Don't mention it."

(TWELVE HOURS times 50 or 70 cents between 10,000 times 10 minus transportation, minus the cantaloupes eaten, minus those who didn't show up today because they got the heaves and the cramps or they got drunk, minus the advance paid to Carrasco, who didn't come back. He's still a hard-working ole boy. See if I can get 'im to train for shipping orders.)

"Joe! Here's someone to see you."

"He's in the can, Mr. Jones."

"Done something wrong, Mr. . . . ?"

"Evans. No, I just came to talk to him about some incident last night."

"He'll be out in a minute. Hey! Son of a bitch! I told you to step on it, Manuel. The boxes over here. The fellow's getting old, you know? I just keep him around to help 'im out, but we get old sometime, you know? Hey, here he comes."

"Joe Uranga? I'm George Evans from . . ."

"No, sir, I'm Joe Durango. Uranga is not working here."

"Damn it, I thought you said Durango, Mr. Evans. I'm sorry . . ."

"Know where I can find him?"

"Yes, sir. He work with Mr. Lynch at the farm. But he don't go by the name of Joe. They call 'im José."

"What's the dif . . . Oh, well, thank you, and sorry to bother you, Mr. Jones."

"No bother . . . Hey! Son of a . . . more boxes over there!"

THE RAIN IS OUT TO MELT God's house, but it can't. It pecks in vain at the window, and when it grows tired, its tears of anger roll down the wall. Then, accepting defeat, it comes in through the

door that opens now and then and sprays the nearby bodies. But
these holed-up men don't care if they get wet. They're there be-
cause they want to be. They're there to take stock of women's legs
and to guess the reason why so-and-so has come so late, as they do
now with Marcela. Everybody looks at her, everybody's thoughts
are on her—the woman who, it seems, has been expecting for-
ever. . . . They don't know if she forgot to make the sign of the
cross when she passed by the holy water or if she refused to. She
merely sits down and begins to wipe her face with a cloth. (I
shouldn't have come. All eyes are on me, they know. Mama was
right when she told me, don't go, but I insisted. Now all I'll be is
a nervous wreck.) "My dear children, have no fear. Set your cares
aside. Let us trust in God, for He knows what He is about." (Yes,
Father, but now the river won't let me cross over. I want to go
with José. I'm very frightened that maybe they're waiting for me
outside and they'll carry me off to the office.) "We know that the
flood can be disastrous for us, but the gospel . . ." (My God, what
am I going to do if they don't let me go home, if they stop me and
ask for José? Dear God, help me . . . .) "And now let us pray,
pray to the Lord that He remove us from danger, that He bestow
on us His blessing. Let us pray. . . ."

The sermon is brief. The priest is just as impatient as the con-
gregation. There is nothing left to say. Everyone knows that their
hopes are bankrupt. Now they all stand, except for Marcela. She
remains seated a little longer because at that moment her legs are
made of rubber and she can no longer move the way she used to.
She now tires a lot. Her feet swell. Her belly is like a swollen river
and makes her feel uncomfortable, now more than usual because
I've been a pest for quite a while now. That's what I think, be-
cause she doesn't even make an effort to stand up. I guess I'm
more of a pest now because I have heard people comment that
when I move I hurt her, and I guess now that I'm more developed
and stronger, it will be that much worse. Undoubtedly that's
what's happening at this very moment. I'm cramping her stomach
real bad because that's what happens when I get ideas. I move
around a lot. I don't want to, but just a moment ago I decided to
sharpen the little bit of memory I've got and to bring together
things that have happened so I can write it all down when I'm
born. And the effort to recall and put it in order makes me move,

just as I'm doing now. My poor mother doesn't know about my faculties. She doesn't know that I have a very precise image of her and what's happening outside. She thinks what she has in her stomach can't feel or hear or think. But she's wrong. She's going to get quite a surprise when she sees I'll be able to write the minute I'm born. It's a real drag for me to be stuck in here, to always be floating in something like a liquid, sticky gum. When I stretch, I right away feel my feet and hands hit against a net. I image that that's what flies feel when they try to get free from a spider's web. I also think about my poor mother. How it must hurt her. I wish I were already born. But she insists no, because she thinks it's better for me, and like all mothers, she doesn't want to see her child suffer. Everything for my child, she says. The fact is I feel bad because I know the suffering she's going through out there, and I can't do anything about it. My hands are tied, and at times I don't get angry with her but with what I hear going on and what I imagine. And my mother's just as stubborn as always. That's why she's refused to give birth to me. I don't want my child to suffer, she says, but I think she's protected me enough. Can you imagine what it must be like to carry a child in your womb for so long? I'm tired of . . . Excuse me, Mama. I'm going to make myself a little more comfortable. Ah . . . ay . . . now I hear the little bells. Get down, kneel . . . That's the way . . . I promise now to remain quiet while the priest drinks the blood of God. If the situation is the same as every Sunday, the church'll be full. Just like always. Like a tired picture that shows everything. The priest up front with his gestures. Dressed the same. The same words. We are all sinners, but the meek will go to heaven. You have to suffer in order to inherit eternal life. That's why Christ loved and suffered. He set an example for us, and you've got to follow it. The children who still haven't learned the movements in order and don't know the responses are probably up front. They don't care much. Nearby'll be the beatas dressed in black hanging around the statues and the dripping candles, deep in prayer. All the same. At the other end, just behind, are the humblest, as though it were the practice of centuries. All the same. The picture of the church and its congregation tells it all. The boring picture is repeated when they go to communion. The line on the right will go first, perhaps because they're surer of salvation, while the other line

waits. The little bell! The little bell is ringing again! My mama
and the others lower their heads when the priest raises the repre-
sentation of the body in the form of a round piece of bread. I
never knew why they do it, I mean, why they lower their heads.
Is it by habit or out of respect? Is it because they're afraid of
the mystery or because they feel guilty at eating the body of
Christ they think they don't deserve? Who knows? I also think
that it's ridiculous to feel my mother beat her chest, something
I also don't understand. It seems like she wants to punish her-
self, to strike her heart because it's beating. Maybe she feels
guilty to be alive or she's renouncing living? Come on, get up,
Mama, wake your limbs up first. Be first just this once. Come
on, beat 'em to it. Look, you've got the same right. Truth is
it no longer matters to you. But it ought to. Look at that girl.
Let me out so I can slap her. Why does she shove in front of you,
pushing you to one side? Does she have greater privilege than
you do even in God's house? But I shouldn't bother you with
my grumblings. I promise to calm down. Now . . . open your
mouth . . . that's it, that's the way. Come on, go on back, but
don't clasp your hands, please, because I don't want you to
fall down like you did last week. Remember, you didn't eat
last night."

Marcela returns to her seat on her legs like butter. After the
priest has given her the host, he tells her to wait for him because
he wants to talk to her. Worried, she goes and kneels in the last
row behind a stocky old man, as though that would erase her fear.
There, on her knees, she prays and (what if I were to come out
right now, quick, without waiting for mass to end? No doubt the
priest already knows and wants to ask me about José. Dear God, I
can't stand it any more . . .).

Outside, the scattered rain continues its pecking while the
congregation gets to its feet. At that moment Marcela notices a
tall man, a blond who comes in without removing his Stetson
hat, and he goes up front as though he were right at home. Then
he comes back with eyes like an eagle that roam from side to side.
She feels a strong shudder go through her, but she hides it, ar-
ranging her veil. When the man notices her, he momentarily
halts in front of her and smiles. Then he winks at her and goes
out. She's left stunned, unable to move.

"Now, Mama. Mass is over. Jump now. Why is your heart beating so hard? What? Is it still raining? How are you going to get home? You can't run. . . . Are you going to sit down and wait? But, no, please don't run. Mamaaa. . . ."

BY THE TIME MARCELA reached home, she was all hunched over, her hands clawing at the air. She was screaming for them to get him off her.

"But, who, my daughter?" a little old lady asked her while Chonito's eyes grew wider.

"The devil," the terrified woman howled.

Whispering a Hail Mary, Vicke quickly made the sign of the cross several times on her forehead and began to sprinkle the room with holy water. After she'd done that, she gave her a spoon of sugar water for the fright and succeeded in calming Marcela down enough so she could say what happened.

"As soon as I came out of church, I was struck by a shadow that kept saying it wasn't going to let me get by. And it laughed and laughed like it was crazy."

"It must be your nerves, ma'am," Chonito stammers.

"Yes, Daughter, it's fear."

"I tell you I saw him. He had different shapes. First it looked like he was going back and forth on a swing just like he was going to knock me down every time he swung by. That was when I began to run, and he turned into a ram and kept butting me with his head. When he saw me fall down, he burst out laughing again. Then he disappeared in . . . du . . . Aaaay! Get him off me! Aaaay, he's coming! Please!"

Marcela begins to beat the air with her hands, running from one room to the next. She knocks the table over and breaks the dishes. Then she crashes into everything in her way. The old woman and Chonito trap her on the bed and struggle with her until they subdue her. The woman's hands are all stiff.

"Please help me! Look at my fingers, Vicke! I can't straighten them!"

Marcela attempts to open her fingers herself, but they gnarl with each other. Then she tries to run away again, but the two pin her down while Vicke talks to her, prays over her, makes the sign of the cross over her paralyzed hands and rubs her whole body. Little by little the hysterical woman calms down until she can at last move her fingers. But her gaze is far off. She doesn't answer their questions. Marcela doesn't open her mouth. She just sits there on the bed like a zombie, her paralyzed eyes on the wall. When they've tried everything in vain, they stretch her body out on the bed. Marcela doesn't resist. Vicke and Chonito think that perhaps after she sleeps a little it will go away, but they don't know the woman's eyes will be dilated for the rest of the day.

The devil withdraws to die laughing. Then, all tired out, he lies down on the wet stones to snore at his leisure.

CHONITO GETS UP from the floor where he'd lain down exhausted after crossing the river and goes directly to the vase full of water. After emptying it, he looks blindly for the leak. When he finally hears the tinkle of the water on pewter, he centers it beneath the leak. He immediately takes the cloth and puts it over the vase because otherwise the sound won't let him sleep. This done, he goes over to Marcela's bed to make sure she's all right. Her deep snoring satisfies him. Great! She's finally fallen asleep. He can't even remember. The woman had cried so much. "I started to think we couldn't control her. She was shaking so much. Poor woman. Not even when I assured her that Mr. José was fine and that he was waiting for her did she feel consoled. It's the first time I see her so, so, I don't know how to explain it, but she was all torn to pieces on the inside. They say that women get that way when they are expecting. I hope to God that's true, because if it isn't, this woman is going crazy. I would swear that she already was when I got here. I sure hope she isn't going to go on being sick this way."

"Ah, how I would like to have a chat with you, Chonito. Thank you for everything you've done. Make you understand why my mama is that way. She's carrying one hundred years, just imagine, Chonito, one hundred years of history in her belly. Her sickness is words that can't come out from here, from inside. They stay stuck in the mouth of her stomach until they make her vomit. Night and day she's enduring this sickness, destined never to get used to it. No, Chonito, Mama is not going crazy. She's sick from words she utters like a sigh in ears that don't retain a thing. And then those same words bounce back, going back into her mouth and lodging there. Then they make her throw up.

That's why my mama's crying, and I hope to God that before I'm born they don't poison me, because they also hurt me. I also feel like my mouth is full of pins. I sure hope I get out of here soon, because this bilious silence bothers me very much. Meanwhile, don't let them come in, if you can help it, Chonito. Don't let the poets sing those glorious epics of life. Cut their balls off for me until I'm born. If they speak to you of deeds, beg the dead to applaud and cover them with leprous kisses. If there is love in their verses, sing ballads to them. If they find beauty in Presidio's valley, tell them about the devil and his cave. Show them how he made love to the Indians. If they inspire you with virtue, Chonito, take them up into the hills, when the people seeking miracles leave legs, arms, and eyes made out of metal. Never a whole body. Never a live body. But rest, Chonito; after all, you can't hear me. Some day soon, I will light a match and burn their feet. Some day they will not sleep because the night will weigh heavily on them, like a ball chained to their feet or like a hard rubber ball. The bodies of the tired laborers will writhe in their beds and their bones will crunch. And the dead will invade their minds, will make them cry, will make them laugh, will drive them mad. Yes, Chonito, someday they will not sleep, they will not sleep, they will not sleep. . . ."

The rain has stopped. Inside, the leaks have grown tired of dripping, dripping. The silence is now overwhelming, enormous. Night, like Marcela's body, also seems to have collapsed with exhaustion. Nothing stirs. Not the stars, not the clouds. Not the moon. Nothing. The houses are coated against the night. Leaden numbness and silence. Only a lost breeze runs its cool hands from time to time over the beards of the poplar outside. Then the tree shivers and answers with the soft sound of a tambourine.

Marcela half opens her eyes, but for a moment she can't see a thing. She can only make out the bodies of Chonito and Vicke sleeping in the room. She's lying on her side because it's been a long time since she could lie on her back. The baby she has tried not to give birth to is like carrying a ton of copper in her belly. Beaten into the shape of a sharp cone. She adjusts her eyes a little more to the dark while she thinks about José, José, how he feels, the Río Grande, there's no way over, mass, the priest, it rained, I cried, I slept, what time is it, it must be three o'clock.

She hates getting up at this time, and she'd like to be able to stay there until dawn, but she knows what's waiting for her outside. The mud, the early morning chill, and then the wet wooden bench. She has to go outside, even if it's only an insignificant trickle. The pressure of the child is great. He makes the bed squeak as she sits up and feels for her sandals with her feet, and when she finds them, she puts them on. Then she covers herself up to her head with the blanket and walks toward the door.

"Ma'am?"

"I'll be right back, Chonito, I'm going outside," she answers him with a low voice.

"Marcela, is that you?" the old woman sits up in bed.

"Yes, I'm going to go to the bathroom."

"Do you want me to go with you?"

"No, Mama, I'll be right back." And she goes right out without waiting for the old woman to insist.

The outhouse with its sheet metal siding is not far, but she has to fight the sticky mud that tries to pull her shoes off. She quickly reaches the door, sensing how wet it's going to be inside. The outhouse is a real sieve. She climbs up to the freezing throne, raises her cape, and then sits down, catching a hand under each buttock. All this discomfort for so little. It's just that the child has slipped way down. "At times it seems like its little head is between my legs. But that's okay. There, there he goes . . . moving again. Go on and move, my child, move around because that's the only way I'm sure that you haven't gone and died on me. It doesn't matter that you hurt me. Move around so I won't worry about you. I don't know what's happened to you, but you no longer move like before. I ought to feel you more, what with how far along I am. Go on . . . that's the way . . . that's the way. . . ."

The woman returns and lies down again. The fetus continues to move with soft, serene movements. She enjoys them. She feels happy because there's life there in her belly. "Don't worry, Mama. I know you're not alone. You can't feel me because I don't want to hurt you. It's just that when I get tired of being all balled up as though I were praying, I've got to stretch. But I do it carefully, now that I've discovered that if I stretch my hands first and then my legs, it hurts you less. That's why you can't even feel me, because I no longer have the habit of kicking at you. Now . . . I'm making myself comfortable because you know, the night has been very long and my head fell asleep. My blood is feeling very heavy. I don't know why I fell asleep that way. Perhaps because your heart was beating so hard or because your guts were growling. You know, that happens a lot to you, since you didn't eat yesterday, don't you remember? "How did you fall asleep? You sure gave us all a scare. Your friend came to see you, and Teléforo almost swam across the river to tell my papa, but you calmed down late into the night. It was nothing but nerves. I felt them like tight bonds here inside. Imagine how I felt, with the boom, boom of your heart going hard in my head and your nerves and guts churning like a flood. Those are the times when I suffer the most, because it isn't true that your heart is in your chest, but rather in your guts. It's beating here in my hands, and I'm doing everything possible not to make the slightest movement. Two days ago I discovered that I can move like a compass. If you lie down on your side, I swing into a vertical position in your belly. If you stand up, I go into a horizontal position. If you make movements I don't understand, I float free. That's why you can't feel me, Mama, and I hope you understand. I'm normal and I'm growing fast. You don't know it, but since I began to exercise my mind, I've noticed the development myself. Ever since I started to think about writing when I'm born. And now this disorder doesn't matter to me. The time will come. What's important now is to let everything fly, to loosen your tongue until the time comes. For the first time I'm happy to be able to see so clearly from here, Mother. There's no need to be on the outside, no need even for it to be daytime, because you communicate it to me. Your soul becomes translucent. When you're happy it turns into a white butterfly, and when you suffer, the little butterfly bleeds all over my body. I tried to talk to Chonito tonight to explain your madness to him, but I don't think he heard me. That's something I don't understand. It seems like some people hear me when I think and others don't. I would like to know if they really can see and hear. I don't know why it's only now that it's occurred to me how slow my life has been. I barely realized today that I've stretched myself out like a very fine thread that goes way back; I was with you in your veins since your childhood. And don't forget, you only gave me your womb so I could grow there, but long ago I was a seed bouncing from womb to womb. Imagine existing one hundred years before being born, looking for a place to take root. But rest now, Mama, the night has been long."

AFTER IT STOPPED RAINING, the night got real nice. It was real pretty, with bunches of stars all over the place. Little by little the clouds had slipped away as though they were afraid, leaving a bundle of bright pinpoints. No doubt about it, the sky looked like one of those beautiful cloaks kings drape their skeletons with.

Downtown, all the guys came out of their houses to see what the hell was happening in the silent town. They were all on foot because their old men wouldn't let them use the car. Besides, you need gas to cruise, and everybody was in the same boat without any, like everything else. The damn rain hadn't allowed them to work all week, so some of the fellows had to be happy with rooking around like the Chinaman on the night of the sixteenth of September celebration. Others had gotten to playing craps for a nickel a throw behind Johnny's Bar—after all, you can't even get feeling good with just a dollar. And if you were hot, you could win a pile and then go play pool for beer. But if not, you were out in the cold, as always happened to those who were already as bad off as sleeves on a vest. Usually, the most undeserving asshole would win at the dice. So no matter how much you snapped your fingers and blew on them and treated them like honeys, they always treated you rotten. Not even Little Joe, or Live Jive, or Silver-Eyed Sixto would give you the time of day. They gave you the cold shoulder, even if you tried to talk them up. Shit, it seemed like the dice were loaded.

Other times the guys wouldn't be making asses out of themselves. By this time they'd be over on the Other Side dancing, ogling the girls, the whole story. It was real cool in the ramadas and whorehouses. Gals walking round and round the plaza like a broken record, chewing gum, waiting for you to go over and talk to them. "Say, chick, let's go get a beer over there where the rubber-lip musicians are. Hey, don't cut me off; I'm short already." If you scored, you'd take her and get her a Coke and talk her up. If you were lucky and she liked you, you could put it to her straight: "Say, let's go where it's dark and get it on." If not, then you could just take it slow, dancing with her. In any case, you'd scored and the idea was to take it easy, to play it cool. But now? Can't do anything; the whole thing's an ugly mess. You're forced to spend your time with a foot on the corner, watching the old folks making the rounds, all sad, all of them frightened that the fucking river will piss all over the place. If that happens, then you and they'll all be in a mess. The damn border patrol are also going back and forth as if that were going to stop the river, but their job is all show because there's nothing for them to take care of. Who's going to cross over here with all that water? Besides, it costs an arm and a leg to cross on the barge. Only the guys that come to the dance from over there in Chuco, Kermit and Odesson have enough money to pay the five bucks to Trompas, who played it smart, buying himself a barge and ferrying people from one side to the other. But on this fucking, worthless night, not even those guys can get over. Only the sky's gorgeous. It's either stay home and snooze or hit the boss lady for the buck she's always got stashed away and you split for the show. Don't be stupid and play it on the craps because then you won't even make it to the movies.

Chale, who's been sleeping all afternoon, gets up and goes to the bathroom. He remembers the date he's got with Jusito, and he starts to get ready. There in front of the mirror, he washes the sleep off his face, and then uses the foam to make himself a beard like Santa's. He takes out the razor, and in a few minutes his cheeks are nice and smooth. His gal likes them like that. Then he smears Parrot gel all over his hair and shapes a neat ducktail. As he bends over he notices his shoes are all scuffed, and right away rubs them against the back of his khakis because there's no time for a speedshine. It's already close to eight o'clock, and that dude is probably already waiting with the chicks. So he quickly slips his pants on, leaving his shirt opened on top so he can sport his hairy chest, and he's ready. "I'm not going to eat, boss lady. I'll be back in a while."

Just when he was about to get into his old man's jalopy, he noticed it had a flat, and he got so upset about it he kicked it until his big toe was sore. After he'd sworn at it for the last time, he took off on foot. His anger didn't go away quickly because he was still thinking about the fiestas he'd missed out on, although he knew full well the danger of crossing the river. He recalled the beating Betabel had gotten, but it had been his own fault that

he'd gotten knifed because why'd he try and go steal the gal away
from that guy out in the open? Yeh, it was all his fault. It's better
you can't get over. You'd just better cool your heels here until the
heat's off. What's the big deal? You can get it on with Mary, man.
Don't be a fucking jerk with her, the dame's got a crush on you,
she really loves you. Otherwise, how come she's put up with so
much? But the guy'd counted on the car to get out of having to
take her to the movies because he was flat broke. The only buck
he had left had gone for gas, and now this fucking flat. Jusito'd
better . . . That damn guy, nothing bothers him. Everything's a
big laugh, and I believe he's going to die crazy. You never know
what he's going to do, what he's going to come out with, what
mess he's going to get into. And that fucking habit of goosing
everybody every time you turn your back really bugs me. And the
stupid things he says. But in any case, the fellow never wimps out
on you. Better the guy backs me up tonight.

When Chale got to the drugstore, jumping puddles, Jusito was
doubled over laughing, and Chale just let him get it out of his
system.

"Uuuh, what a cool dude. Didn't you say the car and me and
that and . . ."

"Never mind, it had more holes than you do, fucker."

"Well, that takes care of that. Now we're gonna be left with
a hard . . ."

"And the chicks?"

"They're already inside. They've been waiting a long time.
Come on, let's go, man. . . ."

"Hold on, dude. I'm broke. Not a . . ."

"Uuuh, what a guy. Here, dude, lookie here. Four big ones."

"Where from?"

"The batteries, dude. I don't think Johnny's tractors'll be start-
ing tomorrow."

"All right, then. Wave to the chicks."

By the time they got to the theater, Jusito and Olga had
French-kissed and he had her peeing her pants laughing. But Mary
cut Chale dead for the way the guy had been misbehaving. So he
gave her lots of bullshit like there was no other chick that made
him feel as good as she did, and as soon as he had some dough
he'd buy her a ring. Then he went on about how his old man

Teléforo did part-time chores for his boss because he could no longer handle the hard work and he himself had to help him out. He told her why he had stood her up the other day—the police'd caught him speeding and since he was stinking drunk, he'd fucked up when they made him stand on one foot. The police'd stripped him even of his underwear, and when he got out, he'd gotten mixed up in Betabel's shit over on the Other Side. In this way he'd calmed his woman down by the time they got to the movies.

Inside, they laughed and laughed at Tom and Jerry. But that's all they watched because by the time Tarzan started beating his chest, with the ape doing the same, the guys had their hands full and their eyes half cocked. They had a great time petting until Jane came on, and that's when the shit started. The guys didn't realize that their hands were in slow motion until they really stopped on the chicks' tits and paid attention. Hot damn, Jane was quite a piece! The chicks got jealous when they saw how their men were all gaping and they put up a stink. Mary told Chale not to be such a pig with his mouth hanging open, but Olga really got upset. She began to scream at them all kinds of dirty words at the top of her voice so that everyone could hear. They had no choice but to go outside and see how to patch things up. Then the four went back in, but everybody was all bent out of shape.

Halfway through the movie the women asked for something to drink just to be bitchy and spiteful, because they knew the dudes were totally broke. Chale didn't know what to answer, but blabbermouth Jusito, who'd promised to cover his eyes when Jane appeared, told Chale to go with him. He saw him laugh and wink. So when the guys went out, the chicks were left dreaming, and when the dudes took their time coming back, they thought they were really going to make it up to them. Surely they were going to bring Cokes and hamburgers and fries, the whole bit. Let 'em sweat, the bastards, so they won't think we're just any piece of ass, right, friend? Yep, you've always got to be firm with those bastards.

They were busy with those thoughts when the guys arrived and plopped down like they hadn't brought a thing. But Jusito set a bag of something on the floor, wrapped in his sweater.

"Where're the Cokes?"

"We've got something better, but you've got to be quiet, because it's a surprise."

"Stupid jerks, you brought sh . . ."

"For sure, right, buddy?"

"That's right, it's . . ."

"You'd better cut the crap. Show us what it is or we're leaving."

"You've got it. Ready, buddy?"

". . ."

"But you've got to close your eyes first. . . ."

When the chicks went along, Jusito raised the container of Kool-Aid and set it on Olga's legs, and when she opened her eyes, Jusito was already almost out the door. Chale also made tracks behind him, and they ducked in the restroom to keel over laughing. The attendant shoved them out because they wouldn't stop laughing. Outside, they continued doubled over with laughter with no thought for their dates. Besides, the night's so rotten the only thing pretty is the fucking sky. With bunches of stars all over the place.

THE DAY DAWNED like Independence Day come late. "The water went over the bridge! It already broke into the fields upstream! It went all over Colorao's fields!" The news spread until it reached every corner of Presidio. The landowners began to curse, yelling for whatever tractors and tools that could be saved. Workers soon began to straggle along, all upset and exhausted by the struggle they'd gone through. There was nothing else to be done; dikes, shovels, and sandbags, bales of alfalfa, and everything humanly thought of had been in vain. The water was rolling over the fields of cotton and late cantaloupe. The water sought room to spread out its stiff tentacles, and when it encountered obstacles larger than itself, it roared at them. Then it swept around them, as though in this way taking on the necessary strength to swallow them up and continue its destruction. The bosses, the owners, turned around, got in their cars, and, their wheels squealing, drove off in a rage. "This year you're not going to get out of the hole, brother, because you didn't insure your crop. They'll come for your new alfalfa packer, the Allis Chalmers and its hoe, also the International that you were using to till with." "Son of a bitch. When you want the fucking water, you don't get it and now . . . goddamn. And all that money I put into repairing the gin . . . all that fucking work for nothing."

All morning there's no end to the line of people going to Sam's Phillips 66. The people from the town come to tank up, getting ready to leave. There's nothing left to do here except shove off to New Mexico or Odesson. "Working for the petroleum companies is what pays the best." "Yes, but what the fuck do I know about machines, and you've got to know how to talk English for those jobs." "Naw, buddy, I know the fellow there, he's a great guy. I'll get you in." The older men who've spent their lives in the fields show up, but they only fill up and leave without a word. They're only thinking about the problems they're going to have away from home—the rent, the shortage of food, the money they're to earn, and what they're going to eat. Then they'll come back here broke. But at least you've stayed alive, right?

On the other side of the street, Nancy's Café is already starting to jump. One by one the trucks filled with the hats of boisterous men begin to arrive. Then Immigration Service jeeps. Only the antennaed car of the sheriff is missing. Between mouthfuls of ham and eggs with coffee: "Damn, you should've seen how the water toppled that tree like a shithouse; the water's pouring all over the fucking place at Johnny's. He tried to save his bulldozer but the bank caved in. That stupid Lencho just let 'er go and he jump off like a scared rabbit. . . . Well, gotta go see if them ole boys done as I told them to. Guess there's nothing else to do but start buyin' Mexican cattle. I hear this guy down by Los Mochis got purty good ones to sell. I'm gonna try and lease some of that Campbell property so I can fatten them carcasses. Six months'll do it. I hear they're paying pretty good prices for beef this year."

Ben, Jr. has another idea: "I'm going to the valley for three months. I'll take the trailers, and I'll get a contract to transport the harvest for Vernes, Inc., and that way I'll recoup a little. After the river goes down, I'll fix the land up and ask the government for a subsidy. The government pays me not to plant. Two hundred twenty thousand tax-free dollars just as a favor. What more can I ask for? Nothing more. That way, the land rests."

The thought makes him generous with the waitress, and he leaves her fifty cents.

"Have a good day, sir."

"You too, ma'am."

THAT MORNING, the old woman Vicke and Chonito got up early with Marcela's cramps, and by the time the sun came out, the house was jumping. The still unborn baby was jabbing hard, and there was no way to stop him. "It must be the blow you got yesterday, Daughter. Don't worry, you've still got time," the woman told her, trying to make her happy. Then she ran back and forth between the kitchen and the living room with cups of mint tea and buttered tortillas, but Marcela refused to eat. "I told you no! I'm already stuffed. Take it away! I don't want it!"

Chonito left them talking. He went off to Teléforo's house. When he got there, he found everybody gathered together. "Carlos's off to California, and I had to get his clothes together. The old man also got up early to help, but what with the damp these days, he hasn't felt well at all. You know how his rheumatism bothers him." Serafina was speaking to Chonito as though he were José's son. . . . It was to be expected. The kid loved his boss more than his own father, and he spent more time here in Presidio than in Ojinaga. Besides, his real father was only interested in the money the boy brought home, and if he didn't, he shoved the shoe box at him, saying, "Hit the street, shithead!" It was difficult to become a clown on those occasions. To make the Americans and the Mexican soldiers hanging around laugh. He just couldn't. He also couldn't stand the other boys who, like insurance agents, followed the poor gringo until his face turned red. When they had got him, three or four hit the ground, looking for more than two feet. And when they saw that the man was no freak, they sat thoughtfully on their boxes. Blond man, earth's mystery, vital fullness, won't you tell us your secret?

The situation had gotten bad the last week, because since José had fled, there was no work. But Chonito had decided to suffer the consequences. More important was the well-being of the Uranga family. So right from the start he told Teléforo that he should count on him to fill sandbags and put up dikes along the river. "Take care of Marcela and Vicke as best you can," José had told him. Let a few days go by and then on Saturday cross the river to report whether the bastards have gone. I'll be at Bernabé's. If anything urgent comes up, count on my compadre, Teléforo."

He kept his word. In the afternoon he went into town. He went to the gas stations, he sat down outside the café, he walked around the hotel, and he even strolled over to the bridge, running the risk they'd nab him. He remembered very well that José had barely crossed over when they'd shown up asking, "Where's José Uranga?" and when they didn't find him, they'd gone back. After a few days they were back in Presidio with an order to arrest him for avoiding the draft. Meanwhile, Chonito came and went with the news, until José at last had decided to move to the other side. He couldn't see himself killing people who shared no blame in the squabbles between politicians. "Talk to Teléforo and tell him to do me the favor tomorrow night. He already knows what he's got to do," he said to him.

Chonito had killed the first hours of the previous night under the soaking wet tents put up to celebrate the national holiday. He had waited until twelve o'clock among the games of dice, clothes raffles, and the shouting of drunks. Then, with the necessary courage, he had crept like a cat along the side of the bridge. Feeling his way, he'd found the boards, because the river was already flying high over them. After an eternal pulling at him, the current had let him cross. At two in the morning, Chonito was a wet shadow sneaking through the town, covered with mud. Then, a hot cup of tea, a woman wrapping him in a sheet, and a mattress stretched out on the floor. Chonito remembered nothing more.

"I only wanted to tell you that tonight is for what Don José asked you to do."

"Fine. Then tell Vicke that I will go for them right after sundown. In a little bit I'll tell Samuel to have the launch ready. But, go on, go have some lunch. Are you sure you don't want anything?"

"No, thanks. I already ate something on the other side. I'd better go see if there's something I can do."

"Okay, buddy, I'll be seeing you. Put 'er there."

"Take care of yourself over there."

"Sure, let's get going. Take care, okay?"

"You, too, Carlos."

THAT NIGHT THEY FOUND the river cresting with chocolate. It looked more like a dark mountain continuously rocking back and forth. Marcela, by contrast, thought about a hunched-up cat with its hair on end, opening its rabid maw without meowing. All she seemed to hear was a soft buzzing like a bumblebee off in the distance.

The woman lowers her head as if looking for something, as if her eyes could stop the sensation of something running down her legs. She feels a warm trickle that begins in the nerves of her head and runs down to her feet. But she doesn't say a thing. She only contemplates a mechanical scene, men in silence, running from the truck to the launch, tossing bundles that Vicke and Chonito had gathered together during the day. It seems that the whole scene is trapped in an enormous shell. Their nerves have turned into cords that cover their eyes, which is why they don't even realize it when light floods them. Not even when they are ready to help the women aboard the launch. Only when Teléforo returns to the truck does he notice the lights growing larger as they approach.

"Hurry up! Get into the launch; they're almost here!" he yells at them; at the same time he starts up the motor of his truck.

The launch man Samuel takes the little old woman in his arms, while Chonito grabs Marcela by the hand to make sure she doesn't trip. But they can't hear a thing. Their guts unclench.

Meanwhile, Teléforo waits for the lights to arrive. "I can take care of it myself. I'll tell them I've just come down to see the river, that's all. Those bastards know who I am. I'll tell them the launch's carrying two friends from Odessa whose mother's sick. That this is their car. What else can they ask? Yes, I'll wait for them here. . . . What? . . . It looks like they're turning the lights off. Who can it be?"

The man waits a moment longer, but nothing happens. He can barely make out the outlines of the car. Then he turns his truck around and drives over to where the lights had been. He drives by slowly, not able to believe there's no one there. He goes back again and then he goes down by the riverbank, but still nothing. He needs to see something, the lights, the outline at least. When he's convinced himself there's nothing, he turns toward home, confused. That's when he hears a loud blow against the windshield. The owl lies flapping its wings at the side of the road. But the man doesn't stop because the sound of the river has become the laughing of a giant. The devil returns to his beloved sierra.

THE FIRST PART of the crossing went by quickly, but the struggling of the launchmen became greater by the middle of the river, and when the launch wouldn't go forward anymore despite their rowing like madmen, they let the water carry them for a while before battling it again.

The little old woman squeezed her daughter's hand every time the mountains of garbage collided with the launch, and she prayed frantically to the saints. By contrast, Marcela's mind was like a dead fish caught in a net. The pain came at intervals, a pain that lasted one eternal minute and then disappeared like the ringing of bells. She seemed suspended in air, beyond human feeling.

"How do you feel, Daughter?"

"Give me some water."

"There isn't any, Daughter."

"I want some water."

"Hold on just a little longer, my child."

Marcela closes her eyes and clamps her legs together as hard as she can. It looks as if she's trying to remove the obstruction that's between her legs.

"Take it away, Vicke."

"I can't, Daughter." The little old woman thinks Marcela's referring to the pain.

"I told you to take it away."

"Calm down, for God's sake, Daughter. You'll see it'll go away soon."

The men row harder. The words of the women give them the superhuman strength that, at another time, they might have run out of. But it's not just that. Marcela's actions seem to indicate that the woman is losing her mind because who in that state could be indifferent to so much pain? No, it can't be natural, they think.

Nor what they now see. The limp body of the woman falls on the little old woman, who screams, startled out of her wits, while she clutches at her. But Marcela's not moving. The men quickly forget about the launch and try to make her come to, but it's no use. Only the dirty water is moving. The water and a newborn in the middle of the river. Over the tops of the trees, over their heads, some cottony clouds begin to wail.

Presidio 1970

O kay, just leave it like that, Son. Tomorrow we'll do a little bit more. We'd better turn in."

"Fine, Papa." And I stood up, putting the hoe over my shoulder.

The two of us walked silently, without speaking, toward the house. There was nothing for us to say. It seemed that the darkness pressed down on our exhausted and sweaty brains, leaving us mute. All you could hear was the grunt of clumps of dirt squashed by the feet of two exhausted men.

When will this all end? I thought, recalling the monotonous and eternal days. Tired days. Days without hope. Poor Papa. He's so old and he still doesn't realize that all the days are the same, without change. That everything boils down to life and death. Surely he hasn't even looked at himself well in the mirror, at the deep lines stamped on his face, at the curved stoop of yesterdays, at the fatigue reflected in his eyes of today.

"The sun sure was hot today, right, Son? It seemed like we were taking a sweat bath."

"Right. That's why I sat down for a good spell under the tree. After all, we weren't making much headway. There's no use in killing ourselves, right?"

He didn't answer. We fell silent again.

That's the way it's always been, Father. This damn land has always ended up with your blood, your sweat. And it hurts me that with every drop of your body part of your soul drains away, a life that is dying in order to live better. I know that your steps point day after day toward an emptiness, and I too am following them. But do you know why I'm doing it? For you, Papa. So you won't be left alone. But now I'm tired, Papa, and I haven't told you I'm leaving. I'm leaving because I'm certain that there's a world better than Presidio . . . Presidio, Texas. Even the name sounds sick to me because I first saw the light of day in Presidio, Texas, which, if you look at it, means under the tiled roof of the jailhouse.

"Tomorrow we'll go back to cleaning, right, Papa?"

"Yes, Son. There's still a little left to do. At least the rows that are going to get watered."

Sure, we'll put some more holes in our shoes, zigzagging like fools between the furrows. We'll pull out the weeds and we'll tramp and we'll walk, and there'll be another line on my old man's forehead. At least right now we'll treat our fatigue with some rest in the emptiness and darkness. Then, we'll get up early next morning as though time had brought something new. As if time had boundaries. How stupid. Life is measured only in terms of effort and action. How dumb are those who consider us jackasses for having roots in "mañana land." But they just don't understand that tomorrow means hope, that today you worked fifteen hours, and that you hope to be able to withstand sixteen. It's the hope of improving yourself, surpassing the limits of the body. It never dies in Presidio. It asserts itself and nurtures like our daily bread, to the point of becoming an eternal parasite. Yes, you've got to hope. . . .

"Why didn't you go to war, Father?"

"Because I don't understand anything about squabbles between countries. Why fight with others if the battle is here inside me, if hunger is my own war? We, Son, are like a pair of dice that have been rolled so much we've gotten round as marbles. And we won't stop rolling until we find a niche. It's that niche we've got to battle and not against ourselves."

But the agents didn't hear you, don't you remember, Father? They came and took you away to another jailhouse without a moment's hesitation, after you'd lost your wife. And now you're paying for the crime of not having killed others, for not having become the enemy of your own people. They refused to understand that for you the fight to live was enough, and you had to serve the sentence. With four more lines on your forehead, with two fallen wings, dragging along the ground, with your back branded, don't you remember, Father? You came back with your soul riddled and with a bleeding heart to walk these lands again. And then you became worn out and got drunk and went mad with the devil's laughter here in Presidio. And after I saw your tragedy, I pulled myself from the clutches and left, do you recall? But now I've come back, after a long time, and do you know why? Because you've died. Yesterday we buried you at last in Presidio's dusty cemetery. I say at last, because we'd grown weary of waking you, and I think you even felt the same way. You must have been tired of being on display to so many people, so much wailing. I only wanted to see you the first day. Then I devoted myself to making the necessary arrangements and to withstanding the condolences. Before then I hadn't realized how many friends you had, all of them faces withered by time, and I thought that life would kill them that way too, just like it did you. After the first day

*of words like a broken record, I devoted myself to my grandmother
Vicke. When I got here, I couldn't say a thing to her, so I let her get it
out of her system against my chest, telling her clumsily not to cry. Then
the two of us went over to contemplate the last vestiges of a scarred
face, a face with fifty years of wrinkles and a heart beaten to death
beneath the skin. "Life always scorned us." That's why I refused to
come back to see you, because you died with your mouth making the
same face of scorn. I'm certain that if you could've spoken to me at
that moment, you would have scolded me. "Do you really think I'm
going to let death make fun of me? Didn't I tell you to bury me with
Mariachi music?" is what you would've said to me. But I also would
have responded with the truth. Life played games with you, Papa. You
died striking at your enemy and only hitting air. I know you couldn't
avenge yourself. That's why you're bitter, Papa, because you were born
with a smoking bitterness in Presidio, a pit of calcinated bones, in Pre-
sidio, "seven pierced letters in Holy Week, jailhouse of elongated time,
a prison suspended in the steam of three o'clock in the afternoon, Pre-
sidio the joke, Presidio the unfortunate, Presidio born old." No, Don
José, you don't have to ask for the children, they were born with wrin-
kles, at three in the afternoon. That's why there aren't, nor ever were,
fevers in Presidio. People came into the world burned, melted down.
The blood of their bodies was forged at one hundred twenty degrees.
And that's why you loved and lived with your blood boiling—hatred
was forged long before you died. And that bitterness from long ago has
fastened onto me. I got it the first day we waked you. That's why I
refused to see you again. Now, three days later, I feel better, although
I've said goodbye to you forever. But, you know, I've decided to stay
because we've got to remove the crown of thorns in Presidio. Yes, we've
got to walk among the cactuses and the mesquites. We've got to endure
the road, remove the crown, and put it on someone else. After that,
we'll go down to the river and wash our wounds, and when we're
clean, we'll return to Presidio, and if we want to keep on going, we'll
have to come back strong, because we'll need the greatest willpower the
soul has to give. Because they will see us and think we're mad and tell
us to go preach down at the riverbank. The people who've put up with
us will understand us, but they will not follow us because they'll be
afraid, and there will be others who'll spit in our faces. They'll tell us
everything's going fine, that the people are happy with their houses and
jobs. But the miracle will take place, and then we'll have to bring them*

together, tell them about the devil that's gotten free and is still on the loose. They'll also have to be told about that famous fort that was born long before 1683 and about so many other things. Yes, we'll have to tell them, but not with suffering and with pardon. A flame has got to be lighted, the one that died with time.

El diablo en Texas

Yo vengo de un pueblito llamado Presidio. Allá en los más remotos
confines de la tierra surge seco y baldío. Cuando quiero contarles
cómo realmente es, no puedo, porque me lo imagino como un vapor
eterno. Quisiera también poderlo fijar en un cuadro por un instante, así
como pintura pero se me puebla la mente de sombras alargadas, som-
bras que me susurran al oído diciéndome que Presidio está muy lejos del
cielo. Que nacer allí es nacer medio muerto; que trabajar allí es moverse
callado a los quehaceres y que no se debe tomar a mal el miedo del turista
cuando llega al pueblito y sale espantado al escuchar el ruido vacío de
almas en pena. Quizás sean estas voces las que nunca me dejan retratar a
mi pueblo como realmente es, porque cuando me hablan me dejan la
cabeza y el alma hechas pedacitos como si hubiera jugado un perro rabioso
conmigo dejando despilfarros de cuerpos arrugados, cuerpos agujereados
como cedazo por donde se filtra el agua que riega los campos verdes de
sudor borracho y risa sofocada por unos miserables uniformes con mapas
del país en el brazo derecho buscando a los que se mojan en el río que
fertiliza plantas de diablos ojos burladores de la gente y de un Santo Niño
que juega a las canicas de rodillas esperando al padre que regrese de
prisión, espantapájaros desconocido, niño esperando debajo de un colum-
pio raptor del viento, niño que escucha suspiros en el agua, en el fortín
tembloroso de aullidos de perros funerarios a pleno medio día y en la noche
el niño muere, la vieja llora, un feto piensa de noche, noche, noche larga
como el infinito, noche pesada, monótona como la historia mentirosa así
como las damas del zumbido, pero éstas tienen razón, la historia no,
porque en los corrales de este lado las vacas flacas de Ojinaga se compran
a muy buen precio para engordarlas a expensas de otros y la iglesia
mientras tanto que se cae de ojos tristes en los días que no hay domingos
así como las casas de queso de chocolate roídas de ratón porque no tienen
cemento y los excusados antiguos tronos de los reyes católicos ahora son de
lámina y los baños al aire libre en pleno invierno arropados en lona para
que no penetren los ojos o en una tina a media sala los sábados para rociar
el piso de tierra, tierra con montes de leña prohibida para todos menos el
inquilino quien conoce la bondad del Señor que tiene tiendas que fían la
comida y gasolina racionada pero en las boticas no se venden medecinas ya
que no hay dotores sólo hojas de laurel, romero, ruda y yerbabuena para
los niños que voltean los ojos legañosos y las madres tienen cuates cuando
comen los chorupes los frijoles con quelites y la carne del diablo con
azadero con trompillo y con empacho la penicilina cura todo mal amén
cuando las trocas cargadas de humillados escupen el sol blasfemo con el

hedor de muerte próxima, olor que penetra, penetra, penetra el espinazo
derretido, doblado, jorobado, abrazando casi casi el melón que si lo comes
te da torzón si no se te suelta el cuerpo se te escapa y la mente se te vuela
con el aire bochornoso pero cuidado porque te empacan en el vagón
refrigerado de la Santa Fe y te llevan a disneylandia mientras el mapa del
gobierno te pregunta si eres legítimo de la tierra sembrada con hermanos
de tus hermanos de tus hermanos amén y el puente de la frontera se cierra
a medianoche pa ponele el candado al infierno aunque por debajo se
escapa todo el río acostumbrado a ser tecolotl y el sol ya ni lo necesitas
porque eres planta, eres tierra infértil, gastada y el diablo está cansado de
reírse en su cama de agua porque el padrecito subió a la sierra a mediodía
en procesión dizque pa desterralo y pa que las puertas se abrieran por todo
el río y se cruzara sin temor y la cruz en la cumbre se bendice al tiempo que
el diablo se prepara para ir al baile y los batos locos no se aguantan
tampoco en las boticas donde hay vitrolas con Elvis Presley Fats Domino
Little Richard and the blob that creeps and you ain't nothing but a hound
dog finding your thrill on Blueberry Hill bailando solos con zapatos
puntiagudos con taps tapping tap tapping chalupas down the street
unpaved no sound carros con colas arrastrando sus dos pipas with fender-
skirts para cubrirse de vergüenza Dios nos libre, que nos libre, las gallinas
dicen en los gallineros de las casas cuando las cantinas cierran y el
pooltable con las buchacas rotas but still ten cents a game after Tarzan
movie over Tarzans wild all over, gritos, golpes en el pecho de Tarzán el
hombre mono que vino a salvar a los pobres indios de una escuela donde
enseñaban a fragmentar los idiomas y el chivero que enseñaba ciencias
porque sabía arrearlas a los pastos secos ya que el agua se la robaron las
bombas traca traca trac toda la santa noche hasta que agarraban aire y se
morían pero el "gin" no se paraba, con su whooooooo sorbía las treilas a la
Chancla y a la Mocha y a la Golondrina nombres puestos por la raza para
indicar sello de posesión prestada a medias mientras todos los inquilinos
orgullosos de ser jefes de las tierras que antes fueron suyas "yo pago
herramientas, veneno, dinero, tú pones la vida y me das la mitad, ¿qué
tal?" pos a toda madre a toda madre te vas y te vas y te vas y no ganas
nada todo el año pero ¿qué tal al levantar la cosecha de tu vida? en tu vida
habías visto mil dólares juntos que duran en un marranito mientras no
pagas cuentas de mil quinientos y te compras una troca sin gasolina para
llevar a tus trabajadores porque ya eres dueño, propietario, sembrador
simbólico y a los menos afortunados los haces ver el día más claro cuando
les pagas parte de la baba que te tocó a ti de la baba que tu jefe te pagó a ti

esclavo sumido, sin saber que le pisaste la cabeza al otro para que viniera por otra, Dios perdónalos, porque al cabo allá en el otro cachete la vida perra, "caray mi amigo, ¿de dónde?" "desde Michoacán" vestido con la ropa hecha de costales de harina y huaraches de hule marca goodyear que nunca conoció Presidio, Presidio bien aventurado, a ti y a vos padre que eres de Presidio, Amén.

Presidio 1883

A VIBORA, ESTIRADA como cola de tigre entre las velas que hace mucho tiempo se apagaron, empieza a retorcerse. Se sonríe la juguetona porque es la dueña del mundo, dueña de esta capilla abandonada, dueña de los ríos, de los dos pueblos situados cara a cara, dueña de la gente. Y esto le da gran satisfacción.

Ahora se desliza por encima de los escapularios y las reliquias, numerosos brazos y piernas y cabezas y toda forma de cuerpos humanos metálicos, y se cuela hasta el suelo. Con la lengua de fuera se arrastra lentamente por la puerta descuartizada hacia afuera y de allí comienza a treparse al techo de la capilla, estrangulando la base de la Santa Cruz. Se detiene en esa posición por un instante para luego ceñirse a la parte superior de la cruz. Ahora enroscada cómodamente, se pone a escudriñar los contornos. "Nada ha cambiado", piensa, "desde que vinieron los frailes siguiendo el río hace mucho años". Recuerda que desde un principio quisieron defraudarla, quitarle el dominio, ese valle que nombraron La Junta de los Ríos. "Pero sólo el tiempo es permanente", piensa. "De esa iglesia y de esa misión, ¿qué ha quedado? Nada".

De allí, de arriba se imagina el valle Presidio-Ojinaga como un pedernal verde delineado por los ríos y se jacta de su imaginación. Después enfoca sobre el laborío de Lynch donde de cuando en cuando brotan cabezas y se sonríe placer. Esta vez las cabezas son como gallos enterradas entre un lago lamoso. De repente se le borra la imagen con el pitido del tren que viene cruzando el puente y observa la víbora como al punto de pasar al lado mexicano se hace una parada momentánea. Después continúa despacio como en cámara lenta y vuelve a sonreír la víbora. ¡Qué imaginación! El río y el tren: una cruz chueca y borracha, una cruz serpiente, una cruz derretida. Pero pronto se cansa del juego a las imágines y se pone a pensar en lo que oyó ayer. Que mañana viene más gente del interior a trabajar los campos de Presidio. ¡Estupendo! Y con el gozo del niño con su nuevo juguete, la víbora se desliza rápido y contenta. Luego empieza el descenso al fondo de la sierra donde se encuentra la cueva.

CHAVA EL IDIOTA NO OYO a los cuatro soldados que venían cantando pero el grito que éstos dieron a las mulas lo hizo que brincara y saliera detrás del mezquite. Luego, como si hubiera visto espantos, tiró la cáscara de plátano que estaba comiendo y salió corriendo con las manos en los oídos. No paró de correr hasta que llegó a la esquina de la viuda Nieves. Los soldados mientras tanto celebraban el susto del idiota a risotadas hasta que había desaparecido. Luego que se les había pasado el ataque de risa el arriero de las mulas ordenó a uno de ellos que fuera a avisar la llegada.

—Tell Ben we got the merchandise and that we'll meet him over there at the fortín.

Sam respondió con una mano en la cachucha. Luego picó espuelas hacia el cercano rancho del terrateniente que se encontraba en las afueras del pueblo. Mientras tanto la carreta siguió hacia el fortín.

Chava se estuvo buen rato arrodillado detrás de la casa de Nieves con los ojos tapados. Entre ave maría purísimas y temblorinas, cantaba de un lindo pescadito que no quería salir del agua porque su mamá le había dicho que si salía, pronto moriría.

Cuando la mujer lo oyó salió de la casa y le dijo que ya se descubriera los ojos y el idiota le respondió con que le dolían los muertos de las mulas y que quería a su mamá.

—Ya hombre ya déjate de cosas, ¿no quieres comer?

— . . . —

—Bueno, si quieres comer, pasa, y ya no te muerdas las uñas que no tienes.

La mujer volvió a entrar y Chava siguió picándose la cara. Trataba de quitarse los pocos pelos de la barba donde la piel estaba para sangrar y así pasó unos instantes de seria concentración mas luego empezó a hablar con sus difuntas, la mamá Pancha, la tía Cuca y la novia Rosario. Entonces decidió proceder por la calle, descalzo y semidesnudo a ciento veinte grados. "Lindo pescadito no quieres venir, a jugar con mi aro, vamos al jardín, mi mamá me ha dicho, que no salga yo". Pero poco a poco fue derritiéndose la canción de Chava en el camino.

No CREA, COMADRE, si le fue bien a Don Ben este año con su cosecha. Por eso va a hacer fiesta. De otra manera no . . .

—Qué va, comadrita. ¿A poco quiere decir que el hombre no tiene corazón?

—No, si no digo que es convenencia, nomás que pos tiene con qué, y nuestros viejos se lo merecen.

—Tiene razón. Ellos sí que echan la lengua.

—Dice Ramón que esta vez se va a lucir en la fiesta que . . .

Así es. Mandó a Chindo que matara tres becerros grandes pa que hubiera suficiente. Quesque va a tener dos cenas . . .

—¿De veras? ¿Y dónde va a ser el fandango después comadre?

—Pos quesque viene gente especial de Marfa. Cuentan que hasta ordenó cinco barriles de cerveza de esa de la estrella.

—Oiga pos ¿que no que iban a hacer el baile allí en el fortín también?

—Parece que no . . . hablando con el trompudo de Jorge, dice que va a tocar en el parque.

—Yo sí que no me la pierdo. Ando reque alborotada y aunque no está mi viejo voy a darme una asomadita. ¿Y usté?

—Ande, si ¿a poco cree que no se me mueve la ala? Si usté va yo la acompaño.

—Ande pues.

Cuando le llego el mensaje a Ben, de inmediato se puso a ensillar el caballo.

—No, Ben, por favor no lo hagas, por caridad de Dios.

—Y de perro muerto,— contestó bruscamente el viejo montándose en el caballo.

La mujer no dijo más y quedó sola con el galope retumbando en los oídos. Cuando el hombre desapareció en la esquina del camino, ella se encerró maldiciendo la ira del esposo. A Rosario le daban ganas de salir a la calle gritándole a la gente que lo colgaran. Mas todavía tenía la esperanza que a Ben se le ablandara el corazón y esto la hizo que se calmara. Después se entretuvo dando órdenes a las criadas que limpiaran las mesas y los manteles de la fiesta. ¡Ah!, y esa cortina maldita que le había ordenado hacer. Sólo Rosario sabía su propósito pues detrás de ella se escondería la maldad del hombre. Que no se le olvidara, le había dicho, pero ella se resistía a sacarla del ropero, como si esta acción fuera a detener la cólera de su viejo. Quizá no viniera por ella, quizá . . .

—Perhaps we should try to . . .

—No. You do as I say.

—Sir, our orders . . . it would be better if . . .

—No.

—Captain Ramsey said some innocent . . .

—You tell the captain I'm going ahead as planned. He'll get the damn thing back tomorrow. Now just help me get it into that room. Los soldados bajaron el cañoncito y lo rodaron hasta el centro del cuarto donde lo quería Ben. Después pidió que lo apuntaran hacia la puerta donde daba el comedor. Los que lo habían traicionado no merecían más que eso, por ladrones. Ya verían cómo pagaban una traición esos cabrones, roba-caballos.

EL ROBA-CABALLOS se llamaba Jacinto y éste nunca pensó en la posibilidad de que lo hubieran delatado así que cuando Lorenzo, el capataz de Ben, cruzó el río para llevarle la invitación, ni siquiera titubeó en aceptarla.

—Pero por qué tanta . . .

—Se merece trato especial, señor Jacinto. El señor Ben me ha mandado expresamente porque se siente muy agradecido. Nadie como usted y sus compañeros le habían ayudado tanto. Eso no se le olvida. Así que llámelos y alllá los espera el fandango. La cena suya es especial, a las ocho.

Lorenzo tenía razón, pensaba Jacinto, aunque al viejo tallado no se le quitaba lo miserable. De otra manera por qué iban a andar robando. Solamente así, robándole, se pagaban ellos mismos las friegas que se llevaban sin nunca recibir sueldo justo. Pero a lo mejor Ben reconocía por fin el valor de sus obreros y con estos pensamientos creyó oportuno invitar a cuanto amigo tenía y para cuando terminó de hacer cuentas ya llevaba veinticinco.

ESA TARDE LA GENTE se hartó de lo lindo en el fortín. Se les hizo raro, sin embargo, que nomás el salón que se usaba para servir estaba abierto. Tampoco pudieron entender por qué otros invitados como Jacinto y sus hombres se habían citado a comer para después. Mientras tanto don Benito, con paso garboso y sonrisa de ángel, caminaba legoneando por entre la gente. Y así, poco a poco se fueron olvidando de las puertas bajo llave. Además la comida estaba tan buena como la cerveza y el baile que seguiría después, ¡caramba!

Con la puesta del sol la gente se escurrió para el parque donde los fronterizos se preparaban para comenzar a tocar y para las ocho el fortín quedaba escueto. Sólo los invitados especiales permanecían esperando su recepción. Mientras tanto Chava, quien no había querido comer, seguía acurrucado detrás de un chaparro cercano como si lo hubieran enraizado. Allí seguía con su temblorina, pensa-

tivo. Se estuvo allí hasta que el fuerte cañonazo lo hizo salir corrien-
do histérico. El el baile, al contrario, la gente ni siquiera oyó los tiros
secos de pistola que terminaban a los que habían quedado vivos. Lo
único que corrió por el baile esa noche, fue el rumor de que un her-
moso galán desconocido había andado bailando con patas de chivo.

"EN ESE TIEMPO la gente sembraba trigo, maíz, cosa asina que se levan-
tara antes de septiembre porque ya nomás llegaba el río y tenían que
abandonar los jacales en las labores y venirse al fortín. El fortín se
ocupaba de pura gente pobre que había perdido su jacal.

"Una vez estaba chica todavía y nosotros sembrábamos allí en la
labor, donde se levantaba más. Teníamos un chilar que se daba muy
regular porque lo lidiábamos muy bien. Cuando no iban unos, iban
otros a comprar el chile barato pero de allí se hacía uno vivir. Lorenzo
tenía una vaca muy dañera. La metía en el corral y sola se salía por
debajo. Iba, hacía el daño, y amanecía otra vez dentro del corral.
Cuando pasaba por el chile regado, hacía quebradero de matas y la
vaca se mantenía gorda porque a nosotros nos fregaba. Pues papá le
reclamó a Lorenzo muchas veces pero nunca quería darse que la vaca
hacía males y siempre decía ¿con qué le probaba? Claro, la prueba era
la huella: papá agarraba la huella hasta entrar el corral pero Lorenzo
no se quería dar. Porque la vaca era de ésas que dan un balde y más de
leche. Mi papá siempre se lo dijo muy claro: mira, vale más que pongas
cuidado porque te la voy a agarrar y me vas a pagar todo el mal que,
anda, mira el destrozo que hace. Mira nomás cómo en el maíz va
arqueando la mazorca. Pues no, siempre ha sido muy diablo Lorenzo.
De todos modos fue mi papá y habló con Fermín que era juez enton-
ces. Fermín fue y le avisó a Lorenzo pero salió con la misma, ¿con qué
me preban? Papá le dijo a Fermín: nosotros tenemos un perro que la
puede agarrar. Yo le echo el perro y te aseguro que una vez que la
agarre, la vaca no vuelve más. Fermín dijo que estaba bien porque ya le
había avisado a Lorenzo que cuidara la vaca o iba a tener que pagar el
daño que había hecho el animal, y había salido con la misma.

"Bueno, pues la sentimos. A mi hermano le hacía más caso que
qué el perro, así que papá le habló y le dijo que andaba la vaca. Le dijo,
échale el perro, y nomás le habló aquél y le echó el perro. No, ¡qué
bárbaro! Le hizo garras el hocico y la hizo volar el alambre. Pero no la
soltó hasta que le habló porque ya de que agarraba a un animal no lo
soltaba.

"Otro día en la mañana se aprontó Lorenzo con un 30-30 a la casa, echándole pestes a papá. Dijo papá: espérame, allí voy. Entonces papá fue y sacó una cuata de dos cañones. Dijo: ándale, a ver quién se va primero. No, se fue para atrás Lorenzo. Y así siguió la cosa".

—En este mundo nadie se va sin pagar las que debe, hija.

    —¿Por qué es mi tío Lorenzo, así, mamá?

    —Porque tiene el diablo metido.

    —Pero él nomás llevó el mensaje, doña Mónica.

    —No es lo único que ha hecho, Eduvijes. Entiéndelo bien, Lorenzo va a pagar todo esto muy caro.

"No te equivoques, hija. No siempre estuvimos necesitados. Este terreno que tiene el Ben era de mi mamá Mónica, de mi tía Paz, de Victoria y Zenobio. Eran los dueños del terreno desde aquí casi hasta el río. Entonces mi tía Paz estaba fuera de sí. Apolonio Varela, casado con la tía Victoria, vivía en Marfa y vinieron para llevarla a lidiar una temporada. La tía tenía una petaquilla y allí guardaba los papeles del terreno y nunca se dieron cuenta de que se habían llevado los papeles. En dos o tres días la señora no quiso aguantar pero allá le hicieron que firmara, vendiéndole al viejo Ben. Todo esto vino a causa de su hijo Lorenzo.

"Entonces tu tío Zenobio y todos pusieron abogado, a don Pancho. Pero le dijeron que no tenían con qué pagarle porque la cosa estaba muy mal. Pues no, les dijo que después le pagaban. Y entonces el abogado de Ben entró por otra parte pero Don Pancho ganó; dijo que podía vender la parte de la tía Paz y hacer lo que le diera la gana, pero lo demás no. Pues se pusieron de acuerdo Ben y Lorenzo, el hijo de la tía. Le untó la mano el viejo, le dio dinero, y lo puso a trabajar en el arroyo. Y cuando fue en la mañana papá para las labores, ya había tumbado Lorenzo el alambre. Entonces le preguntaron para qué y él dijo que porque iba a enderezar la línea. Si en esta vez nos ganaron, a la otra no, dijo. Pues el tío Zenobio, papá y todos creyeron que como iba a echarle bordo para que no entrara el arroyo, a ellos les convenía. El mero bueno fue Lorenzo, el que metió la pata. No se tentó el alma para fregar a la viejita, a su propia mamá loca. Dios lo perdone, hija".

No se supo ni cómo le hicieron para llegar hasta Presidio, pero el caso es que cuando llegaron, llegaron echando grito a caballo. Vinieron del

sur de Texas con una meta: a enterrar a la gente viva y sumirla todavía
más abajo del infierno. Y aunque los invasores habían llegado al
abismo más oscuro de la tierra, supieron ser creativos. En Presidio
descubrieron que la tierra y el hombre tenían posibilidades lucrativas
pero antes había que enterrar a unos. A los pocos meses se fueron
directamente al río para sumir al lanchero, hijo de don Pancho, en el
agua. Primero porque había golpeado a Ben y segundo porque había
intereses más grandes en el transporte de gente. Pero Jesús sólo había
pensado en Rosario su hermana. ¿Qué negocios tenía este gringo
cabrón con ella? ¡Vamos! ¡A volar paloma y a tronar el pico a otra
parte! Así que una noche enterraron a Jesús en agua, llenando la
lancha y el cuerpo de tierra para que los dos se quedaran sumergidos.
La piedra en el pescuezo aseguraría eso. A don Francisco mientras
tanto le sirvió el diploma de abogado para limpiarse la cola, pues el caso
se echó fuera de la corte. Y para el colmo, dentro de un año se le fue la
hija con el gringo. ¡Chingao! ¡Tras de cornao, apaleao! Pero de ahora
en adelante, ¡Cuidado bola e cabrones! Más tarde Santamaría, su
hermano continuó el transporte de gente aun cuando avisaban que
pronto se construiría un puente internacional y que tan pronto se
hiciera, habría que pasar por él. Pero Santamaría con carabina en
mano, seguía sin obedecer la ley porque la gente prefería la lancha.
¿Pasar por la garita y presentar papeles? Vayan mucho a la chingada. El
puente es cosa del diablo. (El puente es el arco iris del diablo: dos patas
de chivo puestas en dos cementerios. El puente es un resbaladizo para
cagarse de risa, ¿que no, Jesús?)

"LOS LYNCHIS TIENEN HISTORIA; los viejos pues. Esos mataron gente a lo
bárbaro. Estos trabajaban unas pobres gentes allí y cuando querían irse
después de un año o más se llevaban su pago. Pos sí te voy a pagar, les
decían, pero luego los sacaban y los mataban. La gente no protestaba
porque no había de comer; estaba muy duro. Nosotros aquí llegamos a
pasarla con una taza de atole y lo que tú quieras. Así es que ¿qué te ibas
a poner a hacer? Seguro que hombres sí había como papá, que ya le
importaba poco matar. Y asina había algunos como él que podían
hacer con cualquiera lo que querían, pero es que pensaban en no dejar
a la familia abandonada. Porque valor cualquiera lo tenía. Papá de lo
que estaba manco de todo eso. Si no nomás mochales el pescuezo y
pasarse pa'l otro lado. Porque aquí no creas que nomás los Lynchis

había. Aquí todavía me acuerdo cómo ese capitán Gray era muy bueno pa poner la bota. Era de los rinchis en ese tiempo. Era muy diablo."

DON PANCHO NO PUDO entender la noticia a pedazos que le daba Chava el idiota, así que mejor concentró en apaciguarle los nervios. Luego que se los calmó, abrió la bodega de la tienda y le puso un sarape sobre los costales de frijol para que se acostara. Por lo menos no andará rondando despavorido el resto de la noche, pensó Francisco. Entonces le echó candado a la puerta y se volvió a su casa-tienda-imprenta, al cabo que la luz del día traería la verdad a la puerta.

Pero la noche se le hizo larga a Pancho. A las pocas horas llegaron a la puerta unos ojos cristalinos de rabia. Reyes manipulaba la carabina como si fuera de papel al tiempo que hacía chorrear el cuento del fortín por la comisura de los labios. Cuando terminó, el viejo lo convidó a que entrara mas Reyes no quiso. Dijo que prefería ir a averiguar la verdad más allá pues a veces era dudosa la palabra de Chindo.

—Está bien pero no vayas a cometer una locura.

—El desgraciado se va a llevar la suya.

—Asegúrate primero, hijo, y paciencia.

—Si nada más a eso voy, porque quiero estar muy segurito.

—Después hablamos. Pero que no se te olvide, Reyes. Mientras vida haya tiempo sobra.

—Está bien, viejo.

Don Pancho se dirigió a su despacho privado y allí, entre libros y alteros de periódicos, se puso a luchar con su cinismo. Meditaba sobre su vida y su carrera—un verdadero desastre. Nada más. Derrota, rotunda derrota y punto. Los periódicos y los libros polvorosos que lo rodeaban eran los últimos vestigios de una lucha en que había sido vencido. ¿Comprobantes de su edad creadora? Hasta la pregunta era necia. Recordaba cómo su abatimiento era el del pueblo; como los dos habían quedado reducidos a un microcosmos insignificante pero repleto de historia. El, por su parte, había sido rechazado por ambos gobiernos a causa de su fuerte sentido de justicia. De los esfuerzos que había hecho en su tiempo por asegurar los derechos básicos del ser humano no había quedado nada y lo único que lo consolaba era desenterrar su verdad, sepultada en polvo. Los números del *Fronterizo* que él había guardado en su despacho lo decían todo. Ojalá que algún día alguien viniera y los leyera, pero eso ya cuando estuviera muerto.

Recordaba muy bien el primer año de práctica, porque fue en ese mismo año cuando se le derrumbó el mundo que había creado en el aire durante sus estudios. La realidad era otra, caramba. La vida se hacía a gritos y a sombrerazos. Pronto se había dado cuenta que la carrera de abogado no era tan ilustre, y menos cuando practicaba en un pueblo de míseras condiciones. Entonces cayó en la cuenta que la mejor manera de ayudar y ayudarse a sí mismo sería por medio del periodismo, y de inmediato circuló *El Fronterizo*, un periodiquito que leían no tanto los que necesitaban leerlo sino otros editores del suroeste. Su negocio cobró vigor cuando para su sorpresa, empezó a recibir periódicos de California, de Trinidad, Colorado, de Laredo, de Nuevo México, y de partes que ni sospechaba hubiera gente mexicana. Con el tiempo la comunicación se hizo una gran voz y un mismo interés: polémicas, denuncias, y protestas relacionadas a la vida de la raza de estos lados. Pronto se habían ido colando sus palabras por los periódicos de México y no había tardado en reconocer el gobierno mexicano el beneficio que Francisco Uranga aportaría al país. Con gran entusiasmo había recibido la nombración de cónsul. ¿Las palabras exactas? "Servir como representante de nuestros paisanos en el extranjero y actuar debidamente en defensa de sus derechos y principios asignados por los tratados entre México y los Estados Unidos". Tan pronto como había recibido el nombramiento, se había puesto a poner en orden de prioridad las tareas a emprender. Primero, aclarar la cuestión de terrenos ultrajados del valle de Presidio y buscar la manera de hacer válidos los reclamos de tierras que se habían ido arrollando como alfombra poco a poco. (Pero recuerda que para entonces ya había sido tarde porque los archivos legales estaban escritos en otra lengua y con otro sello.) Después, seguiría la complicada cuestión de ciudadanía y para esto habría que ponerse en contacto con los demás cónsules del suroeste. En seguida, buscar una manera más eficaz de conseguir la repatriación de todos esos individuos que querían hacerlo y que pensaban que el gobierno mexicano los había abandonado. Otra de las causas, y aquí subrayaba, era combatir la insolencia, por parte de los que se consideraban la ley, de cruzar las fronteras sin ningún permiso previo. Este punto era el de los más sensibles, pues había él experimentado numerosos casos en que el perseguido se sacaba de México para venirle a hacer justicia en corte y en un idioma extraños. Sí, había que aclarar esa ley de extradición tan vilipendiada por el conquistador, aunque sabía que era tarea bastante difícil. En otras ocasiones ocurría lo contrario: el acusado, ante las autoridades mexicanas, no podía comprobar que era ciudadano de los Estados Unidos, aun cuando el tratado decía que el que no se repatriara después de dos años, se consideraría como tal. ¿Y los papeles? Se encontraban en el aire. ¿De dónde eres? De la tierra señor. De donde puedo hacer la vida.

No tardó Pancho Uranga en darse cuenta que él también se encontraba en la misma vorágine. Entre el papelerío y la confusión sentía la vida un mareo y una flotación. Resultó con las manos atadas de frustración, convirtiéndose en una de esas personas que de tanta sabiduría sobre cómo marcha el mundo, se crea una mueca cínica que comunica: pendejos, ¿qué esperaban? ¿El bien de Dios envuelto en una frezada? Entiéndanlo, la humanidad está pudrida por dentro. Y cada vez que resultaba el diablo venciendo, se le enterraba más la espinita y para cuando se la había querido sacar ya le había envenenado el alma. Entonces había tomado la pluma como espada. Aparecieron sus escritos en su propio *Fronterizo, El tucsonense, El hispanoamericano, El Zuriaco, La vox del pueblo,* y cuarenta periódicos más que se publicaban por aquí en ese entonces: "denuncio rotundamente la usurpación de las tierras y apoyo los Gorras Blancas por haber blandido las armas"; "firmo la resolución de la prensa unida hispanoamericana en la que se condena al gobernador de Nuevo México por llamarnos 'greasers' a través de la prensa inglesa de Nueva York y que ahora tiene el garbo de amenazarnos", "protesto expediciones filibusteras por yanquis oportunistas"; "condeno la discriminación en los trabajos, escuelas y establecimientos públicos", "apoyo las defensas hechas por la Alianza Mexicana"; "con rabia y amor lamento la desunión de nuestra raza y lloro por su futuro"; "soy partidario del elemento radical de obreros en San Antonio, California y Nuevo México no porque sé que lograron algo sino porque se comprueba el hecho de que estamos todavía vivos y que siempre tendremos lucha"; "sospecho la justicia y la condena que imparten los jueces y que se rigen por una opinión de testigos prejuiciados; es más, sé que Manuel Verdugo no era culpable. Lo supe después que lo condenaron a muerte en El Paso"; "condeno la venta de esclavos negros en Fayetteville, Missouri"; "sepa el editor de dicho periodiquito en Guadalajara que mis esfuerzos por repatriar a los de nuestra raza son genuinos. Que lo hago porque conozco los sufrimientos padecidos en un país que se considera el mejor ejemplo de la democracia y también le hago ver claramente, con ejemplos, que

nuestra gente aquí no es un montón de tamaleros como usted tan
groseramente nos describe. Esta encuesta que aquí publico contiene la
cantidad de personas de ascendencia mexicana y sepa usted que de
todos los que respondieron, sólo cuatro tienen el oficio de tamaleros y
no porque sean holgazanes sino por la adversa fortuna que les ha
tocado. Numerosas veces he venido apelando al gobierno mexicano
que le conceda el dinero para el transporte a esta gente que quiera
repatriarse así como un pedacito de tierra porque de otra manera ¿cuál
sería la garantía de que podrían vivir mejor si se regresan a México? El
problema radica ahora en que la población china está dispuesta a
contratarse por menos sueldo"; "quiero que sepa el señor, que habla
sin fundamento cuando dice que nosotros los de aquí somos de los más
miserables e ineducados. Sí le concedemos razón que la familia obrera
vive mal, pero eso no significa que somos ineducados. Reconocemos
nuestra realidad y hacemos lo que podemos. Ahora explíqueme, señor
editor, ¿por qué cree usted que esta gente obrera es la que menos ansía
por repatriarse? En otra ocasión me gustaría que usted, en vez de
escupir sinrazones, se pusiera a pensar un poquito más. Nosotros,
colega, no queremos mudarnos de esta tierra que consideramos siem-
pre nuestra y si yo hago el esfuerzo por la repatriación de alguna gente
es porque me mueve la esperanza de que el gobierno mexicano nos
auxilie"; "le advierto al señor Gobernador de Chihuahua que ha dado
muy malos pasos al conceder vastos terrenos a estas compañías colo-
nizadoras pues no hacen más que apoderarse de las riquezas naturales.
Con el tiempo estas compañías seguirán la misma ruta de los grandes
capataces que ahora explotan al pobre sin misericordia"; "denuncio
ante el público los hechos extraviados del cónsul de Paso, Texas por
haber cooperado con el sheriff en la extradición de Rufino Gómez. Los
cien pesos que se le pagaron por debajo de cuerda no le servirán para
aplacar la conciencia después que se le haya juzgado al acusado"; "no
creía que uno de los nuestros (de Laredo) fuera a comentar tan
desfavorablemente sobre la poesía que incluimos en la sección litera-
ria, y mucho menos porque está escrita en un español 'bastardo'.
Lamentamos mucho que estas actitudes prevalezcan tanto. ¿Por qué
se ciega nuestro colega de la realidad? Mejor ¿por qué no se queja el
señor ante el sistema educativo o ante el gobierno federal, quien
prometió respetar nuestro idioma y nuestra cultura? Si hubiera escue-
las donde se enseña en nuestra lengua materna quizás usted no tuviera
razón de lamentarse. Pero esto ya es un ideal. Mejor póngase, gaste sus

energías en asegurar el bienestar de sus hijos que sabe Dios lo necesi-
tan, y no de mostrarnos esa misma actitud de superioridad que
venimos saboreando desde hace mucho tiempo".

Así, con la punta de la pluma, picó crestas sensibles y no tardó para
que ambos gobiernos lo consideraran enemigo de la armonía. Cuando
defendió la causa de Catarino Garza quien, desde Nuevo México,
logró el alzamiento de obreros contra los terratenientes y el gobierno
de Chihuahua, ya no era cónsul. Había sido un milagro que escapase
de la muerte aunque en ese tiempo la hubiese preferido pues ya nada le
importaba. El pueblo que él había defendido con amor ahora le daba la
espalda y era lo que más dolía. Unos, tan pronto como les pagaba bien
la suerte, se le echaban encima. "Viejo revoltoso, déjese de cosas. Hay
prosperidad y usted nos perjudica con sus tonterías. Así que se calla
o . . . " *El Fronterizo* moría una muerte sin gloria. La gente tenía
razón, la historia no se detiene. (La historia corre como el agua. A
veces mansita, otras con el diablo a cuestas, inflada y rabiosa. Después
engendra una mano deforme que estira sus dedos hasta el infinito.
Luego la mano de agua se recoge y se engarruña, dejando un pequeño
hilito por el cauce del Río Grande. Entonces vuelve la gente con su
eterna migración a formar una cruz contorsionada, una miserable cruz
de carne y de agua.) Y porque la historia de mi raza es de río, pensé, me
voy a hacer una lancha para cruzarlos. Esto me ayudará a mantenerme
pero les cobraré solamente a los que puedan pagar. También me dará
la oportunidad de guiar y desviar a la gente por los mejores caminos.
"Vete por aquí y cuídate con tal y tal y si no te da trabajo sigue el río
hasta . . ." Pero antes recogeré mis tiliches, mis libros y me mudaré a
Ojinaga. Haré una casita cerca del río por el otro lado para no dejar
que se borre nuestra historia escrita en el agua. Muchos años después,
cuando perdí a Rosario y me enteré de que iban a construir el puente,
ni me causó sorpresa. Tampoco cuando tuve noticias de que me
habían ahogado a Jesús. Me volvió a sangrar la llaga cuando lo
enterraron casi deshecho y juré que lo vengaría. Pero yo no podía y
pensé que tú lo vengarías, Reyes, por ser su hermano. No te quería
criar para que fueras asesino, no. Las armas vendrían después, y esas
sólo como último recurso. Lo que quería darte primero era educación
de libros pero tampoco de ésos que cuentan historias falsas. Para eso te
pondría a estudiar con Mariana la maestra mía, no con la escuelucha
ésa donde a barrenazos te inculcan la idea de que debes arrancarle las
raíces al idioma que te parió. Después te mandaría allí a Presidio pero

sólo después que ya supieras la verdad, por qué son las cosas como son, cuando ya tuvieras orgullo de ser hijo del pueblo. Pero como tú bien sabes, me resultaste un fracaso. No supe por qué desde niño fuiste así, Reyes. Cuando te mandé con Mariana a los pocos días vino a decirme que la habías golpeado porque ella había hecho lo mismo contigo. No quiso verte la cara jamás. Nomás no quisiste escuela, aunque te costó muchos cintarazos, ¿recuerdas Reyes? Hasta ahora no comprendo como aprendiste lo que sabes. Quizá de mis libros que leías escondido porque nunca te vi aplicado en nada. Eras un holgazán y eras un vago. "Anda, vete a la leña para que vendas y compres o vete a ayudarle a tu tío Santamaría con la lancha," te decía, pero no, resultabas por la tarde con comida, leña y dinero. "¿Y de dónde sacaste ese dinero?" "Vendí pescados al gringo del puente". "¡Ya te he dicho que no te andes metiendo con ellos! ¡Endemoniado muchacho!"

EL TROPEL DE LOS CINCO CABALLOS quedó amortiguado por la arena suelta del río. Los jinetes se aproximaron a la orilla y se fueron sumiendo en el lodo hasta que pudieron alcanzar el agua. El chamaco Reyes quien jugaba distraído, nunca sintió nada por el chapaleo que hacía en el agua. Los hombres se miraban sonriendo, listos para darle un buen susto, pero en ese momento un caballo no aguantó el quisquilleo en el hocico y estornudó. El muchacho saltó como pescado cuando forcejea con el ansuelo mientras que los hombres soltaron la carcajada.

—Miren nomás qué bien dao el cabrón. A ver, acércate. ¿De dónde eres?

—De aquí, de aquella casita que está allá.

—¿Quién es tu padre y qué hace?

—Francisco Uranga, es lanchero.

—¿Conoces bien aquí? ¿Conoces el lugar de los gringos?

—Sí, aquí mataron a mi hermano.

—Y ¿por qué lo mataron?

—No estoy seguro, pero dicen que porque es contra la ley no usar el puente.

—Ah, qué jodidos. Todavía andan conque esa tierra es de ellos. Nomás porque está al otro lado de este maldito charco. Y ¿qué cabrones haces aquí güevoneando?

—Andaba pescando.

—Lo que vas a pescar es un catarro, bruto. ¿Quieres irte con nosotros? ¿Qué dicen muchachos? ¿Nos sirve?

—Pos cómo no, mi jefe.

—Andale pues, ponte la ropa y felicidades.

—No señor, yo no quiero irme con ustedes, ni mi papá . . .

—Píquele, píquele, ¿qué fregaos va a estar haciéndose pendejo aquí?

—A ver, Ramiro. Pásame la buena. Allí tienes. Ahora sí. Oigan, cómo se me hace que éste va a salir bueno.

—El chamaco parece tecolote con tamaña carabinota y con esos ojotes que pela, jefe.

Todos rieron. Reyes no se daba cuenta que en ese momento resucitaba en él su hermano Jesús y que la indignación de medio siglo comenzaría a cristalizarse desde ese mismo día.

"NO TRABAJE EN SHAFTER pero sí cuando estaba chica, Camila mi hermana se casó con Cipriano Alvarado y dijo: No te quedes, vámonos. Pos me consiguió a mí y a mi hermano Chente pero le di bien a entender: no me voy a estar todo el tiempo contigo. Dijo, está bien. Cuando quieras venirte yo te vengo a trae. En ese tiempo en Shafter había mucha gente, mucho dinero porque trabajaban las minas de plata. Los hombres ganaban tanto que hasta a mi hermanito le entró la fiebre, asina chico como estaba. Pero asina les fue a los pobres. Se murieron. Cuando entraban a la mina ya salían de abajo enfermos, los pobres. Yo creo que de eso se murió mi hermanito Chente".

"¿POR QUE TENGO QUE MORIR, Eduvijes? Hermana, sólo tengo doce años. No llores por eso. Tú has hecho lo que puedes. Sólo quiero saber, cómo es la vida cuando creces. No he tenido tiempo de preguntarle a abuelito cómo es cuando ya es viejo uno. Pero tú eres grande. Dime, ¿es bonita la vida como la de los niños? Así la veo yo, Vicke. El año pasado cuando murió mi perro yo sí me sentí muy mal, si vieras, porque tenía los ojos muy tristes y todavía así, meneaba la cola. ¿Tú sabes que los perros mueven la cola cuando están contentos? ¿Es verdad que estaba contento, Vicke? ¿Cuando estaba muriendo? Aun cuando le pegaba meneaba la cola. ¿Así es la gente grande como tú? Yo me sentí muy mal antes de que muriera porque le había pegado yo también. Y antes de morir le prometí que no lo volvería a hacer. Porque yo creo que nadie tiene el derecho de pegarte, de golpearte y si lo hacen, tú debes de pegar también. Porque después te mueres y te vas al cielo sin pagártelas. Bueno, así pensaba yo, Vicke, pero ahora no.

Porque creo que si el perro tiene tanto amor así, la gente ha de tener
más. Digo esto porque yo siento más amor que el perro, Vicke. ¿Es así
con ustedes? ¡Híjole! ¡Pero si estás llorando! No llores, Vicke. Dame un
farito. Nunca he fumado pero ahora tengo ganas de saber cómo es
fumar. A ver, préndemelo. Quisiera que me quitaras esta enfermedad,
Vicke. Esta bola que tengo aquí en el pecho. Me duele mucho. Mira,
tócame aquí. Yo quisiera que me la quitaras. Quiero llorar, Vicke, pero
¿que diría don Jesús? Me daría vergüenza. ¿Qué decía? Que los hom-
bres no lloran. ¿Es verdad eso, hermana? Yo no te diría esto si él
estuviera aquí, pero fíjate, una vez lo encontré detrás de un árbol
llorando. Yo nunca supe por qué, pero si te viera a ti llorando, te
llevaría en su lancha. ¿Te acuerdas, antes que hicieran puente, cómo
llevaba gente de un lado pa'l otro? Yo me divertía mucho con él.
Entonces todos éramos iguales. No es que no séanos, pero ha cam-
biado desde que pusieron el puente. Qué curioso, Vicke. La gente se
siente separada. ¿Que no los puentes son para que haiga menos de eso?
Antes podíamos ir a que los agüelitos sin . . . ¡pa qué son esos papeles,
Vicke? ¿Por qué los piden esos hombres todo el tiempo? ¿Quiénes son?
¿Y el diablo lo has visto, Vicke? ¿Es cierto que estamos en el infierno?
Hace mucho calor aquí pero no es verdá, ¿verdá, Vicke? Me dijo mi
agüelita que el diablo vivía en aquella cueva donde fuimos, ¿te acuer-
das? Yo no lo creo, porque arriba de la sierrita, está bendecido. Pero me
contaron que había venido a hacernos mal, que andaba por los dos
lados del río. Vicke, no me hablas. Me duele mucho el pecho. Tráeme
un trapito caliente por favor. El cigarro no me sirvió. Creía que me
quitaría este dolor. ¿Por qué estoy enfermo, Vicke? ¿Por qué no me lo
quitan por favor? Cuando vuelvas, Vicke, súbeme a la cama. No estoy
a gusto aquí en el piso. Yo no sé pa qué me pusieron aquí abajo. ¡Vicke,
yo no quiero morir!"

LA NOCHE SE ESTIRA larga hasta el infinito. Como un chicle negro y
pegajoso que envuelve el río, los árboles, las labores. Luego llega hasta
los barrios y allí enreda a la gente y la pega fuertemente a las camas, a
los pisos y en dondequiera que se quedaron dormidos. El silencio
también es oscuro y monótono. Luego viene la luna botando al
compás de los violines y entonces el chicle se torna en azogue y pone
lentamente una capa resbalosa sobre el universo. Platino el río, plata
las hojas de los álamos, todo está plateado como una noche de nieve en
otros rumbos.

La plata da dimensión a la noche. La hace larga y la multiplica. La luna no es muerte. La luna es vida para los seres que pululan por el río. Las sombras con la luna cobran vida. Allá está la luna, comiendo tuna, tirando las cáscaras pa . . . dame luna, dame de lo que comes. Tú eres mi vida y mi adoración. Yo soy tu luna. Tu sombra. Soy cuerpo de luz que incendia la noche, que estira la noche. Soy hombre de noche, soy vida de noche. Soy hijo de la llorona y me llamo Reyes, hijos de la tal por cual. Yo soy hermano de Jesús del río.

EN LA PARTE más honda de la cueva situado al fondo de la sierra de la Santa Cruz cae un chorrito de luz sobre el agua estancada de un pequeño lago. La serpiente lo usa como espejo, espejo que ahora refleja una cara humana. La imagen contempla el disfraz, llena de risa; un traje azul oscuro, una cachucha militar para cubrir la cabeza puntiaguda donde se acostumbra ver los cuernos y unas botas aceitosas también pardas. Las botas no sientan bien sobre las patas de gallo pero no importa. Se usarán sólo por unas horas. Como toque final la serpiente "dirige-trenes" descuelga una lamparilla de aceite que ha guardado para la ocasión. Con esto, queda lista para aparecer en la estación del ferrocarril. Después cambiará el disfraz a uno de ranchero pero eso ya cuando esté a punto de recibir las quinientas almas trabajadoras que vienen del interior. Afuera el diablo tomando forma humana monta su burro y lo dirige hacia la estación.

Ferrocarriles de Ultratumba está casi vacío cuando llega. Caso raro, pues siempre hay enjambres de gente esperando los trenes. Quizá por fin han caído en la cuenta de que nunca llegan a tiempo. El taquillero lo confirma. "El tren viene con unos minutos de retraso", dice. Eso dice, pero el diablo sabe muy bien que la palabra 'minuto' no significa nada. Para eso están las advertencias pegadas a las paredes: *en la salida del paraíso los trenes salen a todas horas pero la llegada es cuando Dios quiere.* La otra advertencia que pertenece a la línea del infierno también está subrayada: *en esta línea la salida de los trenes es cuando el hombre quiere y llega cuando menos lo piensa.* Maldita gente pendeja. Parece que nunca lee lo que es obvio.

Es la primera vez que el diablo humanizado ha estado en una estación ferroviaria y siente la misma expectación de pasajero y de espectador. También ha oído que los trenes vienen retrasados, y como no está acostumbrado a esperar, comienza a tener dudas de sí mismo. Ahora no está tan seguro si oyó bien la noticia de que hoy y a esta hora

llegarían los obreros. "No, no es posible que me equivoque. Estoy
segurísimo que los viajeros partieron. De eso nunca hay duda. Pero
quizá . . . ?" Pasa el hombre-diablo a leer las advertencias para ver si
por casualidad la información que contienen le quitan las dudas. "A
ver . . ." Lee . . . pero no saca nada en limpio. "Simples tonterías:"
. . . *en la línea del paraíso no se expenden billetes de ida y vuelta; los niños*
menores de siete años van gratis en los brazos de la madre; no hay rebaja
de precios; solamente las buenas obras se deben llevar de equipaje para no
ser detenidos; se reciben viajeros de cualquier procedencia con tal que
traigan los pasaportes en regla; y el despacho central de billetes está
abierto a todas horas. "¡Tarugadas! ¡Nada más! La línea al paraíso
quebró hace tiempo." El diablo entonces se pasa al anuncio del
infierno: *se admite sin descuento, niños menores no, pasajeros llevarán*
cuanto equipaje gusten pero deben dejar todo menos el alma . . . "¡Ah!
¡Aquí!" . . . *los que viajan por esta línea podrán seguir la del paraíso si*
refrenan su billete ante un sacerdote antes de empalmar con el tren de la
muerte. "¡Hijo de la . . . ! ¿Será posible? ¿Que si el tren se detuvo por
allí, precisamente para eso? ¿Que habría algún aguafiestas desgraciado?
¿Es?"

—El tren llega en carril número cinco.

La poca gente comienza mientras que el disfrazado queda atónito.
Ni siquiera ha oído el tosido del tren.

—Por favor, señoras y señores. Usen precaución. Favor de no
acercarse hasta que haya hecho un alto completo.

El diablo dirige-trenes, lamparilla en mano, sigue a la bola de gente
con tanto entusiasmo que se le ha olvidado hacer el cambio de
vestidura. "Ahora para desviar a los huarachudos", piensa.

Los pasajeros empiezan a bajar. Uno, dos, tres . . . luego dos
. . . luego . . . uno . . . Se pueden contar en la mano. El tren viene
vacío. No, no puede ser. El dirige-trenes no sabe qué pensar y se queda
allí largo rato hasta que ya no baja nadie.

—Pero ¿qué ha pasado con la demás gente?

—Es todo, señor.

—Oiga, espere. Si deben . . .

—Le digo que no hay más y ¡ya no me moleste!

El dirige-trenes enrojece de cólera y entonces hace un berrinche
estrellando la lámpara contra el riel. En seguida se avienta un pedo que
jamás había soboreado ser humano y luego desaparece como rayo por
los cielos. El burro se queda rebuznando por su amo mientras que en la

esquina de la estación el conjunto Los Pepenados cantan: "el diablo se fue a pasear . . . y le dieron chocolate . . . tan caliente se lo dieron que hasta se quemó el garnate . . . pero ay, ja, ja, ja . . . ja ja ja ja . . . pero ay, ja, ja, ja, ja . . . ja ja ja ja ja . . ."

Los quinientos acres de algodón estaban para perderse a causa de la falta de pizcadores. Había sido el primer golpe para Ben, y la situación se puso peor cuando la gente de Presidio pidió el aumento de un centavo más por libra pizcada. No se podía explicar quién había tenido tanta influencia para cortarle el chorro. Además, el "incidente" del fortín era tan insignificante en proporción a los negocios que él hacía, que la misma noche lo había ovidado. Antes, un hecho de justicia como éste no había impedido que el agua corriera mansa y lucrativa. ¿Por qué habría de ser diferente en esta ocasión? ¿Qué habría pasado? ¿Por qué se había negado el gobierno a concederle las quinientas almas que le había pedido? No se lo explicaba. No se explicaba como la excursión que el gobernador Jones, su amigo, había hecho por México, hubiera fracasado.

Sólo Francisco Uranga y su hijo Reyes tenían la respuesta y cuando aquél leyó la noticia en el *Century* de Marfa, se le rodaron las lágrimas. Eran lágrimas de triunfo que había esperado tantos años y eran gozo porque su triunfo había sido doble. La administración mexicana bien sabía el maltrato de sus obreros pero siempre había movidas más beneficiosas y era muy fácil taparle el ojo al macho con dinero. ¡Caramba! Por eso no lo podía creer don Pancho. ¡Hacer arrodillar era casi increíble!

¿Cómo lo había hecho? Cuando se había enterado de que Jones sería, casi por seguro, el siguiente gobernador de Texas, Francisco había ido a estrecharle la mano a Marfa. Allí, el día que había venido a cantinflear frente al público, se había enterado de sus intenciones "internacionales". De inmediato había hecho uso de fraternidades periodísticas y empezó a picar fuerte. Primero les había llegado a los editores de aquí: Rodríguez el del *Zuriago*, Sifuentes el del *Laderense*, Armenta, Armendáriz . . . de allí pa'l real se había convertido la voz en una red que no detuvo fronteras. Fácil había sido. Hacer pública la masacre del fortín y en seguida trazar el plan excursionista de Jones.

Allá esperaron a Jones en cada parada, martillando las mismas preguntas: "¿Es cierto que el mexicano sufre, más que en otro estado, la discriminación en los empleos y establecimientos públicos? ¿Es cierto de la masacre de Presidio? Hago esta pregunta porque tal y tal corrobora que . . . " Después de tres días, el gobernador había llegado aturdido a la capital. En la convención oficial había caído Martínez-Vega, el cónsul de Matamoros, pidiendo la palabra. Primero dio los pormenores y situaciones en las cuales se había enfrentado con dicho gobernador, y en seguida leyó una lista de acusaciones. Finalmente terminó leyendo una resolución firmada por los principales editores de habla hispana en el suroeste. La presión y el escándalo llegaron a tal grado que el mordelón Alcalá tuvo que negarle públicamente la exportación de trabajadores al estado de Texas. Chistoso caso, pensaba Francisco, que semanas antes la raza en Arizona atendiera a la llamada del gobernador arizonense. "Necesitamos el apoyo de todo buen ciudadano para que nuestras cosechas no se pierdan". Los primeros en acudir habían sido los de habla hispana formando tropas de gente los domingos para salvar la cosecha. Paradojas o paradojas. ¡Caray!

Benito recibio las noticias degollando un chivo que cruzó su paso. Luego, como Quijote, corrió a caballo tumbando las carpas que había comprado para la ocasión. Ni en casa pudieron soportarlo esos cinco días.

Sin embargo Benito no se iba a dejar vencer. Mandó a Lorenzo anunciar a los trabajadores de aquí que el aumento pedido se les concedía. Mientras tanto él personalmente iría a pregonar al otro lado que se les pagaría a buen precio la pizca de algodón porque estaba muy necesitado. Después que hizo el hombre la buena oferta en las varias congregaciones, Reyes por otra parte reunió a sus compañeros y les mandó que hicieran público otro aviso contrario, escrito en forma de advertencia: "Se prohibe la cruzada a toda persona que tenga intenciones de trabajar en los campos de Benito. Cualquier acto que apoye la causa de este criminal será castigado con dura pena. El Coyote". El segundo día no aparecía nadie en las labores, excepto Lorenzo quien llegaba con el aviso a casa de su patrón.

—¿Y quién es este Coyote?

—No sé, patrón. Es primera vez que lo oigo mentar por ese apodo. Lo que sí he sabido es que anda rondando un montón de bandoleros hace tiempo y que no se tientan el alma para obtener lo que quieren.

—Conque así es, ¿eh? Bueno. Tú vas a México y anuncias que

pago a cuatro centavos libra pizcada y que concedo completa protección armada.

Después continuó inquiriendo el paradero del Coyote. Ni le importaba quién fuera, nomás quería darle en la madre.

No fue hasta muy tarde ese mismo día que regresó Lorenzo. Este le trajo dos noticias: primero, que había logrado conseguirle veinte pizcadores de noche, pizcadores que estaban un poco inseguros de arrojarse. De todos modos, les había dicho, si se animan vaya uno de ustedes a avisarme que vienen por la noche. La segunda noticia era que el no era otro sino Reyes Uranga su cuñado. ¡Vaya! Reyes el más mansito de todo el atajo de trabajadores. ¿Reyes? Era causa de risa.

Benito no tardó en ponerse en movimiento. Se comunicó de inmediato con el sherife de Marfa para que éste viniera a socorrerlo y para el tercer día ya andaban husmeando las casas y los contornos de Presidio. Luego, cuando no encontraron nada por este lado, los diez rangers cruzaron el río al lado mexicano y se fueron hasta la sierrita donde se suponía que estaba el escondite de Reyes y su banda. Pero tampoco sacaron nada. Así que al día siguiente anunciaban que se iban, preparando la salida a media luz y por la noche regresaron a ver si por casualidad . . . pero Reyes no había tragado el anzuelo.

El cuarto día tampoco pasó nada pero de noche vino un mojado a la casa de Ben para avisarle que vendrían los veinte que se habían reclutado. Mas no sería esta noche sino la siguiente. Así que Ben preparó los costales y los dejó metidos en el tronco del árbol gordo cerca de la bomba de agua. Benito no le dijo a Lorenzo que había venido el mojado por miedo a que el plan se descubriera. Ni éste ni los pizcadores sabían que ellos servirían de anzuelo. La estrategia sería sencilla. Picarle el corazón a Reyes, maltratando un poco a la gente y si tenía güevos, saldría al campo libre, el cabrón. Lo que no supo Benito era que Reyes mismo había ensayado a los pizcadores un día antes. ¿Querían trabajar? Ahora jalan o se ahorcan, les había dicho. Tendrán que cooperar. ¿Que una bala les toque? Ese será su castigo.

Benito sonríe al pasar por el barrio oscuro. Ni perro que le ladre, ¿o es que no los oye? Sonríe con el triunfo en la boca. Esa sonrisa hecha de mueca que no engaña a nadie, que se trasluce como radiografía. Pasa el jinete por los cuadritos de adobe, antipoéticos. Adobes que se hicieron con paja nueva en un tiempo y ahora brotan como inútiles barbas de olote. El que quiera hacer poesía es un mentiroso. Sólo les falta a las casitas una cruz al frente para que sean cementerios. No obstante una que otra se defiende de la muerte con sus florecitas y una barandita al frente. Luego la calle polvorosa, sin brea. Burla, burlados todos, el diablo verde sonríe. El diablo manipula títeres. El diablo juega con la vida humana. Y esa vida humana nunca se dio cuenta cómo se coló por entre ellos. Fue como un aire que se les metió entre las piernas y les echó la zancadilla. Otros cuentan que había sido como un sueño del cual habían despertado sin pantalones. Cuando despertaron se habían puesto a las manos del señor, el que les había prometido alivio y lo había cumplido. Les había dado trabajo en sus mismas tierras y la gente volvió a sentir la vida en las tripas. Después les adelantó la raya y fueron a dejársela otra vez en sus manos. "Que a toda familia se les dé una caja de comida como regalo de Navidad, y cuando se haga la cosecha haré una barbacoa. Pero no se les olvide, voten por mí, voten democrat". En dos años los vasallos habían coronado a un rey que apodaron "diablo verde".

Noche sofocante, noche que oprime, noche que aprieta los gaznates de la gente. Calaveras pálidas de exprimida savia, calaveras perdidas en la tierra seca de los algodonales. Postizas plantas regadas con sudor. Gusanos repletos. Presidio, prisión, infierno. Diablo que se carcajea en silencio. ¡Shhh!

Benito apareció como espanto a la puerta de la casa. Luego pegó los labios a la mampara para llamar quedito . . . ¡Pssst! ¡Lorenzo!

El ladrido del perro dentro del porche le respondió mientras que Benito dio un salto hacia atrás.

—¡Shut up, you bastard!

—Epa, ¿Quién es?

—Soy yo, Ben.

—Wayda momen.

—'Ta bien, Lorenzo. Don't get up. Yo nomás avisarte de pizcadores. Andan cerca del río. Date un vuelta más tarde, ¿okay?

—Okay, Don Benito.

Se alejó el Diablo Verde como sombra.

Lorenzo no se acostó luego. La aparición de Ben a esta hora lo había dejado inquieto, así que salió afuera para fumarse un cigarro. Viejo lángaro, desgraciado. Si no fuera porque me paga bien ya le hubiera aventado el harpa. Los problemas que me acarrea. Algún día voy a amanecer tendidito en el cabrón río, agujerado por mi propia gente. Y es que la gente tiene razón, que les hago mal, pero es que uno está fregado por todos lados. Si el viejo cabrón le ayudara a la pobre gente en vez de la baba que les paga, no tuviera problemas. Chingao. Algún día cambiará, después que yo ya esté bien muerto.

YA EN PLENO CAMPO aparecen diez jinetes y rodean al viejo Ben. Este les comunica lo esencial: los pizcadores andarán en la sección señalada por el álamo gordo pero para estar seguros, esperen a Lorenzo. Este no necesitará pistola para convencerlo de que debe servir de guía. Que no se les vaya a pasar la mano. Después, veremos qué pasa, les dice.

El señor pica espuelas y se pierde en la noche. Ha sido un día muy largo.

EL CHIFLIDO AL OTRO LADO del río hace trizas el silencio. Se va hasta los oídos del lado mexicano. Pronto se echan al río varias figuras y luego se pierden entre el algodonal. Como criminales espantados corren hasta el álamo para coger los costales y se vuelven a sumir en los surcos. Se ciñen los costales a la cintura y empiezan a devorar plantas como peste. Mata tras mata va quedando encuerada. Shas. Shas. Shas. Los costales se van llenando. Se echan el costal al lomo como un chorizo gigante y lo ponen a la orilla del surco.

Esta noche los pizcadores cargan unas orejas larguísimas. Se mueven espantados. Lo peor: no saben si es la espera o no están seguros si el Coyote vendrá. Por eso unos han empezado a mitad de los surcos y se han venido pizcando hacia el río.

Los hombres se arrastran a la luz de la luna. Se cuelan, se retuercen por entre las plantas. Las plantas verdes, con sus motitas blancas parecen arbolitos de Navidad. Los pizcadores quieren treparse hasta la cumbre como si fueran enanos. Pero no pueden escapar la larga cola que los ata a la tierra. Ahora la serpiente, ceñida a la cintura, quiere, con su hocico abierto, tragárselo pero no puede. El pizcador se la tapa con algodón, motitas que la pondrán repleta para que deje en paz a la gente. Las manos, rápidas, rápidas se rasguñan. Quieren despojar el árbol, llevarse esas esperanzas en las bolsas. Quizá algún milagro transformará las motitas en moneditas de oro. Pero todo es inútil. El diablo se las quita. El diablo se multiplica. Después viene otra serpiente tan hambrienta como la otra y otra y otra hasta que alguna noche el bien de Dios les pague la miseria que no merecen. Por ahora los pizcadores platinados seguirán reptando entre mar verde y serpientes blancas. Capullos blancos, puf, billetes verdes. Ojos verdes, dientes verdes. Pudridos, pudrida el alma, verde, verde. Verde mar, cuerpos verdes, verde muerte, descomposición.

LA MUERTE FRESCA entre un ataúd alfombrado es calientita. El cuerpo puede echarse en él, gozar el calor de sábana eléctrica. Pero estos momentos son efímeros porque después se asienta el sereno de la noche y embarga el cuerpo de frío. Es entonces cuando el alma sale con deseos de prolongar la vida. Se desliza por la alfombra como si fuera gato buscando el calor pero todo es inútil; la caja ya no tiene calor ni ternura. Es el alma como una madre que pierde a su hijo en una tormenta y el viento la estira lejos del niño perdido. Así sucede con Vicente. La brisa de la madrugada convierte su alma en humo de cigarro larguísimo y se la lleva soplando hasta el fortín, allí donde tantas otras han sido depositadas.

AFUERA, DETRAS DE LA CHOZA, los señores se aposentaron en cuclillas alrededor de una botella. De acuerdo iban llegando las parejas a la casa del difunto, hombres y mujeres, se separaban y tomaban rumbo distinto. Las señoras pasaban adentro; los hombres seguían haciendo la rueda más grande. Al calor de la botella y la lengua animada de Levario, los hombres se olvidaban a ratos del propósito.

Adentro el olor a cera pega de ramalazo pero después lo amortigua el polvo que se levanta del piso de tierra. No son caras las que se ven ante la luz moribunda de velas. Son cuerpos envueltos de negros vestidos, shales que semejan redes pescadoras. Las mujeres que lograron sentarse ven hacia la nada. Son como momias cansadas de jugar con el rosario. Parecen querer hacer más redondas las cuentas y a ratos, como si les dieran cuerda, empiezan a rezar en alta voz. El murmullo es cosa de minutos; luego entra un silencio de plomo, silencio interrumpido por un mosco gigante y fastidioso. El mosco rodea el cajoncito del muerto dos veces y se para. Vuelve a reinar el silencio. Las mujeres se levantan para salir a coger el aire mientras que otras entran a tomar el mismo lugar en los bancos. Filas enlutadas que contrastan con unas paredes recién encaladas. Roberto, el novio de Eduvijes va y viene, entra y sale, pidiéndoles a los hombres que le ayuden a traer sillas de sus casas porque seguramente vendrá más gente. Gracias a Chito, a Levario, a don Francisco y a Reyes, quienes vinieron y se fueron temprano—todos le han ayudado. La pobrecita de Vicke ni siquiera tuvo tiempo de hacerse su vestido, de barrer, de hacer los arreglos. Pero todos habían cooperado. El cajoncito, puesto sobre dos baldes, lo había donado Levario a pesar de que era tan repugnante. Tenías que conocerlo para aguantarlo. Era de esas personas que sólo necesitan abrir la boca para caer como patada de burro. El anuncio a la puerta de su "fábrica de ataúdes", lo resumía todo: MUERASE AGUSTO . . . CON ATAUDES LOMELI. Pero era de buen corazón. Recuerda Roberto cuando llegó buscando cajón para el angelito:

—¿Quién fue esta vez?

—Chentito, el hermano de Vicke.

—¡Ah! Pues que descanse en paz porque aquí no la tuvo. Nació enfermizo el huerco. Ya casi se moría cuando tenía seis meses y peor que sólo le daban galletitas dulces con café pa comer. A ver, mira aquí, de los mejores. En este sí que se va al cielo a gusto, ¿no?, je, je. Con esta alfombrita puede volar a.t.m. Llévatelo, no te lo cobro y dile a Vicke que muchos días d'estos, ja, ja. No te creas, dile que allá iré a verla por la noche. (Por eso, por hablador y porque eres como eres, caes mal, cabrón. También quizá porque te burlas de la muerte, porque la festejas. Allá irás, vestido de lo mejorcito, con tu botella de tequila para lengonear toda la noche. Así la pasarás, cabrón, hasta que tu Virginia te pare el chorro y te arree borracho a casa. Porque eres un parásito de la muerte me caes mal.)

—Gracias, Levario. Que Dios te los pague.

LA CASUCHA ES CHICA pero la cal le da dimensión a los dos cuartitos. La cortina de percal tapa el boquete donde no hay puerta pero se trasluce como la faz del sacerdote en el confesionario. Vicke, sentada en su cama, observa los movimientos con ojos opacos y luego pasa la mirada a una vela que amenaza apagarse y que esparce el corazón de Jesús por la pared. El Cristo acompaña a Vicke en su dolor, dolor que parpadea al compás de la danzante luz. El Santo Niño, con su lujoso vestidito, también está presente. Ahora Vicke cambia la vista al retrato del angelito muerto y luego a la imagen del Santo Niño. Una, dos, tres veces. Muchas veces, hasta que ambas imágenes se hacen una sola. Estudia, compara. El pelo rizado, la sonrisa, las manitas pegadas. "¡Ay no, no, a la imagen le falta una mano!" Y recuerda que fue el viento de la noche anterior. Recuerda que cuando se volcó la estatua, su hermanito se iba, el pobrecito. Ella lo había levantado del piso, como él había ordenado, y tan pronto como lo había hecho, el niño se había puesto muy platicador. Cuando le trajo el trapo caliente que pedía, le pidió que lo cogiera de la mano y entonces se puso a acordar de cosas. "A ver, Vicke, a que no te acuerdas de esto: allá está la luna . . . ¿cómo es eso que la luna come tuna si es de queso? Yo creo que si fuera verdad ya se había redetido, ¿no crees, Vicke? Allá está el sol bebiendo sotol . . . oye, Vicke, ¿que también las cosas del cielo son como nosotros? Yo por eso no le tengo miedo a la noche, ¿y tú? Cuando sales pa fuera yo no . . . a la víbora de la mar, de la mar, por aquí puedes . . . oye, Vicke, ¿recuerdas la canción del lindo pescadito? . . . en un agua clara que brota la fuente . . . jugar con mi aro . . . mi mamá me ha dicho que no salga yo, porque si yo salgo pronto moriré . . ." Y así había pasado la noche Vicke. Escuchándolo, cantándole, respondiéndole, poniéndole la sonrisita en los labios hasta las horas de la madrugada cuando fue cayendo en sueño. Cuando ya no despertó más y la sonrisa había quedado estampada en su carita, le mandó hablar a Roberto. Su amor vino tan pronto como . . . "Dios mío, dame fuerzas. Sólo quiero saber por qué haces estas cosas con los chiquitos. Tú sabes que son angelitos y que no hacen nada. ¿Por qué te llevas a este muchachito en vez de a mí? Castíganos, mátanos a nosotros los grandes pero no a ellos. ¿Por qué lo haces? ¿Por qué me has dejado sola, sola, sola?"

Los chistes de Levario se hacen más gordos y más borrachos. Se van filtrando por la ventana como si se burlaran de los padres nuestros y de las avemarías. Como cámara de gas, la casucha se sofoca de cuerpos, de cirios, de noche, de náusea. Mareo. Vicke se siente enferma. "La acompaño en su pésame, no. La acompaño en su pésame, no. La acompaño en su pésame, ¡NO! La acompaño en su pésame, ¡NO! ¡NO!" El NO se va haciendo grandote así como dos vejigas infladas. NO. Lentamente se van hinchando en la mente de Vicke hasta que las vejigas no caben en los dos cuartos. Después se derraman por la ventana y se hacen todavía más grandes. Por fin la espina del dolor las revienta. "¡Nooooo!" Empieza a llorar Vicke. Largos llantos intercalados con NO. Afuera la plática cesa para recibir la pena de Vicke por los oídos, pero ya los tapó el licor. ¿No es por eso que se traga en estas ocasiones? ¡Ah, viejos cobardes! ¿Por qué no son tan hombres como las mujeres? ¿Por qué no aguantan a chile pelón, como ellas? Sólo el perro de Levario responde como si estuviera consciente de la angustia. El aullido hace duo al de la mujer.

—¡Shhht! ¡Cállate, perro cabrón!— Levario le da una patada. Este, con la cola entre las patas rodea a los ebrios y luego se echa de nuevo al lado del amo. La plática baja a tono menor.

—Pobre mujer, apenas hace dos años que se le murieron sus viejos, uno tras otro.

—¿Cuando la caminata a Marfa?

—Sí, entonces. Recuerdo también que el chamaco se enfermó mucho. Llevaba la cara abotagada de tanto toser.

—Y ¿qué era?

—Pos no se sabe pero dicen que de allí le vino esto. Otros dicen que cogió algo de las minas cuando estuvo allá.

—Pobre huerco, mejor que ni lo hubieran dejado ir.

—Pobre la Vicke, porque ella siempre lo ha criado.

—Dicen que más temprano vinieron don Benito y doña Rosario a verla.

—¡Ah, Chihuahua! ¿El Patrón?

—Sí, cuando quiere, es buena reata el viejo. Fue el que le hizo a Vicke estos cuartitos en la mera propiedad de él.

—No, pos sí. De eso no hay duda. Yo le ayudé a hacerlos, pero esa vez me dijo quesque iba a hacerlos pa guardar pacas de alfalfa, pero como no se dio . . .

—Ah, pos ai está. Yo oí al revés, que los hizo pa Vicke porque les debía algo a sus difuntos padres.

—¿Sí? ¿Y cómo está eso?

—No se sabe, pero yo creo que sí hay algo porque cuando vinieron los soldados a ella no se la llevaron hasta Paso. Digo, nomás hasta Marfa, pero luego fue el Ben y la trajo a ella y a Chentito.

—Pos quién sabe cómo estará la cosa pero pa que venga a verla, seguro que hay algo . . .

Así se va llenando la noche de vida mientras que adentro los restos de la muerte aletean contra los pechos. Pican, hieren como alfiler. Vicke dormita de agotamiento y sueña garabatos. Un puntito luminoso que se torna murciélago indeciso. Luego desciende hasta el velorio como cometa ciego. Vicke lo ve diminuto al principio pero después se hace más grande, más y más y más hasta que ¡PLAS! Se estrella en su frente. Los aleteos en los ojos y en los brazos la estremecen. El murciélago se va. Abre los ojos la mujer. Levario entra bambaleándose y se dirige al cadáver de Chente. "Dios mío, que salga ese borracho, que se vaya a dormir. Que respete al angelito, por Dios".

El borracho se acerca mientras que los ojos de las señoras quieren detenerlo pero no pueden. Empieza a palpar el cajón. Con gusto sensual pasa los dedos por la pana. No, no es el cuerpo que le movió a acercarse. Es su obra, su cajón. Tan fascinado está que se olvida de que está montado el ataúd sobre dos baldes y se recarga. El cadáver se ladea. El hombre hace el intento de detenerlo pero está borracho. Los dos caen al suelo con un golpe seco.

—¡Aaaaaaay! ¡Por piedad, por favor no me lo golpeen, que le duele! ¡No! ¡Chentito, mi Chentito querido!

Roberto, quien acaba de entrar, acude a ayudarles a las señoras que se acomiden a poner de nuevo el cajón sobre los baldes. Luego coge a Levario del brazo y lo arrastra para afuera.

—Vete ya, Levario. Ya es hora. Y no vuelvas— Es el tono de una voz con rabia refrenada.

—Sssi yyyo nomás quería tocar el cajón. . . .

—Ya te dije. ¡Vete!

La señora Virginia sale avergonzada pidiendo miles de disculpas y se lo lleva a casa. Mientras tanto allí adentro le frotan a Vicke el cuello con alcohol para calmarla. Llora por unos momentos y entonces vuelve a caer en la trampa del sueño.

EL PESO QUE TRAJO REYES se hizo sentir en el campamento. Llegaba del velorio de Chente. Un 'buenas noches, muchachos' y luego silencio. Rufino, alias el grillo, se le acerca.

—¿Qué pasa, jefe? Parece que se le cargó el muertito.

—Pues ¿qué quiere, compa? Pero no es por un angelito más sino porque no le hallo ton ni son a esta perra vida.

—Déjese de cosas, jefe. Mire, aquí le va su preferida.

—Anda pues, échatela.

El Grillo Cantor no iba a recibir premio por esta canción tampoco, pero el corrido de Joaquín Murrieta no se oía mal con el acompañamiento de la guitarra bien afinada.

"Señores, soy mexicano pero comprendo el inglés. Yo lo aprendí por mi hermano, al derecho al revés, y a cualquier americano lo hago temblar a mis pies. Yo me vine . . ." Reyes no escucha ya. La mente de Reyes se desparrama y se le desborda el rencor. El chamaco que acaba de expirar no es más que otro número de muertes ignobles entre las cuales se cuenta su propio hermano Jesús. Por . . .

". . . cantares me he metido, castigando americanos, y al indio noble y sencillo . . ." (Desgraciada vida que no respeta ni a los inocentes. Pero yo no me iré sin cobrárselo muy caro.) "Cuando todavía era un niño, huérfano a mí me dejaron, ni quien me hiciera un cariño y a mi hermano lo mataron . . ." (. . . y mientras haya injusticia, mientras vea caras viejas maltratadas, seguiré, por Dios que seguiré . . .) "ya no es otro mi destino, pon cuidado parroquiano . . ."

—EPA COMPA, que no se le duerma el gallo.

—¿Eh? A chingao, pos sí que se me estaba pegando.

—Uu, ¿a poco se la quiere perder?

—¿Pos si quién dijo miedo? Nomás que ya los años, mi amigo. Como quien dice yo me lo llevé en zapetas, ¿que ya no recuerda? De allí del merito puente. Cabrón, que rejiego se nos puso. Pero ya ve, mire dónde anda ahora.

—¿Qué quiere, hombre? En ese tiempo no sabía ni dónde ponían las gallinas. Pero ahora que veo la cosa más de cerca uno no se aguanta, ¿sabe? A uno le hierve el alma.

—Si vienen, nomás hay que asustarlos. Pa que sepan que aquí pesan. Pero que no se nos pase la mano como a aquel otro. Le rechinaron muy feo los dientes.

Bueno, creo que ya es hora de irnos acercando. De aquí vamos a pata y cuiden esos caballos. Y esperen hasta que cante "El Grillo".

Los DIEZ RANCHEROS, guiados por Lorenzo desmontan también como a cien yardas del álamo. Luego, bajo mando del jefe Chester, le atacan la boca a Lorenzo con un pañuelo y le amarran las manos a la cabeza de la montura. Entonces atan su caballo, junto con los otros, a una durmiente clavada en la esquina de la bomba. En seguida se van escondiendo hasta llegar al álamo y ya allí con el primer tiro al aire, los diez se desparraman por entre los surcos tras la gente.

El Grillo canta. Empiezan a oírse chapaleos en el agua. Reyes y sus hombres cruzan el río como si fuera muy natural. Así llegan hasta el árbol sin preocupación ni prisa y allí escuchan calmados las patadas secas en el cuerpo del que salió corriendo al revés. Umph. Umph. Los pujidos no alteran a los jinetes. Y luego . . .

—¡Aaaagua, muchachos!— grita el Grillo, y entonces empieza la balacera. Los hombres no tiran a pegar pero la sorpresa hace que los azotes de Ben corran espantados dejando el trabajo sin terminar. Eso

quiere Reyes. Después sus hombres sacan los chicotes y se llevan a
Chester y a su pandilla arreando a golpes hasta caer exhaustos.

Lorenzo mientras tanto ha logrado a fuerza de espuelazos que el
caballo reviente la rienda pero no quiere salir a galope porque todavía
tiene las manos atadas. Hace un gran esfuerzo por hablar y pedirles
piedad mas no puede, por el pañuelo. Entonces logra aflojarse el nudo
de las manos pero Rufino lo descubre, y apenas logra picar espuelas
para cuando éste se le apareja y lo tumba a la tierra. Luego lo rueda
barranco abajo y allí lo zambulle sin darse cuenta que el hombre está
mudo. Una, dos, tres, zambullidas. El cuerpo queda flojo. Rufino por
fin lo deja allí para atender a los golpeados.

—Epa, Manuel, ¿qué llevas ai?

—Al viejo Rentería. Todavía no despierta de la zurundiada.

—Pues a ver si le vas echando agua.

Uno por uno los pizcadores se fueron haciendo bola bajo el álamo
gordo, unos no tan golpeados como el viejo, otros solamente con la
boca abierta. Reyes se dirige hacia unos gemidos tirados de panza entre
la acequia. Encuentra a un chamaco tiritando. Le tiende la mano. El
muchacho parece que le cierra el ojo como burla pero está demasiado
morado el golpe para que sea chiste.

—A ver, mira nomás que friega le pusieron. Súbase. Y sepa que
para otra vez no es nomás irse a la brava. No crea que le van a pagar ni
su trabajo ni su paliza. Tenga, pendejo. Echese esta lanita en la bolsa
y . . . búsquele de otro modo.

Pasaron por donde estaba Lorenzo quien seguía todavía como lo
habían dejado en la arena, de panza. El mismo Rufino lo pone boca
arriba . . .

—Oiga, jefe, creo que se nos fue la mano. ¡A qué caray! . . . hijo
de la ching . . . pero si es Lorenzo, compa.

—Pues, ¿qué se le va a hacer? Que Dios lo lleve a él y que a
nosotros nos perdone, compadre.

Allí cerca de presidio donde llaman la Loma Pelona, se levanta el
fortín como un castillo podrido. Es un castillo de adobe sin puertas que
usa el viento como pito de barro y no falta quien pase por allí alguna
noche con pelos de puercoespín y diga: el castillo está espantado. Hay
espíritus y hay diablos que pasan de cuarto en cuarto botando. Los
incrédulos lo niegan diciendo que son mitotes pero lo cierto es que la

historia se intuye. Las leyendas de la gente son las páginas de un libro
que se arrancaron y se echaron a la hoguera . . .

A VER MUCHACHOS, *vamos a darle una porra a don Benito el de las barbas
de chivo. Vamos todos* . . . *¡don Beniiito, don Beniiito, don Beniiito, que
cante don Beniiito, que grite don Beniiito, que ría don Beniiito!* . . .
   —¿*Y por qué se te ocurrió darle porra?*
   —*Porque ayer lo vi pasar con su traje de catrín, con una pata en el
suelo y la otra tocando las barbas blancas del pecho.*
   —*Tiene géneros.*
   —*No, tiene lana y sal el viejito cabroncito de Presidio.*
   —*Otra vez, muchachos, don Beniiito, don beniiito, don benito el de la
tienda* . . .
   —*¡Don beniiito!*
   —*don benito el del grafitti en* . . .
   —*¡Don beniiito!*
   —*en los escusados, en paredes de la calle, en los cheques de banqueros,
en los lomos del ganado* . . .
   —*¡Don beniiito!*
   —*en el cielo y en infierno, en las tierras de los padres de la Vicke que
perdieron en la corte del condado* . . .
   —*¡Don beniiito!*
   —*en los papeles de cuero, don benito el hacendado, don benito el
soldado* . . .
   —*¡Don Beniiito!*
   —*Alabado sea, digamos todos los muertos.*
   —*¡Alabado sea!*
   —*por sus obras y sus bienes, por librarnos el señor.*
   — . . .
   —*Ayer recordé verlo pasar con el pecho tan inflado que se me ocurrió
darle porra. No, quería darle una aporreada si pudiera pero el viejo no
resiste, Dios lo tenga en sus recuerdos cuando muera.*
   —*Espérense, vamos todos a alzar las manos, rezar por él antes de que
venga con nosotros al fortín.*
   —*No, vamos a darle porra otra vez, por su astucia con el pobre, por
sus robos y por los asesinados.*
   —*¡Alto! Cállense por el amor de Dios. Tanta calumnia no soporto.
Era joven, no sabía. Era militar. Hubo guerra, hubo miedo, hubo riña de*

gobiernos, él era sólo un empleado. Le dijeron allá por '63, vente para acá muchacho, donde serpentea el río bravo.

—A la víbora de la mar . . .

—Y le dijo Captain Gray, todos los gatos son pardos, cuida el río de este lado, crúzalo si necesario.

—Por aquí pasó la tropa y se fueron hasta Chihuahua. Don Benito regresó con la gloria de soldado.

—¡Porra muchachos! Benito fue a la guerra . . .

—Montado en una perra, la perra se ensució y Benito le lambió.

—Y luego se coló entre nosotros, conquistó tierra, puso tienda, dio trabajo a todo mundo.

—Cállense gritones, nosotros también tenemos la culpa. ¿Cuántas veces les decía que exigieran sus derechos, que se cuidaran de lobos, que guardaran los papeles.

—Nosotros ¿qué sabíamos de gobierno americano?

—Bien, pero ¿por qué no nos unimos entonces? ¿Por qué? . . . sigan pendejos a ver si le encuentran fin. Cuando se escribió el tratado, se aseguraron derechos de tierras en papel. Después se hicieron reclamos, muchos reclamos, al comité federal. ¿Qué pasó? De mil y pico se aprobaron setenta. El resto se les pagó a dólar y medio el acre. ¿Justicia? Bola e pendejos . . .

—Y usted don Rubén, ¿qué pasó con lo suyo?

—No pos a mí me trajo la larga muy temprano y lo que ya presentía, pasó. Mi pobre vieja, ¿qué iba a hacer? Con tamaña pistolota le hizo la lucha, pero quedó loquita, o mejor dicho, iba quedando. Dios persone al vendido de Lorenzo que también la encandungó. No sé qué tratos se hicieron pero allá en la casa de corte Lorenzo la convinció que traspasara su firma. Ni modo, la vieja pendeja firmó y al rato que ya no es dueña pero que el gobierno va a pagarle todo lo que quitaba. Pero dejemos la cosa, ella no tuvo la culpa y con seguridá que yo hubiera hecho lo mismo . . .

—Si yo bien qui la recuerdo. Yo, cuando vine pa esta tierra, yo trabajé con ella.

—Y tú ¿qué viniste a hacer aquí?

—Pos, siñor, a buscar la vida qui no incontraba en l'otro lado.

—¿De dónde eres tú?

—Soy el tarasco Melchor, siñor. Vengo de muy lejos. Mi dijeron que por acá si vivía mejor.

—Pero si eres bastante joven. ¿Cómo . . .

—Pos, siñor, murí quemadito aquí en el fortín. Nunca pensé murir

tan temprano. Tanto qui le rogué a la virgencita que mi concidiera ver a
mi mamita, pero como ve usté, siñor, no se pudo. Quiría probarle qui sabía
ya escribir y qui estuviera mera orgullosa de mí.

—¿Y qué es ese papel que traes quemado de las puntas, Melchor?

—Pos verá usté, siñor, es una poesía pa mi mamá qui no le mandé.
Cuando me quemaron me la eché a la boca porque era lo único que valía
en mi vida.

—Léela Melchor.

—Ay siñor, nomás no se vaya usté a rir.

—No, hombre, como me voy a reír. Léela, léela, ¿que no, muchachos?

—¡Que lea Melchor! ¡que lea Melchor! ¡que lea Melchor!

—¿Ya ves hombre? Tienes público. Andale. Y por favor alza la cabeza
como si te estuviera oyendo tu mamá.

—Pos ai va. Si llama Magrecita Santa:

"Tú qui en mi desgracia impeñaste todo pa darme consuelo
y darme la friega qui nicisitaba,
tú que le prendites dos velas al santo allá en Igualapa
Cuando jui juyendo muy muy lejos da ti me encontraba,
tú qui eres y juites muy güena y sufrida.
Aceita mis gracias, tamién mis querencias,
pos no puedo darte más que este manojo
de flores cortadas, unas en las siembras
y las más fresquitas allá en la Chinampa,
Acéitalas dulce magrecita güena,
Acéitalas chula magrecita santa.
ora que es tu santo que Dios te bendiga
¿O ya no recuerdas toditas las malas aiciones?
Pos sabes que jue sin pensalo.
Pue qué de querencia
Pue qué de confianza
Porque yo tu nombre lo llevo metido
Como a tu sagrada almita de lirio
Magrecita chula, magrecita güena, magrecita santa.
Has sido güena todita tu vida.
Por todas mis culpas derramaste lágrimas.
Ora que es tu santo sólo puedo darte
este manojito de flores cortadas
unas, en las siembras, y las más fresquitas
allá en la Chinampa

Acéitalas dulce magrecita güena
Acéitalas chula magrecita santa
y abrásame juerte, bendícime muncho
porque ora en tu santo mi espíritu canta . . ."
—¡Que viva Melchor!
—¡Vivaaa! Ahora que cante el indio Melchor. ¡Que cante! Una porra
muchachos . . .
—¡Que cante, que cante, que cante, que cante Melchor, que cante
Melchor, que cante Melchor . . .
"Tzitzi, curapi, tzan en an tzetzas et tzana por su me cuaria . . . ca
que tzan tzin, por tunque lo ña miri curiñaaa . . . flor de canela sospiro y
sospiro porque me acuerdo de tiii . . . sospiro yo, sospiro porque me
acuerdo de tiii, a za guera, aza sentí . . . porque me acuerdo de ti . . ."
—¡Otra! ¡Otra! ¡Otra!
"Ay, ay, ay, ay, tlazita mutzi caraquia, itzle cuicho, itzla cochitl, aim
pero ro quimooo . . . tzama ri cuaria, maqui ni qui ni quia, matzen flor
azul, matze pere tzaratzin, male ña quim pa ña quiii . . . ay, ay, ay,
ay . . . "
— . . . ¿qué decía, señor?
—Que están cantando.
—Ah, sí . . . (las lenguas se confunden, se mutilan como pedazos el
alma) Bonita canción . . . (te barrenan otras con la punta de un lápiz y
luego le dan vuelta para borrarte la tuya tan fácil como si el alma
estuviera en el papel. Luego la lengua se alarga como cuerda y se enreda en
tu cuerpo haciéndote bola como le sucedió al gato.)
—¿Por qué tan serio, joven?
Por nada, nomás estaba pensando . . . (que la justicia es una lengua
hilada de donde se prende la vida y se hace nudos).
—¿Por qué cargas esa cachucha en el pecho?
—Lo hago por costumbre. Traté de detenerme la sangre que me salía.
—¿Que fue pleito?
—No, fue un balazo que me dieron cuando salí corriendo.
—¿Andabas de mojadito?
—No señor, fue cuando se nos puso la cosa tirante el año 30. ¿Se
acuerda cuando a todos nos andaba llevando la trampa de hambre?
—Pos claro que me acuerdo. En esos tiempos anduve yo por Los
Angeles. Decían que nosotros estábamos empeorando la cosa y empezaron
a echarnos de a montón. Yo recuerdo que en agosto del mismo año, salió en
los periódicos que habían echado a 82,000 de allí nomás, pero lo curioso es

que se dieron cuenta muy tarde que nosotros éramos los únicos que no pedíamos ayuda ni nada para comer. Estaba muy confundida la cuestión en esos tiempos. La migra se metía en las casas sin permiso y empezaban a barrer con la gente. Recuerdo del pobre viejo Anselmo, cómo lloró porque lo sacaron de su casa que había habitado más de cincuenta años. Pero esa ya es historia muy larga. Tú, muchacho, dime qué pasó con lo tuyo, pero primero quítate esa cachucha del pecho, parece que estás pidiendo perdón . . . ¡ah caray! ¡Qué tamaño boquetón! Con razón lo traes tapado. A ver cuéntame.

—Pues sucedió que mis padres se emigraron cuando tenía seis años. Mi papá encontró trabajo en el rancho del joven Ben, que antes era de su papá, y se sintió feliz aunque yo tuviera que ayudarle después de la escuela. Así estuvo la vida hasta el 31 como usted lo cuenta. Se les puso a los del gobierno que éramos estorbos aunque decían que nos echaban porque nos tenían compasión. Lo que no querían entender era que estaba peor allá. Un día se metieron a la casa y revisaron papeles. Mi papá se había emigrado bien pero le dijeron que yo era ilegal y que tendría que irme al país donde había nacido, a México. Y si no, pues toda la familia tendría que regresar. Mi mamá imploró, lloró y mi papá rezongó pero fue inútil. A mí tanto que me gustaba la escuela. Pues de todos modos me fui a quedar con los abuelos pero no pude aguantar. Después de seis semanas, y a pesar de la advertencia de mi abuela, me vine tempranito a cruzar el río (Güelita, me voy para el otro lado. No muchacho, no cruces el río. Seco está el prado a los dos lados, no cruces. ¿Que no ves que bajo el agua las arañas una red te van tejiendo? ¿Que no ves que las sanguijuelas verdes te calarán en los huesos?) Era todavía oscuro pero así con todo el miedo me arrojé solito . . . (Sombras frondosas, como peces moribundos . . . chapaleos en el agua . . . huellas que se ahogan.) Mi güelita no quería dejarme venir y todo el camino parecía que la oía decirme que me devolviera . . . (Verdes sombras, tus pupilas con el color de los mares . . . el sauce te está llorando con sus lágrimas amargas . . . ¡regrésateee!) Pero de todos modos crucé como un eco en las montañas. Parecía que todo estaba contra mí porque tan pronto como crucé, empezó a ponerse más oscuro y a relampaguear . . . (Se me nublaron los ojos, de nubes grises y negro cielo . . . tembló la tierra bajo los pies, quebrose el cielo en pedazos, machetazos luminosos.) Entonces sí que me asusté porque si llovía no iba a poder seguir y yo creo que fue el miedo el que me hizo continuar, aunque sabía que no podría protegerme si me agarraba el agua a medio camino y me desorientaría. Pues así fue. Me pescó la lluvia cuando apenas iba a

media labor . . . (pedradas en el rostro, fustigazos en la espalda. ¡Corre!
¡Refúgiate! ¡Regrésateee!) y lo peor del caso es que pronto se convirtió en
granizo y me puso bien moretoneado. (Lágrimas, lluvia, munición de hielo.
¡Clemencia!) La cachucha para nada me ayudó y como loco empecé a
correr llorando. Ni siquiera me acuerdo como di con el árbol (bajo el sauce
triste tiritaba mientras que las gotas en las hojas de las plantas aplau-
dían). Allí me hice pelotita y lloré mucho tiempo hasta que me quedé
dormido. Por la mañana me puse otra vez a caminar pero llevaba un peso
bruto en el alma, como si todo el mundo se burlara de mí. Y cuando llegué,
lloré en los brazos de mi mamá como un niño. (Y tú, mamita, tú le diste
forma al tiempo sondeando la transparencia del mar. Te gustaba recoger
las aguas de lagunas y de ríos en tus pupilas redondas. Y aunque los ríos no
corrían como antes, te recreabas con el viavén de tu silla. ¡Te acuerdas que
te picaba las costillas y que así llenabas los arroyos de tu piel? Risa de agua
multiforme rebosando tus enaguas de percal. Vida sin medida. Mares
pululantes. Cielo transparente que se arrulla en tu regazo.)
   —*Ya me lo imagino. Pero entonces ¿cómo te balacearon si no fue en*
esa ocasión?
   —*Ah, pues fue más luego cuando me puse a trabajar, como ya no iba*
a la escuela. Andaba solo limipiando en la labor cuando aparecieron los
chotas. Los mismos. Yo creo que si no hubiera sido por esta cachucha no
me hubieran reconocido. El caso es que de inmediato vinieron hacia mí.
Nomás les dije que cuando menos me dejaran ir a traer mi ropa y a
despedirme. Pues dijeron que estaba bien y me echaron al carro. Me
llevaron hasta la casa y me esperaron en el carro hasta que arreglara todo
y aunque mis padres armaron un lío, de nada sirvió. Al salir noté que uno
de los chotas estaba tomando agua de uno de los grifos que estaba un poco
retirado. El otro parecía dormitar sentado en el carro. Entonces no sé qué
me pasó pero se me ocurrió correr aun sabiendo que no podría escapar. El
que tomaba agua me vio y disparó para asustarme pero después se echó a
correr y al ver que no me alcanzaba se hincó para no fallar. Yo como tonto
di la vuelta como para encararme con él y de repente sentí un friíto cerca
del corazón. Pero no sentí dolor sino una sorpresa grande. Recuerdo que
actué como un miedoso porque ya cuando los dos vinieron a ponerme las
esposas, yo ya les ofrecía las manos juntitas. Después así esposado recogí
mi cachucha y me la puse en el corazón. Me ayudaron a levantarme y
caminé con ellos al carro pero las piernas me decían que no. Yo creo que
con la cachucha quería tapar el boquete por donde se me iba la vida. ¡Pero

cómo se puede guardar la vida en una cachucha? Todos los que vamos a morir somos chistosos, ¿no cree usted?

—Es cierto. Pero ¿qué haces tú aquí, si no eres de Presidio?

—Soy del mundo, señor. Como la muerte. Que importa ser de aquí o de allá. La ignorancia es grande y es igual. También la pobreza. La realidad es el agujero que traigo aquí, señor.

—La realidad soy yo, señores.

—¿Y quién eres tú?

—Soy Jesús del río, soy de agua.

—Estás loco, eres de tierra como nosotros.

—Ni de cenizas ni de barro. Viví del agua y morí en el agua. Todo soy de agua.

—¿Y por qué estás en el fortín si eres de agua?

—Porque el fortín es de vidrio, es aquario.

—Sí, cómo no, loquito. Un aquario con puertas de adobe gastado. Eres ridículo.

—No, las puertas son de voces.

—¿Nuestras?

—No, del diablo.

—No es cierto, son las nuestras. Son llantos, son silbidos de hombres que quieren cruzar el río. Te hablan a ti, Jesús.

—No, son las sirenas del mar. Me quieren, por eso me llaman.

—Sí, te quieren. Muerto.

—No, me quieren para que cuente cuentos de hadas.

—Mitotes tuyos, Jesús. ¿Para qué van a querer idioteces?

—Porque mis cuentos son la verdad. Yo también soy sirena.

—¿Por qué dices eso Jesús?

—Porque mi cuerpo está en Presidio, pero mi alma en el río.

—¿Que no se fue al cielo?

—No, porque se me seca y quiero que siga viviendo.

—¿En un infierno como éste?

—Sí, para que aplaque las llamas.

—¿Pero cómo, dime tú, vas a lograrlo si estás muerto?

—Voy a resucitar, me llamaré José.

—¿Tu hijo?

—No, el de mi hermano Reyes, y ya me voy cantando señores: "Es mi orgullo haber nacido en el barrio más humilde . . . (este hombre es un loco de atar, ojalá que se calle pronto) . . . y el día que el pueblo me falle, ese día voy a morir."

Los pocos turistas que por casualidad se cuelan a Presidio en busca
de cosas viejas, tienen la suerte de hallar una reliquia güera llamada
Mack. Este se supone ser el experto de la historia de Presidio, del fortín
y de Ben Lynch. Así que para cuando salen de Nancy's Cafe ya
quedaron enterados del número de colgadas, de cogidas y de todas esas
cosas que es capaz de hacer el hombre. Lo demás es fácil. Por unos
dólares organiza la excursión al fortín. Ya allí, los hace formar un
semicírculo antes de entrar para que . . . pero mejor que te lo cuente
el viejo cabrón . . .

"Yes siree, old ben came to this part of the country from his dad's in
Alabama. Guess he got tired of driving them dark folks over there and
so headed fer San Antone. Ben was still young then and I guess them
wild hairs of his stood up when he heard 'bout the trouble with
Mexicans. The story 'bout the slaughter at the Alamo made him mad
a plenty. Now I ain't sure when he get to San Antone but I know he
arrive too late. Musta been a sight when he ride into town. You should
see a picture of him, here, see? Big, and tall in the saddle, with all that
fair hair a bristling in the wind. Anyway, he got there a day after all
this happened and he sure got burnt up when he hear about Crockett
and Bowie died. Couldn't do nothing about it, though, just get mad
over the whole mess. He wasn't received good either by Mrs. Caulder
because she got a patio full of dead stinking . . . bodies, so she give
him a piece of her mind thinking he had took part in the killing. But
he told her different and help her get rid of most of the carcasses.
Young Ben was a hell of a cowpoke. He was a pretty happy-go-lucky
kid them years but I ain't saying he had no sense in him. He was
hardworking and never give his boss reason to talk. He was a tough
hombre those years; sure he could sing and yodel, but people sure
wasn't going to mistake him for no sissy. He could fight damned near
anybody and boy, could he ride. He could ride broncs till they spilt
over tired as hell. And them bulls, you would a think he was born on
'em. But his rough and tough ways don't mean he wasn't brought
up right. Hell no. His folks reared him good. They tell him 'bout the
Lord, and the right living, and all that 'bout being a loyal and proud
man. Sure he was ornery—a few fights once in a while but who ain't
when you're that age? And specially when you come to a town
of . . . people with different folkways and no care fer law and order. I
mean, you know, he come to San Antone fer that there reason. He

learned pretty quick how to deal with 'em in the canteenas and he wouldn't let no man beat 'im. And he already know 'bout how conniving these critters can be with knife and all, you know what I mean. Fact I heard the reason there ain't no Indians in this part of the country no more is 'cause these folks beat 'em at their own game. The first time he fight, he fight five of them at once and he licked 'em clean. And when he whipped 'em pretty good, that's when he got his reputation. He didn't need no gun; the bastards would disappear like shitflies . . . pardon the expression . . . and after that they would turn yeller and run. O yea, they knew what he stood fer. Anyway, guess it was about that time that things started getting pretty stinky down the Rio Grand and they start organizing the Texas brigade and other lawful organizations to clear the mess. You know, horse stealing, cattle rustling, killing white folks. People nowadays don't pay much attention to the service these constabulary, Texas Rangers they call 'em, give to their country. Remember there wasn't no law to protect the citizenry so they take it in their own hands. Sometimes when there wasn't no courthouse judge around, a noose on a tree was enough fer 'em. Hell, with all these desperados running wild, they had to do something, hoosegow or no hoosegow. Sure, they made some mistakes, but hanging innocent people was rare. And although they crossed the border and followed them outlaws clear to hell, there was not enough of them to clear up the mess. Anyway, to make a long story short, the Rangers went recruitin' by way of San Antone and they hear of Ben's reputation soon enough. In fact, they found that the only bad habit he had was seeñoritas and tobacco chewing so they hired him. But first they talk to his boss directly and of course there wasn't no problem. Mixin' with them don't spoil 'im. So he pack his saddlebags with dried beef and off he goes (come a ti yi yippi yippi yea, come a ti yi yippi yippi yea, tis cloudy in the west and looks like rain and my old slickers in the wagon again . . . on a ten-dollar horse and a forty-dollar saddle . . .) I ain't sure what good he done over the Valley by the Rio Grand, but next thing, he show up in Presidio. It was about the time the government start getting pretty worried about border troubles so they start moving soldiers up and down the river. Ha, ha, but I cain't figure why they sent soldiers to Presidio 'cause it was just a poor Mexican settlement and there was no white folks yet. All they find was poor people and a few savages, Jumanos, they call them. They say the name's Mexican which means humans, and I guess that's true,

he, 'cause they sure as hell didn't cause no trouble. That's funny.
Sometimes you cain't tell the difference between Mexicans and
Indians. They mix up pretty good, ha, and they sent the whole
company to fight and there was none to fight. Truth is, they only find
a forteen built of adobe by Spanish soldiers, long time before, and it
look like it never been used; yea, this one here you're seeing. They say
it was a custom to build them everywhere they went, just like the
Alamo in San Antone, but this one here wasn't no beauty. Sure
doesn't look like it can even hold water out . . . fact you probably
could blow at it and it'd fall. Anyway, they find themselves this
Presidio del Norte with nothing to do so they move up to Marfa sixty
miles away where there was white folks already. But Ben stayed 'cause
he was smart. He know what he was doing but you know, this is where
the story become different. I mean, Ben was different. He changed, no
doubt about it, 'cause he married a seeñorita. By this time he was
pretty savvy in the language and took to marrying. Of course she was
different, too, educated, pretty, clean—you know what I mean. But I
ain't saying he was a turncoat though. He still loved law and order.
He always done good like he used to. He never quit being a ranger
either and he would run anybody out of town that give him reason to.
One night when he was a courting Rosary, he got pistolwhipped pretty
bad by his brothers but he got even soon enough. But that's what I
mean, he become different 'cause he didn't hold no grudge. He learn
how to love these people. I guess that's what love does to you, get soft
in the guts. Anyway, he was a well-respected feller by the community
and of course they couldn't help it 'cause he was kind to them. He
gave 'em work and food, everything, and of course they look up to him
like a daddy. He learned how to handle 'em and I say this 'cause next
thing, he own a hell of a lot of farmland and longhorns. Fact he even
take over the forteen and use it as a office once his business went good
and the soldiers had move out. He started using a lot of Mexican help
and from here he would pay 'em with all them wads of bills. Yup, Ben
was a good old critter with a big heart, you have to admire a guy like
him. Sh . . . Hell, he even make big barbacoas and invite the whole
lot of them to eat. He was fair if they do the job but if they fail or trick
him, boy, he would turn meaner than a . . . angry mama bear. It ain't
no bu . . . lie either. But people remember more than good deeds. For
example, he never forget Paz, the old lady that sell him the land. He

done a lot of favors fer her, and even after she died, he took in her daughter Vicke once she lost her husband. Anyway, people remember old Ben Lynch. He was hardworking, kind, lawabiding, etcetera and all them qualities that an hombre should have. And I ain't saying all about him is true though. But damned near all ot it . . . Okay folks, let's go in . . ."

"MI PAPA TRABAJABA en Ojinaga en una labor, rentada a medias y levantaba mucho trigo. Ya se nos acabó la necesidad porque trabajaba mamá haciendo tortillas y lavaba ropa pa darnos comida a los que estábamos chicos. Entonces él agarró esa labor y ya se nos acabó el hambre. Levantaba frijol, calabazas, lentejas y todo iba alzando. Cuando nos vinimos hacía muy poco que había levantado el maíz, unas mazorcas grandotas y hizo una trofa grande allí junto de la casa. Hizo una testera grande con palos pa echarle maíz. Pos bastante dejamos cuando vino Pancho Villa. No logramos nada. Nos vinimos porque los caballos de Pancho se lo comieron. Una pérdida bárbara. Dejamos las garras que teníamos, las chanclas que teníamos, porque no teníamos zapatos, camas y todo se quedó. No vinimos nomás de con una burra, con una angarilla y una bandeja grande llena de masa que habíamos amasado pa hacer pan. Eso fue lo que sacamos y vinimos a hacer tortillas al campo donde se acampó toda la gente; también sacamos una esquilia y un sartén y unas cucharas nomás.

"Pasando todo la burra se fue adelante con los triques y nosotros atrás. Pa cuando salimos a la orilla de río, ya nos daba l'agua muy arriba porque creció el río. Pos todos los que sabían nadar se retiraron y los que no pos se quedaron allá. Anda, si fue un desgarriate esa tarde. El hermano de Carmen Chávez cuando se soltó el tiroteo fuerte allá en el pueblo entonces se vino él y otro. Hicieron una balsa pos sin saber cómo se hacía. Hicieron la balsa pa tirarse al río y sí lo hicieron pero se 'hogaron. No, si fue un desgarriate bárbaro. Nosotros cruzamos por-que la casa de nosotros estaba arriba de la loma. Allí nomás bajaba uno y allí estaba el río. Pasó mucha gente y se acampó en el bosque. Unos ganaron pa una parte y otros para otra. Se desparramó la gente y nosotros nos vinimos pa Puerto Rico a vivir".

"CUANDO VINO LA REVOLUCION de 1910, los soldados agarraban a la gente y la metían de soldado así que los que vivían en Ojinaga, casi todos se fueron pa'l otro lao. Y nosotros como no teníamos trabajo pos andábamos de vagos, como luego dicen, sueltos. Estaba poco dura la cosa así que nos manteníamos pescando. Estaba muy bajo el río, el agua muy clara y limpia y donde había hondables nos metíamos con horquillas a hacerle ruido al pescao pa echarlo fuera pa fisgarlo en las horquillas, cuando salía pa afuera de lo hondo. Ese día que nos agarraron allí andábamos.

"Nos vinimos en la mañana yo, Francisco mi hermano, que estaba de este tamaño, Francisco Brito mi primo y Chamalía Heredia un tío mío. Nos metimos al río hechos ala, en forma de ala, y con las horquillas le hacíamos ruido al pescado. Mi tío no se metió sino que se subió al barranco porque de arriba del barranco se veía el pescado si salía o no, tan clara así estaba l'agua, y de allí nos decía si salía el pescado. Y a poco rato allí en el mero frente de Quivira oímos un tropel de caballos. Era una avanzada que iba de Ojinaga pa donde estaban peleando en el Mulato. Entonces Chamalía nos preguntó si les hablaba pero yo le dije que no porque como andaba la revolución pos no podía uno saber qué podrían hacernos. Bueno, pues éste les habló; les pegó un grito y ellos se dejaron venir. Nomás llegaron y luego luego, con los rifles en la mano, agarraron a Chamalía. Luego nos dijeron a nosotros que saliéramos pero nos encaminamos pa'l otro lao (y a mí me podía mucho, por ejemplo, que no fuera y que me llevaran a mi hermano, tan chico; Francisco estaba chamaco de a tiro) pero nos agarraron a tiros. Tuvimos que salirnos y nomás pasamos y nos amarraron. Nos trataron muy mal. Nos decían que éramos maderistas y que estábamos pasándoles parque a los maderistas. Eduardo Salinas, el jefe de ellos, les ordenó que nos amarraran con las sogas de los caballos. Nos mancornaron y nos echaron descalzos por arriba de los mesquites. Entonces dijo que nos iban a fusilar. Allí en Quivira arriba de la loma estaba un camposanto y les ordenó que nos llevaran a la loma pa matarnos allí. Nos acusaban de algo que ni cuenta nos dábamos. Sí sabíamos de la revolución pero no andábamos. Pos nos llevaron hasta allí y todos se fueron rumbo al Mulato menos dos. Ellos se quedaron con nosotros en la loma. Estaba un solón muy fuerte y nosotros descalzos y todo lo que usted quiera. Pos se pusieron de acuerdo y llevaron a Francisco, como era el más chico, a que nos pasara la ropa y después nos vistieron allí en la loma. Aunque tenían orden de que nos mataran, no lo hicieron, y uno de ellos sí nos hizo una movida muy buena. Porque ora verá que en el otro lao nos juntábamos todos los muchachos en la noche a pelear de mentiritas. Unos de Loma Pelona y otros del Terronal. Poníamos lumbre en las palmillas y todo eso pa pelear con tizones prendidos. Unos eran maderistas y otros eran gobiernistas. A mí los muchachos maderistas me pusieron de capitán esa noche. Entonces de un papel hacíamos cheques pa pagarles a los solados y como me tocó a mí ser jefe, parece hecho adrede que traía todos esos papeles en la bolsa del pantalón. Allí tenía escrito el valor del dinero cuando nos agarraron.

"Si yo estoy viendo porque Dios es muy grande. Entonces pos yo estaba muy apurado pero ni remedio. El soldado que fue a trae la ropa, me esculcó y me sacó todo lo que traía, en la bolsa. Pero ése no lo presentó ni se lo enseñó a ninguno, si no, no estaba contando. Fíjese nomás, cómo estaría yo. ¡Ay, Chihuahua! Pero no dije nada, nomás me hice como que estaba muy enojao y les echaba. Bueno pues nos remitieron a Ojinaga y nomás nos vieron presos y mujeres y soldados nos dijeron barbaridad y media. Después nos soltaron y nos echaron a la cárcel y esa noche allí dormimos. Nos tuvieron el día siguiente también. Para esto, mi abuelito Cleto Heredia, que era sherife del condado de Presidio, se dio cuenta de que nos echaron tiros pa'l otro lao y les apretó. Pos a los tres días nos echaron fuera y hasta nos ofrecieron un salvo-conducto pa'l otro lao. Entonces, viendo a aquellos que estaban tan enojados, le dije a mi tío Chamalía: vamos a darnos, vamos a darnos de alta con los maderistas. Y así lo hicimos. Así fue como entré yo a la revolución.

"Cuando fregaron a Madero, me vine con Villa. Anduve en las armas hasta el 15. Del 15 me salí y me trasladé al otro lado pero siempre trabajando por el partido hasta el 20 que ya se arregló todo. Trabajé con la cuestión de Villa en muchas formas: llevaba parque, vestuario, bueno, hacía de todo. Tenía labor pa que no se me notara; estaba yo en medio de la labor, cerca del río y allí sembraba. A Hipólito, hermano de Villa, yo lo pasé a los Estados Unidos. Vivía él en San Antonio pero lo vigilaban hasta no poder estar en casa. Y nomás ponga cuidado hasta donde son los americanos de convencieros. Por cuestión de dinero y todo lo que usted quiera, ellos mismos lo sacaron hasta tráemelo hasta Marfa donde lo recibí. Yo lo tuve en mi casa a él y a otros generales y de allí los marché en la noche hasta juntarlos con los Villistas. Así seguí trabajando hasta el 20 que se acabó la revolución, con mi gente, de acuerdo con él, y cuando

teníamos que ir a verlo pasábamos el río en la noche. Así andábamos
pa allá y pa acá.

"En esa tomada de Chihuahua, Villa fue muy diablo. Era muy
sagaz. Dimos un ataque primero y no pudimos entrar. Como era la
capital del estado, estaban todos los soldados reconcentrados allí.
Entonces éste pensó hacer una llamada falsa. Así que agarramos al
telegrafista de Villahumada y le exigió él que formara una llamada a
Juárez, como que era de Chihuahua, diciendo que pedían auxilio de
tropas para Chihuahua. Fue trampa porque entonces llamó a Juárez y
mandaron unos trenes de soldados. Cuando ya venían, les pegamos,
los fregamos. Entonces éste hizo la llamada que iba a atacar Chihua-
hua y volteó y le pegó a Juárez y la tomó. Fue muy importante porque
ya quedó Chihuahua cercada por dondequiera; la única salida era de
Ojinaga porque aquí habíamos cuatro gatos. Cuando ya se dio cuenta
el gobernador se vino con millonarios y tropas. Todos vinieron a dar
aquí.

"Nosotros que éramos unos cuantos aquí andábamos por las lomas
con reses y cuando veníamos pa Ojinaga no sabíamos que estaban los
contrarios adentro del pueblo. Nomás que Luis Cortez mi cuñado y
otros hombres de Presidio, pasaron por la Junta y nos avisaron. Esos
fueron los que nos libertaron la vida.

"Pocos días después nos juntamos con la gente que Villa había
mandado adelante, como dos mil, y mientras tanto las tropas de
Ojinaga eran un hervidero. Los contrarios, como no cabían, se despa-
rramaron pa las labores o pa'l Mulato. Bueno, pues primero avanza-
mos sobre los del Mulato y los agarramos en la puerta del cañoncito
pero muchos se escaparon pa'l otro lao por El Polvo. Les salimos en el
arroyo del Alamo y allí nos topamos a pelear. Otro día en la tarde
rodeamos Ojinaga pero era un gentío bárbaro. No pudimos hacer
nada. Eramos unos cuatro gatos como luego dicen pa ocho mil hom-
bres. Pues resulta que dimos tres ataques, pero no . . . fíjese que había
unos hoyos muy grandes parejitos de costales de arena donde estaban
parados toda la gente. Nos mataron mucha gente. Salíamos pa atrás
derrotaos. Y luego a los tres días llegó Villa con su gente. Maclovio
Herrera, Rosalío Hernández y otros. Bueno, con toda esa gente
todavía no les competimos. Pero Villa era muy diablo y me acuerdo
como si fuera ahorita, que llegó muy enojado por haber metido la
gente en esa forma. Y es que estaba muy dura la cosa. Fíjese que todos
los álamos los tenían tumbaos y luego tenían alambres de pico por si

entraba la gente a caballo. Bueno nos dijo claramente: no les dé cuidado, muchachos. Pa mañana, siendo Dios servido, para esta misma hora, tenemos que ir a comer de la cena que van a cenar ellos. Tenemos que agarralos antes de la cena. Dicho y hecho, como así fue. Ordenó a todos, que ya venían como ala, los echó a pie. Uno que otro oficial venía tras de la gente a caballo pero eso era pa cuando el ataque, con la orden de que el que diera pie atrás, era macheteao. Así que no había quién corriera. Nomás se perdió la mira y a todos les dijeron la seña y la contraseña. Esta era la seña, del cuerpo destapao, sin sombrero, el sombrero aquí y el brazo arremangao y luego la contraseña. Hubo muchos que agarraron la seña pero la contraseña no y todo ése que no la daba, abajo.

"En todo caso, parece hecho adrede que cuando se metió el sol se vino un viento con mucho polvo que ni la mano se veía. Así que pa cuando supieron los contrarios ya estábamos sobre de ellos. Y me acuerdo como si esto fuera ahora, comimos la cena de ellos. Ahora verá que después en la noche nos pusimos a hacer café pa tomar y corría cerca de allí un arroyito donde cogimos el agua. Y todos los del cuartel bebimos café pero otro día nos dimos cuenta que era sangre con la que hicimos café. Corría, estaba corriendo porque en el hoyo grande cayó mucha gente. Cuando habían salido corriendo, pos muchos cayeron allí muertos y heridos. Venía corriendo mucha sangre y de allí agarramos.

"Otro día en la mañana amanecimos a ver cuántos muertos había allí y pa voltearlos. Anduvieron guayines, carros de mula, levantando gente del mismo pueblo. Los acarrearon y los echaron allí donde está el tanque, la herradura que le nombraban. Allí había un hoyo muy hondo y estaba tapado de puros difuntos. Todo el santo día anduvieron acarreando gente en cantidad . . . No, si no crea, está larga la historia . . ."

Presidio 1942

EL CONEJO, HECHO BOLA sobre sí mismo, duerme placentero. No sabe por qué esta vez sueña tan bonito. Como una sonrisa de bebé disfruta el paisaje alineado de lechuga. Contento está el conejo pues se sueña comiendo, así hincado y sin preocupación. ¡Caray! lo difícil que está la vida por allá especialmente cuando vienen los humanos alborotados a echarle pajuelazos. Trocas esparciendo su luz en busca de sus orejas y de repente, zas . . . zas . . . zas. Pobres hermanos conejos. Unos sirven de festín a los perros, otros a los lobos. Pero esta noche el conejo de la luna se repliega sobre sí mismo como feto contento, y sueña . . .

La luna se viste de amargura y saña. Malhumorada está porque no ha llovido y porque por todos rumbos el universo está ardiendo. El Río Grande ya sólo es un charco, las plantas se queman, y la gente, partículas secas, empiezan a brotar por el río. La luna los odia cuando no puede detenerlos, cuando no hay agua suficiente para taparles el pico. Por eso también está enojada la luna. Porque la gente no cesa de traficar. Por eso gruñe.

—¡Salte! ¡Vete, desgraciado mantenido!

El aposento del conejo se estremece con el grito de la luna y lo hace que pegue el brinco hasta la tierra. Luego, sobresaltado, sale corriendo como si oyera ladrar los perros detrás de los matorrales. De pronto siente un leve dolor cerca de la cola. Se imagina una bala menudita que lentamente le va dejando un hormigueo de pierna cruzada por todo el cuerpo. No puede levantarse. Hace el intento de menear la cabeza y parece que no la tiene. Ahora, hasta los ojos siente pesados. ¿Estará soñando? Medio recuerda que muy entrada la noche le vino el cansancio y se echó allí cerca de la cueva para recobrar un poco las energías pero no recuerda cuando le venció el sueño. Y ahora la sensación extraña. El parálisis que sintió antes, le ha llegado a la lengua. Trata de ver en derredor pero sólo se topa la vista con su cuerpo, a punto de reventar. La hinchazón es extrema. Ya no sabe qué pensar, no sabe si todavía está soñando o si anduvo en la luna. Tampoco está seguro si fue balazo el que sintió en la cadera o simplemente cayó tan fuerte desde arriba que su cuerpo se lastimó. Ahora entre párpados borrosos sólo discierne la víbora aproximarse con movimientos rituales. La víbora de la sierrita de la Santa Cruz se le acerca con la boca sumamente abierta y él no está seguro si se carcajea la serpiente en silencio o quiere decirle algo al oído. Mientras tanto lo único que repite su mente sonámbula es un cuento de un ratoncito pequeño que sin malicia se sentó al frente de su agujero cuando apareció un gato zalamero ofreciéndole todo tipo de delicias, y luego el ratoncito había salido solamente para ser devora . . . zzzzzzzzz.

HAY COSAS que se repiten como los sueños y mi padre, como tantos otros hombres, necesita de ellos para tolerar la vida. Esta mañana se ha despertado soñando sonrisas. Con el mismo espíritu se levanta del piso y va a sentarse al lado de un enorme vientre que parece derramar la cama. Contempla a mi mamá con ternura pero ella ni se mueve, ni siquiera siente un moyote que, prendido a su mejilla, insiste en extraerle otro bocadito más de sangre. Después que se lo espanta, mi papá se casca unos zapatos torcidos que remedan el rechinar de la puerta. Al salir, lo saludan unos golpecitos leves en el pantalón. Es la cola cariñosa de Chango.

El perro no necesitará el "ven, vamos a ver el amanecer" porque lo seguirá como lo ha hecho siempre, y los dos caminarán juntos hasta los algodonales. Irán al mismo sitio donde papá José nos ha llevado a soñar tantas veces y allí se sentará hasta que se ponga borracho de Dios. Entonces empezará su cuerpo-embudo a sorber los mil colores que nacen en el horizonte. Pero pronto se disuelve el paño mágico y las nubes quedarán completamente desvestidas, preparadas para recibir al rey.

Mi papá siempre ha creído que las nubes son pobres ninfas burladas. Piensa así porque cuando el sol se destapa la cara, de inmediato comienza a volverse loco de risa. Y así, a risa y risa, a vuelta y vuelta el sol le inyecta las energías necesarias para vivir. Pero también se burla de él y la risa se convierte en saña de perro que se quiere arrancar la cola. Y sólo cuando papá se entera de que se está tatemando vivo, baja los pies a la tierra. Entonces, meneando la cabeza sin poder creerlo, le hablará a su Chango: "yo no sería como él, amigo. Sí amanecería con los huesos jóvenes y agradecería mi fortuna pero no quemaría ni me burlaría ni me volvería loco de rabia". Luego rumbo a casa, seguirá con el sueño de que algún día vivirá en un reino igual y que algún día dormirá en la casa del Pintor . . . a su manera.

José, después de haber celebrado el amanecer, entró de buen humor y antes de pasar al lavamanos, dio un beso de pichón a su amada encinta, quien estaba preparándole el almuerzo. Ella le respondió con una sonrisa poco forzada.

—¿Cómo amaneció mi chorriada?

—Bien . . .

—¿Otra vez el latoso ése que trae allí?

Marcela meneó la cabeza.

—Ai verá lo que va a salir. Entonces se le va a olvidar todo esto.

—Ojalá y Dios te oiga José. Sólo quiero que nazca bien.

La mujer tenía razón por preocuparse. Tres años a puro muele y muele y nada, hasta que por fin había logrado el embarazo. La alegría sin embargo había durado poco, pues desde un principio había comenzado a sufrir. Y ahora nueve meses después, conque llega retrasado. La viejita Vicke, su mamá, andaba preocupada también y por eso había dejado de trabajar en la casa de Rocha. Ahora el quehacer de lavar y planchar la ropa lo hacía aquí.

Después de desayunar en silencio, ella con el amargo sabor en la boca, él con el buen humor que trae el sábado, José le dio otro beso.

—Cuídate mucho, José. Cuídate del sol.

—Pierda cuidado, mi vieja— y salió.

ESA MAÑANA el sol descubrió las casas de chocolate con una grande llamarada de tal modo que a los humos que despedían los cañones de las cocinas ni siquiera se les permitió perfilarse. Este día quemaría el sol y la gente, ardida ya, estaría lista para dar fin a la semana al puro medio día. Poco a poco los cantos de los pájaros se fueron haciendo un fuerte chillido de coraje: después las chicharras continuarían su canto para terminar en autodestrucción—insectos cuyos cuerpos se encontraban engarrotados a los arbustos.

A lo lejos se veían trocas y carros llenos de trabajadores dirigiéndose hacia las diferentes partes de los laboríos. Teléforo el compadre de José, hacía lo mismo: se fue pitando de casa en casa, recogiendo a los que andaban bajo su mando.

Teléforo depositó a los limpiadores en la sección de algodón menos sucia y al ver éstos lo limpio de los surcos, se les subió el ánimo. De inmediato se hincaron a la orilla para sacarle filo a los azadones enérgicamente y cuando oyeron a Teléforo darle instrucciones a su hijo que se encargara de la supervisión mientras él fuera a echarle un vistazo a los mojados que traía trabajando cerca del río, apenas pudieron contener el entusiasmo. El Chale era reata y cuando quería les hacía la parada. Pero ahora les hablaba en tono serio.

—Orale ésos, ya oyeron el jefe, ¿qué nel? Así que nada de perra. Aviéntensen o si no, los reporto.

—Uuuu, que zura el bato, vamos a empelotarlo pa que no se madereye el güey— brincó el Jusito, mientras que las mujeres se enrojecieron y pronto se escurrieron por los zurcos. ¡Chamaco descarado! ¡No tiene pelos en la lengua!

El Chale, al notar el enojo en las caras de los otros, soltó la carcajada.

—Puros mitotes, ésos. ¿A poco me creyeron? Este bato no está lurio ni come lumbre, ésos. Llévensela suave, al cabo no te dan premios.

Lentamente fueron entrando y al poco rato se vieron puras cabecitas gorrudas en medio de los algodonales. Tampoco tardaron en descubrir el engaño; la maldita carrijuela se entretejía por las plantas a modo de ni siquiera dejar cruzar. Una sola mata de esa fastidiosa enredadera servía para hacer bola a todo el mundo. Los azadones venían sobrando; había que gatear por debajo y arrancar la raíz con la mano. Y así se pasaba el día, sepultado en un laberinto como si se fuera un borracho que no encuentra la puerta de la casa. A las cansadas aparecían los cuerpos en las orillas, cuerpos empapados con caras que escupen, que tosen, que tiran los azadones sobre la acequia y se dirigen al árbol cercano. Luego eternos movimientos de cabeza, hacia donde debe aparecer el socorro—la troca amarilla del viejo que trae la raya. Pero no se va nada y entonces la vista se clava en los pechos húmedos femeninos, como si de allí brotara el ánimo más grande del mundo. Los viejos enclenques, al contrario, piensan en cómo hacerle esta vez pa que alcance el cheque mientras que las mujeres milagrosamente ponen zapatos nuevos en los huercos después de haber calculado los biles atrasados de dos a tres semanas. Cabrones chamacos. Tienen patas de fierro. Más adelantito, la pacota de jóvenes saborean el baño frío y las cervezas.

LA ESCENA SE REPITE a la orilla del río. Con una excepción: Leocadio el cacarizo está furioso. La audiencia, que por lo general aplaude su don creativo, ahora se burla de él porque sus cuentos tienen la tendencia de terminar demasiado fantásticos o pendejos. Hoy no han podido tragar la historia verdadera del hombre que era tan fuerte que podía quebrase los piloncillos en la frente. Por eso está enojado.

—No se fije en esta bola de groseros, compadre; sígale.

—No, que vayan al jodido. Se creen que son muy sabios los . . .

—Le digo que no se fije. Yo sé que usted no anda con esas pendejadas de libros.

—Pos usté sabe bien, compa, que aunque no tenemos escuela estamos más al alba que toda esa plebe, ¿verdá? Nomás dígame qué quiere saber, compa, a ver si no sé.

—Pos sabe, siempre he querido saber cómo empezamos los humanos. Nunca estuve claro en eso. ¿Cómo empieza todo ese mitote, compa?

—Pos ora verá. Dicen quesque estaba muy oscuro y todo y ai tiene usté que Diosito en ese tiempo se sentía muy solo y añídale que no había nada de luz. Pero yo creo que la pelada verdá es que no tenía nada que hacer y un día nomás por curiosidá se puso a soplar así como cuando le sopla uno a los hormigueros pa que se enojen las hormigas, ¿sabe? Y pos dijo, a jodido, y se reculó pa atrás. Y es que se le prendió el sol en la cara y casi lo dejaba tuerto. Ai tiene usté que le gustó lo que había salido del soplo y le siguió con una luna y a ésta le puso arete pa decoración. Se le puso buena la cosa, ¿sabe cómo, compa? Entonces todo alborotado empezó con la tierra y le echó agua. La prueba ai está, compa, este río que pasa por aquí. Luego . . .

—Párele ai, compa. ¿Usté dice que se aventó todo esto solo?

—Así como se lo digo, por Dios santito.

—Oiga, pos tendrá tamañas manotas como las de Lencho, ¿no cree usté?

—No, señor, si nomás tenía que pensalo, le soplaba y era todo.

—¡A jodido! ¿Me quiere usté decir que lo hizo con la pura cabeza?

—Sí.

—Ai sí que voló puntos.

—Así es la cosa. Dijo, voy a pensar en el sol y ¡puf!, ai lo tiene, bien redondote y caliente como un jodido. ¿Y las estrellas?, ni más ni menos. Pero fíjese, compadre, que todavía le faltaba lo bueno. ¿Qué cree usté que faltaba?

—Pos los animales.

—No, hombre, nosotros. Los jumanos.

—Párele, párele ai. ¿Y qué cree que somos, compa? Puros cabrones animales. Y si no lo quiere creer, fíjese en la cara del Chango Pérez. Si no es animal, está encartao cuando menos.

—No, hombre, no le mueva a eso. Ese ya es otro cuento . . . pero usté se me está adelantando, compa. Déjeme seguile.

—Ande pues.

—Resulta que en ese tiempo andaban las víboras paradas.

—¡Ah jijo!

—No se asuste, compa, que no picaban. A Diosito menos porque él las había echado al mundo asina como le digo. Ai tiene usté que en ese mismito tiempo pensó hacer el hombre, pero con éste si tuvo más batalla. Aquí sí tuvo que usar las manos. Agarró un pedazo de zoquete por donde pasaba l'agua pa regar el jardín y le sopló. ¿Y qué cree usté que pasó?

—Pos le salió una mujer.

—No, compa, le salió un machote así, del pelo de Sansón, y . . .

—Oiga, compadre, cómo se me hace que me está reburujiando las cartas.

—No, si así jue.

—Pos yo creo que está todo confundío.

—No se mande, compa. Es confundido.

—Dispénseme, confundillo. Este . . . ¿que no jue mujer la que hizo primero?

—No, si pa allá voy. Dijo Diosito, hay que hacerle compañera a este macho, y le sacó una costilla con las manos.

—No, compa, esto ya huele mal. Es puro pedo suyo. ¿Cómo cabrones . . . ?

—Si ni pestañeó, yo creo que ni cuenta se dio porque ¿no se acuerda usté que en primer lugar nomás tenía que soplar?

—Pos . . . está poco chillona, si usté me pregunta.

—Y si usté cree que el machote que se aventó estaba bien hecho, debiera ver la hembra.

—Sí pero fue al rev . . .

—Se aventó un cuerote como los que hace Lencho. Ya usté se imagina y pa peor remedio, imagínese usté los dos empelota.

—Está bien, si usté dice que así jue, está bien. Pero de todos modos que me la ponga, está jodida la cosa. ¿Cómo iban a resistir usté sabe qué?

—Ai voy pa allá, pero no se me adelante. Diosito entonces puso las hermosas criaturas en ese jardín que le llaman el paraíso, y allí mero ni el diablo entraba. Si no digo que no había diablo pero Diosito ya les había pitado. Y ya se los haiga si le hacen caso, les dijo, y ellos obedecían la orden.

—¿Y qué comían allí, compa?

—Ah pa eso, Dios le sopló a un árbol de manzanas.

—¿Y a poco se la pasaban comiendo manzanas?

—No, eso no, porque era pecado pero las hojas eran tan buenas y tan dulces como las mismitas manzanas.

—¿Y a poco se pasaban todo el tiempo comiendo? Yo creo que coj . . .

—Usted no me deja hablar, compa. Cállese y espérese hasta que termine. Después puede hacerme preguntas.

—Está bien, compadre, no se enoje. La cosa es que me la está haciendo un poco dura pa tragar. Andele, sígale, no se enoje.

—Resulta que como estaban en el paraíso no tenían deseo de nada, usté sabe de . . .

—Sí, de coger.

—Un aburrimiento de a chingal. Hasta que vino una de esas víboras y le dijo a la mujer: cómete una manzana y verás qué bonitos se te ponen los cachetes. Y la mujer vanidosa . . .

—¿Pos no me dijo que estaba criada como con leche de burro?

—Sí, pero le faltaba color. Pero lo importante es que la víbora era el enemigo de Diosito. Era el mero diablo. Y ai tiene usté que la tentó.

—¿Dónde le tentó, compa?

—Chingao, compadre. No puede uno platicar en serio con usté. No se haga pendejo. Quiero decir que se la conchabó a que se comiera una manzana. Entonces Diosito se puso de muy mal pelo y los echó de allí. Desde entonces tuvieron todas las cosas que nosotros tenemos, los problemas, los gustos, los deseos.

—Usté dice que pudieron . . .

—Sí, entonces sí. Se desataron y empezaron a echar cría.

—Pos me va a perdonar y yo sé que se va a enojar, pero no me la pega. No me trago esa parte de la víbora. Eso de echárselo a la víbora y pior a la mujer pos nomás no. ¿Cómo cabrones cree usté que se iba a aguantar un garañón sin curiosear la cosa, prencipalmente cuando andaban empelotados? Dispénseme pero no se lo creo.

—Pues entonces vaya usté al cabrón, compadre. Ya no me pida que le cuente nada, y si quiere saber algo, vaya a otra parte. Conmigo no cuenta y se acabó. Yo ya me voy.

—Espere, compa, no se vaya tan enchilado. Usté no sabe discutir como la gente educada. Luego luego se enchila.

—Vaya usté a la chingada, compadre. . . .

TARDES CALLADAS. Uniformes rayados. Por las tardes se frotan las quemaduras. Las líneas blancas de sudor que se secó en las camisas huelen mal pero no importa. La gente se las deja puestas para comer la primera comida caliente del día. Las cabezas de fiebre comen calladas, los movimientos lentos como si estuvieran viviendo en una eterna monotonía. Pero luego el sol se va apagando y poco a poco los cuerpos resucitan; los jóvenes, como el Chale y el Jusito salen a los billares, a la botica, al mono, al otro cachete para gastar las cinco lanas que les quedó. Los viejos al contrario se van a hacer las compras de la semana y a pagar lo que quedaron a deber. Luego con su six-pack se regresan a la casa contentos de aire fresco, soltando una lengua que todo el día estuvo gorda y seca. Y por allí cerca, detrás de los mezquites y los guames, por el arroyo, y por el llano, los chamacos corren y gritan, palpando la vida. Juegan a los encantados, a la roña, a la víbora de la mar mientras que por otras partes voces viejas, voces apagadas, voces y más voces siguen negando la muerte.

Entra la noche gigante y negra. Con sus pasos sordos y un deseo de estrangular. La gente recula. Los moyotes chillones les dicen al oído que ya es hora de meter las sillas. Una por una las lucecitas cuadradas brotan como magia; las casitas de adobe también se engarruñan, se encogen con la noche. Sólo así podrán resistir su peso.

DICEN QUE PEDRO el tragaplumas nació con un corazón muy grande y que por eso tenía que respirar con la boca abierta. Que no le cabía, dicen, pero creo que eso era sólo parte de la razón. Pedro había nacido con la boca lista para reírse y la cosa más insignificante, el chiste más malo, lo hacía soltar la carcajada. La única vez que cerró la boca fue cuando se tragó las plumas. Le pegaron fuerte y alto a la pelota destripada y Pedro la logró coger: con la boca. Y aun así, después se rió. Por eso yo creo que no había en él lugar para tragedia.

Tampoco puedo creer que su corazón fuera capaz de reventarse. Y es que su corazón era de risa, una risa líquida que se escurría por los pantalones. Por eso después de la escuela, todos se iban a refrescar a la botica. Lo arrinconaban para que no pudiera levantarse, y entonces empezaban los chistes. Ratos después, se levantaba toda la tropa con Pedro en medio, para que no lo viera la gente. Porque la risa líquida ya se había desahogado. Otras veces por la calle:

—A que no se lo picas.

—A que sí . . .

Y se acercaba Pedro muy despichadito por detrás del señor.
Después salía corriendo. Meado de risa.

Esta noche de sábado la plebe cierra la cantina. Pero esta noche,
aunque quedan picados, no sacan cerveza. Muy simple. No hay lana.
Ni el Nalgas desparramadas que siempre trae de no se sabe dónde, ni el
Chango gorila que lo mantiene no se sabe quién, ni el Güero desca-
rapelao, que siempre saca del calcetín. Y aun así, el pueblo apagado no
puede convencerlos de que ya es hora de descontarse.

—Que se traiga el Louie la guitarra y nos vamos a las lomas.

—No, que se traiga a su hermana.

—La tuya, hijo 'e tu . . .

—Orale pues, ésos. Achirápense.

Es el mago quien habla, el Nalgas. Se apaciguan.

—Yo no sé ustedes, pero a mí ya me lleva la trampa de hambre.
Necesito refinar.

—Si, pero todo está cerrado.

—Entonces tenemos un problema, ¿no? ¿Qué les parece?

Silencio. Todos esperan las sabias palabras del Nalgas.

—Al pollero, vamos a pegale.

Los ojos de todos se abren un poco más y pronto se traza el plan.
Aventar a uno de ellos enfrente del gallinero del gringo, entrar y
esperar con la mano extendida hasta que la gallina se suba. Eso es,
esperar como momia para que no se alboroten, y listo. Sales, le tuerces
el pescuezo, y ya. Fácil. Pero ¿quién va? Silencio. No hay héroes
. . . Después, uno por uno voltea hacia el carro. El Tragaplumas está
dormido. Como siempre con la boca abierta.

—¡Pedrooo!— grita el Louie lo más fuerte posible. Después, lo
demás es fácil.

—Yo voy— consiente medio dormido.

Se detienen bastante retirado, sin apagar el motor. Por todos lados
ladran los perros. Y por todos lados la gente duerme como siempre.
Muerta.

Se baja Pedro bambaleándose. Pronto se lo traga la oscuridad.
Mientras tanto la espera en el carro es peor que el riesgo del Traga-
plumas. Los minutos son horas, escopetazos, degüellos, muerte, hasta
que por fin aparece la silueta y un bulto colgando al lado. Le abren la
puerta y sube, jadeando. Pronto no queda más que el chirrido de las
llantas en la esquina de la calle. Todos aguantan el deseo de hablar
hasta que por fin dan vuelta en un callejón.

—¿Cómo te fue?

—Bien, pero nomás pude traer una.

La palpa el Chango.

—Oye ¡qué chingona está!

La pesa el Louie,

—Oye, de veras.

La levanta el Güero de las patas,

—¡Hijo de la madre, te trajiste el gallo!

Y en cinco minutos Pedro vacía toda la cerveza que trae en el cuerpo. Esa misma noche también le atacan la boca de plumas de gallo. Dizque para que se meara más. Pero nadie pudo creer que se le reventara el corazón.

EL SORBETE DE LOS TUBOS estremece el cuerpo sentado en cuclillas y hasta ahora no había sentido el peso de la inclinada cabeza posada sobre el pecho. Chonito echa un vistazo medio dormido al agua corriente para cerciorarse de que no está soñando pero ve la acequia seca. Se habrá acabado el agua en el río, piensa, al momento que endereza el cuerpo tullido de cansancio. No se puede imaginar que se haya quedado dormido tanto tiempo, que ni siquiera el sol lo haya despertado. Un leve escalofrío le pasa por el cuerpo haciéndose dirigirse hacia el bulto que hace la camisa y el sombrero. Luego coge la pala para ir a la otra orilla con grandes esperanzas de que se haya terminado de regar la melga. Pero no necesita; José su amo se acerca.

—¿Qué pasó, Chonito, ya estuvo?

—Yo creo que no, don José, se paró la pompa.

—Ya sé. De allá vengo. Cuando venía pa acá no la oí, así que me fui a ver. Ya empezó otra vez. Yo creo que mañana acabamos ¿no?

—Sí señor, nomás que no se acabe l'agua.

—Ai te traigo un lonchecito pa que te aguantes hasta el mediodía y . . .

—Pero ¿que no va a jalar usté en lo del viejo?

—Sí, pero voy a poner al chamaco de Leyva que la cuide. Le arreglo la presilla y los tubos nomás pa que la cuide. Al cabo es poco.

—Pos si usté quiere yo . . .

—No, hombre, los cabrones chotas andan como hormigas. Vale más que te vayas a mediodía y me esperes en el otro lado. Después que me paguen voy y cambio el cheque y te pago.

—Como ¿a qué hora lo veo, señor?
—Me esperas allí en el álamo como a las tres.
—Está bien, patrón.
—Y cuídate porque . . .
—No se preocupe, don José, en eso ya estoy bien quemao.
—Bueno, allá te veo más tarde.

En un instante José desaparece en el mar algodonero del río mientras que Chonito vuelve a sentarse en el borde, esta vez para ponerse las botas torcidas llenas de misericordia mientras que las nalgas se refrescan con la tierra húmeda. El chamaco, a pesar de que ésta es la tercer noche de insomnio que ha pasado, no hace por irse a dormir en alguna sombra cercana. Se siente feliz porque esta vez su amo va a fregar pato. No se cansa de contemplar los cuarenta acres de plantas bien cargaditas de fruto. Quisiera que el señor José se hubiera estado aquí a su lado para compartir con él los preciosos capullos que empiezan a revantar, verlos besar el agua. Pero Chonito sabe que es mucho pedir. José el enamorado de una tierra que ya no es de él, José el de las piernas arqueadas tiene que ser más que inquilino. Por eso se ha ido a unir con el grupo de limpiadores que dirige Teléforo.

DE PRESIDIO sólo el recuerdo de las nubes y del diablo. Flaco éste, gordotas aquéllas, ambos se resbalan por el cielo burlándose de la gente, de los animales, de las plantas. Nunca llueve en Presidio y el estruendo que sale de la garganta de esas nubes sólo sirve para llenar el hueco de silencio por un instante, pero ni siquiera el eco en la sierrita de la Santa Cruz sirve para asustar al diablo. El sinvergüenza nunca se olvida del pueblo. Con su mano firme aplasta los chaparros y la hierba mal crecida. Con las dos exprime las aguas del Río Grande que antes fue y lo reduce a espejismo, a charco.

Pero el patas de chivo no es todo maldad. Tiene un columpio muy largo en la cumbre de la sierra y de vez en cuando aparece en los bailes como galán. Otras veces aparece en forma de burro y se deja montar hasta que los chamacos descubren, con un palo, que no tiene culo y entonces desaparece, dejando el olfato de cologne francés. Sin embargo, la broma que prefiere más es la del gato y el ratón jugando a las escondidas. El chiste es de cuidar la gota de agua que divide dos tierras, como si no fuera la misma. El gato patrullero, con ceño fruncido, espera en acoso al ratón, cuya defensa carga en el estómago en forma de hambre. Brinca el ratón el charco y empieza la pesquisa ridícula mientras que el diablo se rueda por el suelo a carcajadas.

EL SOL SE LO BEBE, lo quema. El sol se ríe porque lo marchita. Las plantas, como él, se sienten inútiles, sin saber qué hacer, mientras que el sol bebe sediento hasta chupar la última gota.

Chonito quiere llorar pero no puede. Le duele la garganta, aun cuando está entre el agua hasta el pescuezo. Sabe que no debe moverse porque se le va el agua y tiembla de miedo. Gime. Mientras tanto el chamaco se está convirtiendo en vapor.

Sigue en su misma posición y revive de nuevo el incidente. Había sido rápido. Después que se había ido don José, se había reclinado sobre la pala y de inmediato lo había vencido el sueño. Los jeeps de la migra lo habían despertado y como bocabierta se había puesto a ver la pesquisa sin fijarse en el boquete de la acequia por donde se estaba colando el agua. Parecía como si nunca hubiera visto esa escena—de oír el "aaaagua" de los mojados y luego un montón de cabezas voladas hacia el río. ¿Cuántas veces había presenciado el espectáculo, pataleadas de viejos y niños o de algún accidente como el del mes pasado? Había volado el avión patrullero muy bajito, hasta nivel de cabeza y zas. El señor a caballo había perdido la cabeza muy finito. Quesque por la noche la anda buscando todavía. O de la semana pasada cuando encontraron al chicuelo regordito, flotando en la acequia. Dicen que el chota quería nomás asustarlo con las zambullidas porque seguía cruce y cruce.

Después que se había pasado todo el fandango, se había fijado en el agua que se salía, y al principio no se alteró pero luego le entraron ansias y empezó a palear como loco. El agua se llevaba la tierra y el agujero se hacía más grande. Paleó hasta que le sangraron las ampollas y luego, sin encontrar salida, se había quitado los zapatos, se había metido al agua y se había atravesado en el boquete. Y así había que esperar a don José, quien no tardaría en volver, ya que era cerca de la una.

La angustia y todo se le calma cuando piensa en lo hombre que es. Todo puede hacer ya aunque apenas tiene doce años—el azadón, la pala, la pizca, el empaque, todo. Y porque sabe que lo puede hacer como los grandes, siente orgullo. Pero luego vuelve a la situación en que se encuentra y siente vergüenza. ¿Qué irá a decir don José? Por bruto. El agua está muy escasa y si el viejo la ve corriendo por el camino, se va a enojar. Qué bruto, se me durmió el gallo.

Ahora vuelve a sentir sueño por el agua fresca que le corre entre los brazos, las piernas, el pescuezo. El murmullo del agua lo arrulla pero resiste porque se siente muy raro, algo así como flotando en el aire, como que no hay fin a la espera. Como aquella vez cuando por casualidad había empezado a marchar el tractor. No había sabido qué hacer sino dar vueltas y más vueltas en círculo hasta que se le acabara la gasolina. Había pasado una eternidad borracha hasta que se le había ocurrido chocarlo contra una treila. Después había salido corriendo hasta su casa. Pero esa vez había encontrado salida. No como ahora. Ahora tendría que esperar y esperar y esperar . . .

José necesita dar grandes estrujones a Chonito enroscado para poder volverlo en sí, y cuando por fin abre los ojos, suelta el llanto. Entonces se desahoga el muchacho entumecido en el pecho del hombre. Pero después que se le ha pasado el susto a José, no puede contener una sonrisa y el chamaco, al notarlo, para de llorar y se desprende bruscamente. Luego sale corriendo hacia el río. Mientras tanto las carcajadas lo siguen golpeando y no cesa la burla hasta que llega a las orillas del río.

El DIABLO SE PONE JUGUETON pero por el momento no se le ocurre nada; sólo contemplar su cuerpo en el espejo. Desnudo así, se ve que no tiene sexo. Ni pelos. De frente su sexo parece un bizcochito de niña recién nacida. Da la vuelta y no se encuentra al ano. Quiere ahora pensar en algún símil, en alguna metáfora para su bello cuerpo pero no puede encontrar una "feliz comparación". Piensa y piensa y lo único que le viene es una serie de interrogantes. Esta incapacidad le molesta tanto que lo pone de mal humor y entonces busca otra manera de deleitarse. De inmediato se mete en un traje de payaso y se contempla en el espejo de nuevo. ¡Bah! El juego es demasiado pueril. No le vale afuera. Debe ponerse más serio con sus bromas; tiene que seguir burlándose de la vida humana.

Ahora se arquea las cejas puntiagudas con un negro pincel y en seguida estira el brazo para rascar azul de cielo. Este se lo talla en las pupilas. Como último toque a la parte superior del cuerpo, se casca una peluca rubia y un sombrero tejano. Luego busca un traje para cubrirse lo demás y encuentra el verde oscuro, su preferido. Cuando ya se lo puso, a pujidos se mete unas botas que le cubren las patas de gallo. ¡Ah! Allí está. De paso se guiña el ojo en el lago que usa como espejo. Ya afuera, se monta en su columpio . . . pero . . . ¡momento! ¡Por poco se le olvida! Sin embargo, hay tiempo todavía. De manera que no se preocupa. Se cimbrea alto, alto, hasta que alcanza una estrella. De inmediato la arranca y se la prende donde debe palpitar el corazón. ¡Listo! El diablo está listo para seguir su chiste eterno.

CUANDO QUIERES LLEGAR A PRESIDIO te vas por un camino apretado de guames y mezquites. Con el aire pegado a las pestañas y una mente retrasada, el cuerpo se te suelta y se te cae en una noria que nunca terminó de escarbarse. O te resbalas por un embudo. Antes de caer te sientas en la cumbre de la loma para divisar, al fondo, las cagarrutas de chiva: casas que resaltan como huérfanas entre los vastos terrenos agrícolas. Casas de adobe maltratado, casas que piden misericordia a Dios. Casas: zapatos viejos que se abandonaron a un sol que engarruña todo. Tú como borracho te sueltas de la cumbre y luego te dejas resbalar por un camino que parte a Presidio en dos. A paso de rueda, Johnny's Bar, Texaco, Ron's Lumber, Halper's (al que le barrenaron la sien para hacerlo que soltara la lana), Phillip's 66, Juárez General Store. A paso de rueda.

—¿Y el centro? ¿Y la vida?

—Ah, pues éste es Presidio, señor. No pregunte más que no sabría decile. ¿Que qué? Ah, sí. La gente la encuentra en la orilla del río, entre lo verde, por debajo del puente, por encima.

—And what's across the border? Mexico?

—Sí, señor, Ojinaga. (Presidio partido en dos hace tiempo.)

—¿Reyes Uranga?

—La segunda casa con gallinero. Pero de día no vive allí, sólo de noche.

—¿Y el joven?

—¿José? Oh, ése ya es otra cosa. Si no está en casa, pos búsquelo en lo verde del melón, de la lechuga, del algodón, entre un costal, o sobre una pala al mediodía de tacos y kool-aid. Quizás en la empacadora. Oiga y ¿quién es usté?

—George Evans de Marfa. Quiero habla con él, ¿entiende?

—¿Que anda mal?

—No no. Nomás habla.

—Entonces si así es lo encontrará entre vagones congelados del

Santa Fe jugando a la pelota en el packing shed de Jones entre manos
grietudas, pantalonudas, garzoludas, sudadas.

—¿Dónde?

—¿Que dónde está? Pues mire, sigue el mismo camino hasta afuera
y allí donde están los corrales de las vacas, allí mero está la empacadora
de Jones.

—Muchas gracias.

—De nada.

(DOCE HORAS por 50 por 70 centavos entre 10,000 por 10 menos
transporte, menos los melones que se comen, menos los que no
vinieron hoy porque les dio vómito y torzón o se emborracharon,
menos el adelanto de Carrasco que no regresó. He's still a hardwork-
ing ole boy. See if I can get 'im to train for shipping orders.)

—Joe! Here's someone to see you.

—He's in the toledo, Mr. Jones.

—Done something wrong, Mr. . . .

—Evans. No, I just came to talk to him about some incident last
night.

—He'll be out in a minute. Hey! Son of a bitch! I told you . . . más
rápido, Manuel. Cajones aquee. The fellow's getting old, you know? I
just keep him around to help 'im out, but we get old sometime, you
know? Hey, here he comes.

—Joe Uranga? I'm George Evans from . . .

—No sir, I'm Joe Durango. Uranga is not working here.

—Damn it, I thought you said Durango, Mr. Evans. I'm sorry . . .

—Know where I can find him?

—Yes sir. He work with Mr. Lynch at the farm. But he don't go by
the name of Joe. They call 'im José.

—What's the dif . . . oh well, thank you, and sorry to bother you,
Mr. Jones.

—No bother . . . Hey! Son of a . . . more cajones over there!

LA LLUVIA QUIERE DERRETIR la casa de Dios pero no puede. Picotea la
ventana inútilmente y cuando se cansa, desliza sus lágrimas de rabia
por la pared. Luego, para conformarse en su derrota, entra por la
puerta que de vez en cuando se abre y rocía a los cuerpos cercanos.
Pero a estos hombres atrincherados tampoco les importa que los moje.
Están allí por gusto. Están para pasar revista de las piernas y para

adivinar la razón por qué ha llegado tarde tal y tal, como ahora lo hacen con Marcela. Todos la miran, todos la piensan—la mujer que espera eternamente . . . No se sabe si al pasar por el agua bendita se le olvidó hacerse la cruz o no quiso; sólo toma asiento y empieza a limpiarse la cara con un paño. (No debía haber venido. Todos los ojos me ven, saben. Bien me lo dijo mamá, no vayas, pero yo insistí. Ahora lo que voy a pasar aquí son puros nervios.) "Queridos hijos míos, no hay que temer, dejad de preocuparos. Tengamos confianza en Dios, él sabe lo que hace". (Sí padre, pero ahora el río no me va a dejar pasar. Yo quiero irme con José. Tengo mucho miedo de que me estén esperando afuera y me lleven a la oficina.) "Sabemos que la creciente puede ser desastrosa para nosotros pero el evangelio . . ." (Dios mío, ¿qué voy a hacer si no me dejan ir a casa, si me detienen y me preguntan por José? Dios mío, ayúdame . . .) "Y ahora recemos, roguémosle al Señor que nos saque de peligro, que nos eche la bendición. Oremos . . ."

Ha sido breve el sermón. El cura siente la misma impaciencia de la congregación. No hay más que decir; todos saben que sus esperanzas quedaron en bancarrota. Ahora se ponen de pie, menos Marcela. Se queda sentada un ratito más porque en estos momentos sus piernas son de hule y porque ya no se puede mover como antes. Ya se cansa mucho. Se le hinchan los pies. Su vientre de río crecido la hace sentirse muy incómoda, ahora más que de costumbre porque "ya hace bastante rato que le estoy dando lata. Eso digo yo porque ni siquiera hace el esfuerzo de pararse. Juzgo que ahora la molesto más porque he oído comentar que cuando me muevo la lastimo, y me imagino que ahora que estoy más desarrollado y más fuerte será un tanto peor. Sin duda que eso estará pasando en este momento; le estaré torciendo el estómago de lo lindo porque así me pasa cuando se me ocurren cosas. Me muevo mucho. Yo no quiero hacerlo pero hace poco decidí afilar la poca memoria que tengo y acumular cosas que han pasado para escribirlo todo cuando nazca. Y el esfuerzo por recordar y ponerlo en orden me hace moverme, como ahora lo estoy haciendo. Mi pobre mamá no sabe de mis facultades; no sabe que tengo una imagen bastante precisa de ella y de lo que ocurre afuera. Piensa que lo que trae en el estómago no siente, ni oye, ni piensa. Pero está equivocada. La sorpresa que se llevará cuando pueda escribir tan pronto como nazca. Es algo fastidioso para mí estar metido aquí, estar flotando siempre como en un chicle líquido y pegajoso. Cuando me estiro siento de inmediato pegar los pies y las manos contra una red. Me imagino que así se sienten las moscas cuando quieren despegarse de la telaraña. También pienso en mi pobre mamá. Lo que le duele. Yo quisiera ya haber nacido pero ella insiste en que no, porque cree que así es mejor para mí y como todos los sentimientos de una madre, no quiere ver sufrir a su hijo. Todo por mi hijo, dice. El caso es que yo me siento mal porque sé de los sufrimientos que ella pasa allá afuera y no puedo hacer nada. Estoy con las manos atadas y a veces no me enojo con ella sino con lo que oigo que está pasando y lo que imagino. Y mi mamá con el mismo tesón. Por eso ha resistido parirme. No quiero que mi hijo sufra, dice, pero yo creo que ya bastó de protección. ¿Se imaginan ustedes lo que será cargar un niño en el vientre tanto tiempo? Yo ya me cansé de . . . perdón mamá. Voy a acomodarme un poco . . . ah . . . ay . . . ya ya oí las campanitas. Ponte, ponte de rodillas . . . así, así . . . Ahora prometo quedarme quietecito mientras que el padre se toma la sangre de Dios. Si la situación es igual que todos los domingos, la iglesia estará llenita. Y común. Como un retrato cansado que todo representa. El padre al frente con sus ademanes. Vestido igual. Palabras iguales. Todos somos pecadores pero los humildes iremos al cielo. Hay que sufrir para ganar la vida perdurable. Cristo por eso amó y sufrió. El nos puso el ejemplo y hay que imitarlo. Al frente estarán los niños que todavía no aprenden los movimientos en orden ni saben los responsos. Poco les importa. Cerca estarán las beatas vestidas de negro pegadas a las estatuas y a las velas que chorrean, sumidas en oración. Igual. Al otro extremo, mero atrás, estarán los más humildes, como si fuera costumbre de siglos. Igual. El retrato de la iglesia y su congregación sugiere todo. El retrato fastidioso se repite al comulgar. La línea de derecha irá primero, quizá por estar más seguros de la salvación mientras que la otra línea espera. ¡La campanita! ¡Suena otra vez la campanita! Mi mamá y todos agachan la cabeza cuando el padre levanta la representación del cuerpo en pan redondo. Nunca supe por qué lo hace, digo, por qué agachan la cabeza. ¿Será por costumbre o por respeto? ¿Será por el miedo al misterio o por sentir culpa de comerse el cuerpo de Cristo que no creen merecer? Quién sabe. También pienso que es ridículo sentir los golpes que se da mi mamá en el pecho, algo que tampoco entiendo. Parece que quiere castigarse, golpearse el corazón porque le late. ¿Acaso se siente culpable de estar viva o reniega de estarlo? Levántate ya mamá, desentumécete primero. Siquiera esta vez sé tú primera. Andale, gánales. Mira que tú

tienes el mismo derecho. La verdad es que ya no te importa. Pero debe.
Mira esa niña. Déjame salir para darle una bofetada. ¿Por qué se te
adelanta y te hace a un lado? ¿Que tiene también más privilegio que tú
aun en la casa de Dios? Pero no debo molestarte con estos berrinches.
Te prometo calmarme. Ahora . . . abre la boca . . . así, así. Anda, ya
regrésate pero no entrelaces las manos por favor porque no quiero que
te caigas como la semana pasada. Recuerda que anoche no comiste".

Marcela se regresa al asiento con piernas de mantequilla. Después
que el cura le ha dado la hostia, le ha dicho que la espere porque quiere
hablarle. Ella, consternada, se ha ido a arrodillar en la última fila detrás
de un viejo robusto como si esto fuera a quitarle el miedo. Allí, de
rodillas, reza y (¿que si me saliera ahorita, rápido, sin esperar que se
acabe la misa? Sin duda el padre ya sabe y quiere preguntarme por José.
Dios mío, ya no aguanto más . . .)

Afuera, el agua menudita sigue picoteando mientras que la con-
gregación se pone de pie. En ese momento nota Marcela a un señor
alto, güero que entra sin quitarse el sombrero stetson y se pasa hasta el
frente como si ésta fuera su casa. Luego se regresa con unos ojos de
águila que se columpian de lado a lado. Ella siente un fuerte estreme-
cimiento pero lo disfraza, componiéndose el velo. Cuando el señor la
nota, se detiene momentáneamente frente a ella y le sonríe. Luego le
guiña el ojo y sale. Ella queda pasmada sin poderse mover.

"Ya mamá. Ya se acabó la misa. Salte ya. ¿Por qué te late tanto el
corazón? Que, ¿qué? ¿Está lloviendo todavía? ¿Cómo le vas a hacer
para llegar a casa? No puedes correr . . . ¿Te sientas a esperar? Pero
no . . . por favor no corras. Mamáaa. . . ."

YA CUANDO LLEGO a casa, Marcela venía agazapándose y echando
manoteadas al aire. Gritaba que se lo quitaran.

—Pero, ¿a quién hija?— le preguntaba la viejita mientras que
Chonito hacía los ojos más redondos.

—¡El diablo!— aulló la mujer aterrorizada.

Con el ave maría purísima en la boca, Vicke pronto le hizo unas
crucecitas en la frente y empezó a rociar el cuarto de agua bendita.
Luego que hubo hecho esto le dio una cucharada de azúcar para el
susto, y de esta manera fue calmándola lo suficiente para que les dijera
lo que había pasado.

—Luego, luego que salí de la iglesia se me pegó una sombra que me
repetía que no me iba a dejar pasar. Y se reía y se reía como loca.

—Han de ser los nervios, señora— balbuceaba Chonito.

—Sí, hija. Es el miedo.

—Les digo que lo vi. Tenía diferentes formas. Primero parecía como que se estaba columpiando y me quería tumbar cada vez que se mecía. Fue cuando empecé a correr y entonces él se hizo borrego y a topetes me traía por delante. Cuando me vio caer en el suelo se volvió a reír. Después desapareció en . . . pol . . . ¡Aaaay! ¡Quítenmelo! ¡Aaaay viene! ¡Por favor!

Comienza a manotear Marcela, echándose a correr de un cuarto a otro. Se vuelca la mesa y quiebra los trastes. Luego barre con todo lo que se le pone en frente. La viejita y Chonito la atrapan sobre la cama y allí forcejean con ella hasta dominarla. La mujer tiene las manos engarruñadas.

—¡Por favor, ayúdame! ¡Mírame los dedos, Vicke! ¡No puedo estirarlos!

Marcela trata de extendérselos ella misma pero se la traban los dedos unos con otros. Entonces intenta salir corriendo de nuevo pero los dos la sujetan con fuerza mientras que Vicke le habla, le reza, le hace cruces sobre las manos paralizadas y le soba todo el cuerpo. Poco a poco se va calmando la mujer histérica hasta que por fin puede mover los dedos. Pero la vista se llena de lejanía. No contesta a las preguntas. No reacciona a nada aun cuando la viejita trata de darle caldo con su propia mano. Marcela no abre la boca; sólo se queda sentada en la cama como zombie, los ojos paralizados en la pared. Cuando todo ha resultado unútil, tienden el cuerpo sobre la cama. Marcela no resiste. Piensan Vicke y Chonito que quizá con una dormidita se le pase pero no saben que la mujer mantendrá los ojos dilatados el resto del día.

El diablo se retira para morirse de gusto. Luego, cansado se acuesta sobre las piedras húmedas para roncar a sus anchas.

Chonito se levanta del piso donde rendido ha quedado después de pasar el río y va directamente a la cazuela llena de agua. Luego que la vació afuera, vuelve a buscar el gotero a ciegas. Cuando por fin escucha el tin sobre el peltre lo centraliza debajo de la gota. En seguida, saca el paño y lo pone sobre la cazuela porque de otra manera el sonido no lo va a dejar dormir. Hecho esto, se acerca a la cama de Marcela para cerciorarse de que está bien. Los profundos ronquidos lo dejan satisfecho. ¡Vaya! Por fin ha quedado dormida. El ni se acuerda. Tanto que había llorado la mujer. "Ya se me hacía que no la controlábamos. La tembladera que se cargaba. Pobre señora, ni siquiera cuando le aseguré que el señor José estaba bien y que la estaba esperando, se consolaba. Es la primera vez que la veo tan, tan, no sé cómo explicarlo, pero estaba hecha pedazos por dentro. Dicen que las mujeres cuando están esperando se ponen así. Quiera Dios que sea verdad porque si no, esta mujer se nos está volviendo loca. Juraría que ya estaba cuando llegué. Ojalá que no le vaya a seguir ese mal".

"Ah, cómo quisiera platicar contigo Chonito. Darte las gracias por todo lo que has hecho. Hacerte comprender por qué mi mamá está así. Es que trae cien años, fíjate Chonito, cien años de historia indignada en la panza. Su enfermedad es de palabras que no pueden salir de aquí, de sus entrañas. Se quedan pegadas en la boca del estómago hasta hacerla vomitar. Día y noche allí la tienes con ese mal, destinada a nunca acostumbrarse. No, Chonito, mamá no está volviéndose loca. Está enferma de palabras que pronuncia como suspiro en oídos que no retienen nada. Y entonces esas mismas palabras se retachan hacia atrás, entrando de nuevo por la boca y aposentándose aquí. Luego la hacen que devuelva el estómago. Por eso llora mi mamá y quiera Dios que antes de nacer no me vayan a envenenar porque también a mí me hieren. También yo siento la boca como si la tuviera llena de alfileres. Ojalá que salga pronto de aquí porque me fastidia mucho este silencio de hiel. Mientras tanto Chonito, si puedes, no los dejes entrar. No dejes cantar a los poetas esas épicas gloriosas de la vida. Córtales los güevos por mí, mientras yo nazca. Si te hablan de hazañas, pídeles a los muertos que aplaudan y los cubran de besos leprosos; si hay amor en sus versos, cántales corridos; si belleza encuentran en el valle de Presidio, cuéntales del diablo y de su cueva. Muéstrales como se hizo el amor con los indios. Si de virtud se inspiran, Chonito, llévalos arriba, donde la gente de los milagros deja piernas, brazos y unos ojos de metal. Nunca un cuerpo entero. Nunca un cuerpo vivo. Pero descansa, Chonito, al cabo que ni me oyes. Algún día y ya pronto, encenderé la chispa, les quemaré los pies. Algún día no dormirán porque la noche les pesará mucho, como una pelota atada a los pies con una cadena o como pelota de hule muerto. Los cuerpos de los trabajadores cansados se retorcerán en sus lechos, rechinarán sus huesos. Y los muertos les invadirán la mente, los harán llorar, los harán reír, los volverán locos. Sí Chonito, algún día no dormirán, no dormirán, no dormirán . . ."

Ha cesado de llover. Adentro los goteros se cansaron de cae y cae.

Ahora el silencio se hace aplastante, enorme. La noche, como el
cuerpo de Marcela, pareció también caer exhausta. Nada se mueve.
Ni las estrellas, ni las nubes. Ni la luna. Nada. Las casas están emba-
durnadas contra la noche. Engarrotamiento y silencio de plomo. Sólo
un vientecito desorientado pasa sus manos frescas por las barbas del
álamo afuera de vez en cuando. Entonces el árbol siente el escalofrío y
responde con un leve sonido de pandereta.

Marcela entreabre los ojos pero no ve nada por el momento. Sólo
adivina los bultos de Chonito y Vicke durmiendo esparcidos en el
cuartito. Está acostada de lado porque ya hace mucho que no puede
ponerse de espaldas. Ni lucha le hace. El bebé que ha resistido parir es
como traer una tonelada de cobre en la panza. Fraguado en forma de
cono puntiagudo. Acostumbra un poco más los ojos a la oscuridad
mientras piensa en José, José, cómo estará, el río grande, no hay pase,
misa, el padre, llovió, lloré, dormí, qué hora, serán las tres.

Detesta levantarse a estas horas y quisiera poder aguantarse hasta
que amanezca porque sabe lo que le espera afuera. El zoquetal, el
fríto, y luego el asiento de madera mojado. Tiene que salir aunque sea
sólo un chorrito insignificante. La presión del niño es mucha. Hace
rechinar la cama al incorporarse y busca las chanclas con los mismos
pies y cuando los encuentra, se los casca. Luego se cubre hasta la
cabeza con la cobija y camina hacia la puerta.

—¿Señora?

—Ahorita vengo, Chonito, voy afuera— le contesta en voz baja.

—Marcela, ¿eres tú?— la viejita se sienta en la cama.

—Sí, voy a hacer aguas.

—¿Quieres que vaya contigo?

—No mamá, si horita vengo— y sale de inmediato sin esperar la
insistencia de la viejita.

El excusado de lámina no está lejos pero tiene que pelear con el
lodo pegajoso que quiere robarle los zapatos. Pronto se pone a la
puerta, anticipando lo mojado que estará adentro. La casita es un
verdadero cedazo. Se sube al helado trono, se levanta la capa y luego se
sienta, atrapando las manos debajo de cada nalga. Toda esta incomo-
didad para tan poca cosa. Es que el niño ya anda muy abajo. "A veces
parece que traigo la cabecita entre las piernas. Pero no le hace . . . ya,
ai va . . . se está moviendo otra vez. Muévete, m'ijo, muévete porque
sólo así estoy segura de que no te me has muerto. No importa que me
duelas. Muévete para que no me preocupes. No sé qué te ha pasado

pero ya no te mueves como antes. Debiera sentirte más, con lo avanzada que estoy. Andale . . . así . . . así . . ."

La mujer regresa y se vuelve a acostar. El feto se sigue moviendo con unos movimientos suaves, serenos. Ella los disfruta. Se siente feliz porque allí en sus entrañas hay vida. "No te preocupes mamá. Sé que no estás sola. No me sientes porque no quiero causarte daño. Nomás cuando me canso de estar así como si estuviera rezando engarruñado, me tengo que estirar. Pero lo hago con cuidado, ahora que he descubierto que si estiro las manos primero y luego las piernas, es menos dolor para ti. Por eso ya no me sientes, porque ya no acostumbro patalearte. Ahora . . . me estoy acomodando porque sabes, la noche ha sido muy larga y he estado de cabeza dormido. Ya me estaba pesando mucho la sangre. No sé por qué me quedé dormido así. Quizá porque tu corazón latía demasiado fuerte o porque te gruñían las tripas. Sabes, esto te sucede a ti muchas veces, como ayer que no cenaste, ¿recuerdas? ¿Cómo te quedaste dormida? El susto que nos diste a todos. Vino tu comadre a verte y Teléforo casi cruzaba el río para avisar a papá pero entrada la noche te tranquilizaste. Eran puros nervios. Yo los sentí tan apretados como cuerdas aquí dentro. Imagínate como estaba yo, con el tun, tun, de tu corazón a prisa en mi cabeza, y tus nervios y tus tripas revolcándose como creciente. Estos son los momentos cuando sufro yo más, porque tu corazón no es verdad que está en el pecho, sino en el vientre. Aquí lo tengo palpitando entre mis manos y yo hago lo posible por hacer el menor movimiento. Hace días descubrí que me puedo mover como un compás; si te acuestas de lado, me atravieso en tu vientre en posición vertical; si te paras me pongo en posición horizontal; si haces movimientos que no entiendo, me dejo flotar sin resistir. Por eso no me sientes mamá, y ojalá que comprendas. Estoy normal, voy creciendo rápido. No sabes, pero desde que empecé a ejercitar la mente, noté yo mismo el desarrollo. Desde que me puse a pensar en escribir cuando naciera. Y ahora no me importa este desorden. Ya vendrá el tiempo. Ahora lo que importa es dejar todo volar, soltar la lengua hasta que llegue el tiempo. Por primera vez estoy contento de poder ver tan claro desde aquí madre. No hay necesidad de estar fuera ni que sea de día porque tú me lo comunicas. A ti se te trasluce el alma. Cuando estás alegre se te vuelve mariposa blanca y cuando sufres, la mariposita sangra bañándome todo el cuerpo. Esta noche quise hablar con Chonito y explicarle tu locura, pero creo que no me oyó. Esta es una cosa que no entiendo. Parece que unas gentes me oyen cuando pienso y otras no. Yo quisiera saber si de veras tienen sentidos, si de veras oyen. No sé por qué no ha sido hasta ahora que se me haya ocurrido lo lento que ha sido mi vida. Apenas hoy me doy cuenta que yo me extiendo como un hilito muy fino hasta muy atrás, desde tu niñez yo te llevaba en mis venas. Acuérdate también que tú sólo me diste tu vientre para que allí creciera pero que mucho antes, ya venía semilla volando brincando de vientre en vientre. Imagínate cien años de existencia antes de nacer, buscando donde pegar mis raíces. Pero ya descansa, mamá, que la noche ha sido larga".

DESPUES QUE SE DESCONTO l'agua, la nochi se puso buti suave. Muy de aquella se puso, con fregales de estrellas por todas madres. Poco a poco las nubes se vían escurrido como si tenían escame hasta dejar un friego de alfileres aluminados. Simón, el cielo parecía una cuilca calota como ésas que usan los reyes pa taparse el esqueleto.

Downtown toda la raza jue saliendo de los chantes, a ver qué fregaos taba pasando en el pueblo escueto. Todas iban a patín porque los jefitos no vían cooperao con las ranflas. Además se necesita gota pa dar el round y también está escasa de a madre como todo el borlo. La pinchi lluvia no vía dejado camellar toda la semana así que unos batos tenían que contentarse con milal como el chinito la nochi del diciséis. Los otros se vían ponido a tirar crape de a nicle detrás de a que Johnny's Bar, al cabo que con un bola ni siquiera te ponías feeling. Y si la traías parada pos podías hacer roncha y luego te ibas a jugar pool por beeria. Pero si no, pos quedabas brujo de a madre y como siempre, así pasaba con los que andaban más jodidos que las mangas de un chaleco. En los cabrones dados el bato más zura siempre salía ganando. Así que aunque les tronaras los dedos de a madre y les soplaras y los trataras como jainas, siempre vinían las jodidas burras. Ni siquiera little Joe, ni Fiva la viva, ni Sixto el ojo de plata te hacían caso. Te tiraban a loco aunque les periquearas. Chingao, parecía que los dados taban loaded.

En otras veces los batos no estaban aquí haciéndose pendejos solos. A esta hora andaban en el Otro tirando chancla, watchando las rucas, cavuleando todo el pedo. En las ramadas y los congales todo bien de aquella. Chavas dando güelta y güelta en la plaza como disco rayado, mascando goma, esperando que te les acercaras y les cantaras. "Esa, vamos a echarnos una cartita allí donde están los trompas de hule;

ésa no me corte que estoy chaparro". Después si pegabas, te la llevabas
y le apañabas una coca y le tirabas líneas de aquella. Si tenías suerte y le
caibas bien a la chava tú le podías cai a la brava: "Esa vamos a lo
oscurito pa tirar pichón". Si nel, pos te la llevabas suave nomás tirando
chancla. De todos modos vías pegado y el borlote era calmala, llevár-
tela suave. ¿Pero horita? Ni qué pelarle, ta de a madre gacho el pedo. A
güevo te la pasas con una pata en la esquina, watchando a los rucos
dando el round, todos agüitados, todos escamaos que el jodido río se
suelte meando por todos laos. Entonces sí, se joden ellos y tú también.
Los cabrones chotas también andan güelta y güelta como si eso iba a
detenelo, pero lo suyo es puro pedo porque no tienen ni qué chingaos
cuidar. ¿Quién va a pasar pa acá con toda esa agua? Además te cuesta
un güevo cruzar en el chalán. Nomás los batos que vienen al borlo de
allá del Chuco, Kermit, y el Odesson train lana pa pabuleale cinco
grandes al Trompas que se jugó chango y se apañó la lanchita pa estar
pase y pase gente pa'l Otro. Pero esta noche jodida, raspa, ni esos
pasan. Nomás el cielo está suave. O te quedas en el chante a aplastar
oreja a le cais a la jefita con el bola que siempre tiene escondido y te
pelas al show. Pero no seas pendejo; no te vayas a jugarlo en los crapes
porque ni al mono vas a poder ir.

El Chale que ha estado bonkeado toda la tarde, se levanta y se va al
toliro. Recuerda el date que tienen él y Jusito y se pone a alistar. Allí
frente al espejo se quita la güeva remojándose la máscara y luego con la
lija se hace una barba blanca como Santo Clos. Saca la zura y al recle le
quedan los cachetes bien lisos. A su jaina le gustan así. Ahora se
embarra la greña con grasa Parrot y se hace un ducktail padre. Al
agacharse se da cola que los calcos tan bien cateados y de volada se los
pasa por detrás de los Khakis porque no hay tiempo pa'l speedshine. Ya
van a ser las eight y aquel bato ya estará esperando con las rucas. Así
que pronto se deja cai el zurrón, dejándose la lisa desabrochada de
arriba pa esportear su pecho peludo, y listo. "No voy a refinar jefita. Ai
la watcho al recle".

Cuando se iba a subir a la carcacha del jefito, se fijó que estaba
ponchada y se caldeó tanto que la agarró a patadas hasta que le dolió el
dedo gordo. Después que le echó la última madre le puso el bato en el
dodge patitas. El agüite no se le calmó de volada porque pensaba
todavía en las fiestas que iba a perder aunque sabía bien el peligro de
cruzar. Recordó la chinga que le vían ponido al Betabel pero él vía
tenido la culpa que lo filerearan porque ¿cómo se pone a tumbale la

ruca a aquel bato así a la brava? Simón, él vía tenido la culpa. Ta mejor
que no puedas pasar. Mejor calmantes montes aquí hasta que se
apacigüe el pedo. ¿Qué le pelas? Aquí tienes pichón con la Mary, ése.
No seas jodido con ella, la ruca ta encanicada, te quiere chingos. Si no,
¿cómo te ha aguantado tanto? Pero el bato vía contado con la ranfla pa
sacarse de llevala al mono porque andaba bruja. El único bola que le
vía quedado se le vía ido en gota y ahora la mugre ponchada. Valía más
que el Jusito . . . a este bato jodido nada le agüita. Toda es pura pinchi
risa y yo creo que así lurio va a morir. Nunca sabes qué va a hacer, con
qué va a salir, en qué pedo te va a meter. Y esa desgraciada costumbre
de andar picando chiclosos cada vez que das la espalda me agüita de a
madre. Y las pendejadas que dice, pero eso sí, el bato nunca se te raja
en ninguna parte. Vale más que esta noche me aliviane el bato.

Cuando llegó el Chale a la botica brincando charcos, al Jusito le
agarró una risota de poco pelo y el Chale nomás lo dejó que se curara a
gusto.

—Uuu, qué bato éste. ¿Pos no que la ranfla y que yo y que . . .

—Nel ése, taba más agujerada que usté, jodido.

—Pos ya la chingamos. Hora vamos a quedar con el . . .

—¿Y las jainas?

—Ai stán adentro ése. Hace friego que nos calman. Vamos a
ponele, carnal . . .

—Espérate ése. Ando bruja. Ni un . . .

—Uuu, qué bato. Aquí camarón, wátchele. Cuatro lanotas.

—¿De dónde . . . ?

—Las baterías ése. Cro que los traitores del Johnny no van a
estariar mañana.

—Orale, pues. Capea a las rucas.

Pa cuando llegaron a las vistas el Jusito y la Olga ya se vían
prendido varios de lengua y la llevaba meándose de risa pero la Mary
cortó gacho al Chale por el mal porte del bato. Así que éste le jue
cantando que no vía otra chava que lo haciera sentir más de aquélla
que ella y que tan pronto como tenía lana le iba a apañar la man-
cuerna. Después le siguió con que su jefito Teléforo se la pasaba
cascareando con el viejo porque ya no podía ponele duro al jale y él
tenía que alivianalo. Le teoricó el pedo de por qué la vía dejado parada
el otro día—la jura lo vía pescado speeding y como andaba bien
marrano, vía chisquiado de a madre cuando les quiso pintar el cuatro.
Hasta los chonteados le vían quitado en el tabique y después cuando

salió se vía metido en el pedo del Betabel allá en el Otro. De esta forma
alivianó a su chava pa cuando llegaron al mono.

Adentro, garraron chingo de patada con el Tom and Jerry pero
nomás eso watcharon porque pa cuando empezó Tarzán a echarse
jodazos en el pecho y el cabrón chango haciendo la misma, los batos
tenían las manos llenas y un ojo torcido. Pasaron muy buen tiempo
pichoneando de aquella hasta que apareció la Jane y jue cuando
empezó todo el borlote. Los batos no se daban cola que sus baisas se
vían ponido en slow motion hasta que se vían parado a la brava. ¡Hijo
de la chingada, la Jane taba buenota de a madre! Las chavas se
resintieron cuando vieron la curadota que se estaban dando los batos y
las dos protestaron. La Mary le dijo al Chale que no juera tan
descarado y boca abierta, pero la Olga sí se jue grande. Empezó a
gritarles fregadera y media en voz alta pa que oyeran todos. Entonces
no hubo más remedio que salir ajuera pa averiguar y arreglar el pedo.
Después entraron otra vez los cuatro pero todos venían de mal humor.

A medio mono las rucas pidieron algo pa tomar nomás de cabronas
y vengativas porque sabían que los batos andaban raspas. El Chale no
supo qué contestar pero el cabrón perico del Jusito, que vía prometido
taparse los ojos cuando apareciera Jane, le dijo al Chale que juera con
él. Este lo vio rirse y cerrale un ojo. Pos cuando ellos salieron las chavas
se quedaron haciéndose ilusiones y cuando los batos duraron mucho
pa venir, pensaron que a la brava querían quedar bien con ellas. Que
con seguro van a trai cokes y hamborgas y papas y todo el pedo. Que
sufran los cabrones pa que no crean que semos cualquieras, ¿que no
carnala? Simón, hay que ponerse dura todo el tiempo con estos
jodidos.

En eso estaban cuando llegaron los batos y se aplastaron así como
que no traiban nada. Pero el Jusito puso un bultote de poca madre en
el piso y lo traiba envuelto en su suera.

—¿Ontán las cokes?

—Traimos otra cosa mejor ésas, pero hay que calmala porque es
sospresa.

—Tan lurios, trajieron m . . .

—A la brava, ¿que no, carnal?

—Simón, es . . .

—Vale más que se la corten. Destapen lo que train o nos vamos.

—Orale pues. ¿Tas listo, carnal?

— . . .

—Pero tienen que cerrar los ojos primero . . .

Cuando las chavas siguieron la línea el Jusito levantó el garrafón de Kool-Aid y se lo puso en las piernas a la Olga y pa cuando abrió los ojos la ruca, el Jusito ya estaba casi a la puerta. El Chale también salió hecho madre tras de él y se metieron al toliro pa agarrar chingos de patada. El ruco que cuida el pedo allí los sacó a pushones porque no paraban de rirse. Allá ajuera siguieron cagándose de risa sin pensar en sus jainas, al cabo que esta nochi jodida, raspa, lo único que tiene de bonito es el cabrón cielo. Con fregales de estrellas por todas madres.

EL DIA AMANECIO como un Grito de Dolores retrasado. ¡Ya voló el puente! ¡El agua ya reventó en la labor de arriba! ¡Ya se metió a las labores del Colorao! La noticia se fue encadenando hasta que llegó a todos los rincones de Presidio. Los dueños empezaron a echar madres, que sacaran los tractores y las herramientas que pudieran salvar. Pronto empezaron a hormiguear trabajadores alborotados, abatidos con la lucha que habían hecho. No se pudo más, presas, palas y costales llenos de arena, pacas de alfalfa, y todo lo que humanamente se había pensado resultaba inútil. El agua fue arrollando los plantíos de algodón y de melón tardío. El agua buscaba espacio para estrechar sus tentáculos entumecidos y cuando encontraba obstáculos más grandes que ellos, les bramaba. Luego los rodeaba lentamente, como si así cobrara fuerzas necesarias para después engullirlos y continuar su despojo. Los señores grandes, los dueños, entonces daban una media vuelta, se montaban en sus vehículos y con un rechinar de llantas se alejaban rabiosos. "Este año te vas a quedar en el hoyo, hermano, porque no aseguraste tu cosecha. Vendrán por tu nueva empacadora de alfalfa, por el Allis Chalmers y su arado, lo mismo que el International que usabas para el disco". "Son of a bitch. When you want the fucking water you don't get it and now . . . goddamn. And all that money I put into repairing the gin . . . all that fucking work for nothing".

Toda la mañana la visita a Sam's Phillips 66 es interminable. La gente del pueblo viene y tankea, alistándose pa salir. Ya no hay más que hacer aquí, sino ponele pa Nuevo México o pa'l Odessón. "El jale en las compañías de petróleo son las que más te pagan". "Sí, pero yo qué jodidos sé de máquinas y tienes que saber bastante totacha pa esos jales". "Nel carnal, yo conozco el bato de esta companía, es a toda madre. Yo te acomodo". Los más viejos que han dado la vida entera a la labor también vienen pero sólo echan gasolina y se van sin decir palabra. Piensan sólo en la pela que van a llevar, la renta, las malpasadas, el dinero que van a ganar y que se van a comer. Luego regresarán otra vez aquí raspa. Pero cuando menos has vivido, ¿que no?

Al otro lado de la calle, Nancy's Cafe también empieza a animarse. Una por una van llegando las trocas sombrerudas y excitadas. Luego los jeeps de la migra. Sólo falta el carro antenudo del sherife. Entre bocadones de ham and eggs con café, "Damn, you should a seen how that water topple that tree like a shithouse; the water's pouring all over the fucking place at Johnny's, tried to save his bulldozer but the bank caved in. That stupid Lencho just let 'er go and he jump off like a scared rabbit . . . Well, gotta go see if them ole boys done as I told 'em to. Guess there's nothing else to do but start buyin' Mexican cattle. I hear this guy down by los Mochis got purty good ones to sell. I'm gonna try and lease some of that Campbell property so I can fatten them carcasses. Six months'll do it. I hear they're payin' pretty good price for beef this year."

Ben Jr. tiene otra idea: "Me voy por tres meses al valle, me llevo las trailers, consigo contrato para transportar las cosechas de Vernes, Inc., y me recupero un poco. Después que se baje el río, compongo las tierras y reclamo al gobierno la reducción. El gobierno me paga por no sembrar. 220,000 dólares tax-free por hacerme un favor. ¿Qué más quiero? No puedo pedir más. Así las tierras descansan".

El pensamiento lo hace generoso con la mesera y le deja cincuenta centavos.

—Have a good day, sir.

—You too, ma'am.

Esa mañana la viejita Vicke y Chonito se levantaron temprano con los pujidos de Marcela y ya para cuando el sol salió, la casa estaba animada. El que estaba para nacer venía tocando con punzadas fuertes y no había manera de detenerlo. —Debe ser el golpe que llevaste ayer, hija. No creas, si todavía te falta tiempo— le decía la señora, en un esfuerzo por conformarla. Luego carrereaba de la cocina a la sala con tazas de yerbabuena y tortillas frotadas de mantequilla pero Marcela las rechazaba. —¡Te dije que ya no quiero! Ya me tienes empanzada con tanto mugrero. ¡Llévatelo, no lo quiero!

Chonito las dejó hablando. El salía para la casa de Teléforo. Cuando llegó, encontró a todo mundo en rejuego. —Es que Carlos se va pa California, y tuve que arreglarle la ropa. El viejo también se levantó temprano pa ayudar pero con la humedá de estos días no se ha sentido bien. Ya sabes lo que sufre con las riumas— La comadre Serafina le hablaba al muchacho como si fuera hijo de José . . . Era de esperarse. El chamaco quería a su amo más que al propio papá y se pasaba más tiempo aquí en Presidio que en Ojinaga. Además, a su papá sólo le importaba el dinero que el muchacho traía a casa, y si no, le alistaba el cajoncito de shine y "¡a la calle, güevón!" Era difícil transformarse en payaso en esas ocasiones. Hacer reír a los güeros y a los soldaditos mexicanos que rondaban el zumbido. Nomás no podía. Tampoco toleraba a los otros muchachos que, como agentes de seguros, seguían al pobre gringo hasta que se le ponía la cara roja. Luego que vencían, se lanzaban tres o cuatro al suelo, buscándole más de dos pies, y al ver que el señor era un ser normal, se sentaban en sus cajoncitos pensativos. Hombre güero, enigma de la tierra, plenitud vital, ¿cómo no das a saber tu secreto?

La última semana se le había puesto mal la situación porque desde que José había huido, no había trabajado. Pero estaba decidido a sufrir las consecuencias. Más importante era el bienestar de la familia Uranga. Así que desde un principio le había dicho a Teléforo que no contara con él para llenar sacos de arena y hacer presas en el río.

—Cuida a Marcela y a Vicke lo mejor que puedas— le había dicho José. —Que pasen unos días y el sábado cruzas para que me enteres si los cabrones ya se fueron. Estaré en la casa de Bernabé y si hay urgencia cuenta con Teléforo, mi compa.

Había cumplido a la letra. Por las tardes se iba al pueblo. Se metía en las gasolineras, se sentaba afuera del café, paseaba por el hotel y hasta se daba la vuelta al puente, arriesgándose a que lo pescaran. Recuerda muy bien que apenas había cruzado José, cuando habían llegado con "dónde José Uranga" y cuando no lo habían encontrado, se habían regresado. A los pocos días ya estaban en Presidio con orden de arrestarlo por evadir el servicio militar. Mientras tanto Chonito iba y venía con las noticias hasta que por fin había decidido José mudarse al otro lado. El no podía verse matando gentes que nada de culpa tenían en los pleitos de políticos. —Habla con Teléforo y dile que mañana por la noche me haga el favor. El ya sabe lo que debe hacer—le había dicho.

Chonito había matado las primeras horas de la noche anterior debajo de las carpas mojadas que celebraban las fiestas patrias. Entre

juegos de dados, remates de ropa y gritería de borrachos, había espe-
rado hasta llegarse las doce. Luego, con el valor necesario, había
pasado como gato prendido al costado del puente. A tientas se había
ido encontrando las tablas porque el río ya volaba por arriba. Después
de un eterno jalar de greñas, la corriente lo había permitido cruzar. A
las dos de la mañana Chonito era una sombra mojada que se colaba
por el pueblo embadurnado de zoquete. Luego un té caliente, una
señora enredándolo con una sábana y una colcha tendida en el piso.
Chonito no recordaba más.

—Nomás quería avisarle a usté que esta noche es el encargo de
don José.

—Muy bien. Entonces dile a Vicke que allá iré a recogerlas
despuesito que se haiga metido el sol. Al rato le aviso a Samuel que se
aliste con la lancha. Pero anda, vente a almorzar. ¿Estás seguro que no
quieres?

—No, gracias. Si ya comí allá. Mejor me voy a ver en qué puedo
ayudar.

—Ese carnalito, ai nos watchamos. Póngala ai.

—Pues que le vaya bien por allá.

—Simón, a ver si nos alivianamos. Pásela suave, ¿eh?

—También usté Carlos.

De noche se encontraron con un río lomudo de chocolate. Parecía
más bien una montaña prieta en continuo vaivén. Marcela al contra-
rio se imaginó un gato engrifado que abría el hocico rabioso sin
maullar. Lo único que parecía oír era un leve zumbido de abejón en
lejanía.

La mujer baja la cabeza como si buscara algo, como si la vista fuera
a detenerle la sensación de algo que le chorrea por las piernas. Siente
un arroyito caliente que empieza desde los nervios de la cabeza y baja
hasta los pies. Pero no dice nada. Sólo mira una escena mecánica,
hombres sin diálogo que corren de la troca a la lancha, echando bultos
que acumularon Vicke y Chonito durante el día. Parece que la escena
toda está encarcelada entre una enorme concha de rumores. Los
nervios, hechos cuerda, les tapan los ojos y por eso cuando quedan
inundados por la luz de unos faroles ni cuenta se dan. Ni siquiera
cuando están para subir a las mujeres. Sólo cuando Teléforo vuelve a
la troca es cuando nota el par de luces que se viene haciendo más
grande.

—¡Pronto! ¡Súbanse a la lancha que viene alguien!— les grita, a la vez que echa a andar el motor de su troca.

Samuel el lanchero toma a la viejita en los brazos mientras que Chonito coge a Marcela de la mano para estar seguro de que no tropiece. Se mueven los remos con furia esperando la bala de pistola en el estómago. Pero no se oye nada. Las tripas se desanudan.

Mientras, Teléforo espera que lleguen las luces. "Bien me las arreglo. Les digo que vine a darle la vuelta al río y es todo. Saben los cabrones quién soy. Les digo que la lancha lleva a dos amigos de Odessa que tienen a su madre enferma. Que el carro que está allí es el de ellos. ¿Qué más pueden preguntar? Sí, aquí los espero . . . ¿Qué? . . . Parece que se están apagando. ¿Quién debe ser?"

El hombre espera un momento más pero nada sucede. Apenas distingue el bulto del auto. Entonces da la vuelta a su troca y se dirige hacia donde habían estado las luces. Pasa despacio y no puede creer que no haya nada allí. Regresa otra vez y se va hasta la orilla del río y tampoco. A fuerza quiere ver algo, las luces, el bulto por lo menos. Cuando se convence de que no hay nada, perplejo sale rumbo a casa. Es entonces que oye el fuerte golpe contra el parabrisas. La lechuza queda pataleando al lado del camino. Pero el hombre no se detiene porque el rumor del río ahora se convierte en una carcajada de gigante. El diablo regresa a su sierrita querida.

LA PRIMERA PARTE de la cruzada se avanzó con suma rapidez pero el forcejeo de los lancheros se fue haciendo más duro al llegar a medio río, y cuando ya no se movía la lancha a despecho de que remaban como locos, dejaban que el agua se los llevara un momento para luego seguir luchando.

La viejita apretaba la mano de su hija cada vez que pegaban los montes de basura contra la lancha y se comía los santos. Marcela al contrario llevaba la mente como pescado muerto en una red. El dolor le venía a intervalos, dolor que le duraba un minuto eterno y luego desaparecía como vibración de campanas. Ella permanecía indiferente. Parecía estar suspendida en el aire, más allá de la emoción humana.

—¿Cómo te sientes, hija?

—Dame agua.

—No hay agua hija.

—Quiero agua.

—Aguántate un poco más hijita.

Marcela cierra los ojos y aprieta juntas las piernas lo más fuerte posible. Parece querer quitarse la obstrucción que trae entre las piernas.

—Quítamelo, Vicke.

—No puedo, hija—. La viejita piensa que Marcela se refiere al dolor.

—Te digo que me lo quites.

—Por el amor de Dios cálmate, hija. Verás que pronto se te quita.

Los hombres reman más duro. Las palabras de las mujeres les sacan fuerzas sobrehumanas que en otra ocasión ya se hubieran acabado, mas no es sólo eso; las acciones de Marcela parecen indicar que la mujer va perdiendo la cabeza porque, ¿quién en ese estado pudiera sentir la indiferencia a tal dolor? No, no puede ser natural, piensan.

Tampoco lo que ahora ven. El cuerpo suelto de la mujer cae sobre la viejita quien grita despavorida, al tiempo que ésta la estruja. Pero Marcela ni se mueve. Los hombres pronto se olvidan de la lancha y buscan la manera de poder volverla en sí pero ya todo es inútil; solamente el agua sucia tiene movimiento. El agua y un recién nacido a medio río. Sobre las copas de los árboles, sobre las cabezas, unas nubes de algodón desmenuzado sueltan el llanto.

Presidio 1970

Ya déjalo así, hijo. Mañana haremos un poco más. Vale más reco-
gernos.
—Está bien, apá— y me enderecé, a la vez echándome el azadón en
el lomo.

Nos fuimos los dos caminando hacia la casa taciturnos y silenciosos.
No teníamos nada que decir. Parecía que la oscuridad nos apresaba los
cerebros fatigados y sudorosos, dejándonos mudos. Sólo se escuchaba el
quejido de terrones aplastados por los pies de dos hombres exhaustos.

¿Cuándo terminará esto? pensaba, recordando los días monótonos y
eternos. Días cansados. Días sin esperanza. Pobre papá. Es tan viejo y aún
no se da cuenta que todos los días son iguales, sin cambio. Que todo se
reduce a existencia y muerte. Seguramente ni siquiera se ha fijado bien en
el espejo, en las hondas líneas estampadas en su cara, en la joroba
encorvada de ayeres, en la fatiga reflejada en sus ojos de hoy.

—Qué sol tan perro hizo hoy, ¿no hijo? Parecía que nos habíamos
dado un baño de sudor.

—Pues sí. Por eso me senté buen rato bajo el árbol . . . al cabo poco se
avanza. ¿De qué sirve matarnos?

No me respondió. Volvimos a quedar mudos.

Así ha ocurrido siempre, padre. Siempre se ha quedado esta tierra
maldita con tu sangre, con tu sudor. Y me duele que en cada gota de tu
cuerpo vaya parte de tu alma, de una vida que muere para vivir mejor. Yo
sé que tus pasos apuntan a un vacío día tras día y yo los sigo también. Pero
¿sabes por qué lo hago? Por ti papá. Por no dejarte solo. Pero ya me cansé
papá, y no te he dicho que me voy. Me voy porque estoy seguro de que hay
otro mundo mejor que Presidio . . . presidio, tejas. Hasta el nombre me
suena enfermo para haber visto la luz primero, bajo tejas de presidio.

—Mañana vamos a seguir limpiando, ¿no papá?

—Sí, hijo. Hay que hacer un poco más. Cuando menos las melgas que
se van a regar.

Claro, haríamos más agujeros en los zapatos, zigzaguearíamos como
locos por los camellones. Quitaríamos yerba y pisotearíamos y caminarí-
amos y aparecería otra línea en la frente de mi viejo. Por lo pronto ahora,
nos curaríamos las fatigas con descanso de vacío y oscuridad; después nos
levantaríamos temprano por la mañana como si fuera algo nuevo en el
tiempo. Como si el tiempo tuviera límites. Qué pendejadas. La vida se
mide sólo a base de esfuerzo y de acción. Qué brutos los que nos consideran
güevones por tener raíces en la "tierra del mañana". Pero es que no
comprendan que mañana significa esperanza, que hoy se trabajó quince

horas y que hay esperanza de aguantar diecisiete. Es esperanza de mejorarse, sobrepasando los límites del cuerpo. En Presidio nunca muere. Se afirma y se hace sustento como pan de cada día, hasta el punto de convertirse en parásito eterno. Sí, hay que tener esperanza . . .

—¿Por qué no fuiste a la guerra, padre?

—Porque no entiendo de riñas entre países. ¿Para qué pelear con otros si la lucha la traigo aquí dentro, si el hambre es mi propia guerra? Nosotros, hijo, somos como un par de dados que de tanto rodar hemos tomado forma de canica. Y no cesaremos de rodar hasta que encontremos un hueco. Es ese hueco con el cual debemos luchar y no contra nosotros mismos.

Pero los agentes no te escucharon, ¿te acuerdas, padre? Vinieron y te llevaron sin pestañear a otro presidio, después de que habías perdido a tu mujer. Y ahora pagabas el crimen de no dar muerte a otros, por no hacerte enemigo de tu barro. No quisieron entender que para ti la lucha por vivir bastaba y tuviste que cumplir la sentencia. Con cuatro líneas más en tu frente, con dos alas caídas, arrastrando por el suelo, con una marca estampada sobre tu espalda, ¿te acuerdas, padre? Regresaste con el alma agujereada y con corazón sangriento para luego volver a caminar por esas tierras. Y después te cansaste y te emborrachaste y te volviste loco de risa endiablada aquí en Presidio. Y luego que vi tu tragedia me arranqué de las garras y me fui, ¿te acuerdas? Pero ahora he regresado, después de mucho tiempo, y ¿sabes por qué? Porque te has muerto. Ayer por fin te enterramos en el polvoroso cementerio de Presidio. Digo que por fin, pues ya nos estábamos cansando de velarte y yo creo que hasta tú mismo sentías igual. Ya estarías cansado de estar expuesto a tanta gente, a tantos gemidos. Yo sólo quise verte el primer día. Después me dediqué a hacer los arreglos necesarios y a soportar condolencias. Hasta entonces no me enteré de los amigos que tenías, todos ellos caras marchitas de tiempo y pensé que así los mataría la vida también, como a ti. Después del primer día de palabras rayadas como un disco, me dediqué a mi abuela Vicke. Cuando llegué no le pude decir nada así que la dejé que se desahogara en mi pecho diciéndole torpemente que no llorara. Entonces los dos caminamos para contemplar los últimos vestigios de una cara cicatrizada, un rostro de cincuenta años arrugados; debajo de la piel un corazón reventado a golpes—la vida siempre nos tuvo desprecio. Por eso no quise volver a verte, porque moriste con el mismo gesto de desprecio en la boca. Estoy seguro que si me hubieras podido hablar en ese momento, me hubieras regañado. —¿A poco crees que voy a dejar burlarme de la muerte? ¿Que no te dije que me enterraras con mariachis?— me hubieras dicho. Por eso sientes rencor, papá, porque naciste en un rencor humeante, en un hoyo de huesos calcinados, en Presidio—siete letras taladradas en semana santa, presidio del tiempo prolongado, presidio suspendido en un vapor a las tres de la tarde, presidio la burla, presidio mal aventurado, presidio nacido viejo. No, don José, no había que buscarle amaneceres a Presidio, no había que preguntar por los niños, la gente nació con arrugas, a las tres de la tarde. Por eso no existían ni existen fiebres en Presidio. La gente parió quemada, derretida. La sangre de sus cuerpos está hecha a ciento veinte grados. Y tú por eso amaste y viviste con la sangre hirviendo—el odio ya estaba soldado desde mucho antes que tú murieras. Y ese rencor que viene desde muy atrás ahora se me ha pegado. Se me pegó desde el primer día que te velamos. Por eso no quise volver a verte. Ahora, tres días después, me siento mejor aunque me haya despedido de ti para siempre. Pero sabes, he decidido quedarme porque hay que quitar la corona de espinas en Presidio. Sí, habrá que caminar por los cactos y los mesquites. Habrá que aguantar el camino, quitar la corona y ponérsela a otro. Después, ir hasta el río y lavarse las llagas, y ya cuando se está limpio habrá que regresar a Presidio y el que quiera seguir tendrá que regresar fuerte porque necesitará la voluntad más grande que emana del alma. Porque lo verán y lo creerán loco y le dirán que se vaya a predicar a las orillas del río. La gente que ha sufrido con él lo comprenderá pero no lo seguirá porque tendrá miedo, y habrá otros que le escupirán la cara. Le dirán que todo corre muy bien, que la gente está contenta con sus casas y trabajos. Pero el milagro obrará y entonces necesitará reunirlos, contarles del diablo que se desató y que todavía anda suelto. También habrá que decirles de ese famoso fortín que nació mucho antes de 1683 y de tantas otras cosas. Sí, habrá que contar, pero no con sufrimiento y con perdón. Habrá que encender la llama, la que murió con el tiempo.

Bibliography

Bibliography of Works
By and About Aristeo Brito

Charles Tatum

Works by Brito

El diablo en Texas. Tucson: Editorial Peregrinos, 1976.
Cuentos i poemas. Washington, D.C.: Fomento Literario, 1974.
"El lenguaje tropológico en *Peregrinos de Aztlán.*" *La Luz* 1.2 (May 1975): 42-43.

Works about Brito

Alarcón, Justo S. "La metamorfosis del diablo en *El diablo en Texas* de Aristeo Brito." In Francisco Jiménez, ed. *The Identification and Analysis of Chicano Literature.* Jamaica, NY: Bilingual Press, 1979. 253-267.

Barrón, Pepe, introd. *Cuentos i poemas de Aristeo Brito.* Chapbook of *Fomento Literario* 1.4 (Spring 1974). Washington, DC: Congreso Nacional de Asuntos Colegiales, 1974. iii-iv.

Cota-Cárdenas, Margarita. Review of *El diablo en Texas,* by Aristeo Brito. *Revista Iberoamericana* 108-109 (July-December 1979): 693-695.

Eger, Ernestina N. Review of *El diablo en Texas,* by Aristeo Brito. *Latin American Literary Review* 5.10 (Spring-Summer 1977): 162-165.

Febles, Jorge M. Review of *Cuentos i poemas de Aristeo Brito. Revista Chicano-Riqueña* 5.4 (Fall 1977): 56-58.

——. Review of *El diablo en Texas,* by Aristeo Brito. *Revista Chicano-Riqueña* 5.4 (Fall 1977): 55-56.

Lewis, Marvin. "*El diablo en Texas:* Structure and Meaning." In Francisco Jiménez, ed. *The Identification and Analysis of Chicano Literature.* Jamaica, NY: Bilingual Press, 1979. 247-252.

——. Review of *El diablo en Texas,* by Aristeo Brito. *Revista Chicano-Riqueña* 6.3 (Summer 1978): 70-71.

Martínez, Julio, and Francisco Lomelí, eds. *Chicano Literature. A Reference Guide.* Westport, CT: Greenwood Press, 1985. 77-83.

Rodríguez, Juan. "Comments on *El diablo en Texas.*" *Carta Abierta* 5 (October 1976): iv.

Rodríguez del Pino, Salvador. *La novela chicana escrita en español: cinco autores comprometidos.* Ypsilanti, MI: Bilingual Press, 1982. 91-115.

_____ . "Lo mexicano en la novela chicana; un ejemplo: *El diablo en Texas.*" In Francisco Jiménez, ed. *The Identification and Analysis of Chicano Literature.* Jamaica, NY: Bilingual Press, 1979. 365-373.

Tatum, Charles. Review of *El diablo en Texas*, by Aristeo Brito. *World Literature Today* 51.4 (Autumn 1977): 592-593.

_____ . *Chicano Literature.* Boston: G. K. Hall, 1982. 131-132.

_____ . *Literatura chicana.* México, D.F.: Secretaría de Educación Pública, 1985. 189-191.

Vega, Sara de la, and Carmen Salazar Parr. "Lectura No. 8: Aristeo Brito." In *Avanzando.* New York: John Wiley, 1978. 41.